W9-CXO-230

FabJob Guide to
Become an Image Consultant

TAG GOULET AND RACHEL GUREVICH

FABJOB GUIDE TO BECOME AN IMAGE CONSULTANT

Editors: Tag Goulet and Rachel Gurevich

ISBN: 978-1-897286-81-4

Copyright Notice: This edition copyright © 2011 by FabJob Inc. All rights reserved. No part of this work may be reproduced or distributed in any form or by any means (including photocopying, recording, online or email) without the written permission of the publisher. (First edition copyright © 2003 by FabJob Inc.)

Library and Archives Canada Cataloguing in Publication

Goulet, Therese, 1959-
FabJob Guide to become an image consultant / Tag Goulet and
Rachel Gurevich.

Includes bibliographical references.
ISBN 978-1-897286-81-4

1. Image consultants--Vocational guidance.
I. Gurevich, Rachel   II. Title.   III. Title: Image consultant.
IV. Title: Become an image consultant.

HF5389.G62 2011   650.1'3'023   C2011-900010-5

Important Disclaimer: Although every effort has been made to ensure this guide is free from errors, this publication is sold with the understanding that the authors, editors, and publisher are not responsible for the results of any action taken on the basis of information in this work, nor for any errors or omissions. The publishers, and the authors and editors, expressly disclaim all and any liability to any person, whether a purchaser of this publication or not, in respect of anything and of the consequences of anything done or omitted to be done by any such person in reliance, whether whole or partial, upon the whole or any part of the contents of this publication. If expert advice is required, services of a competent professional person should be sought.

About the Websites Mentioned in this Guide: Although we aim to provide the information you need within the guide, we have also included a number of websites because readers have told us they appreciate knowing about sources of additional information. (**TIP:** Don't include a period at the end of a web address when you type it into your browser.) Due to the constant development of the Internet, websites can change. Any websites mentioned in this guide are included for the convenience of readers only. We are not responsible for the content of any sites except FabJob.com.

FabJob Inc.
19 Horizon View Court
Calgary, Alberta, Canada T3Z 3M5

FabJob Inc.
4616 25th Avenue NE, #224
Seattle, Washington, USA 98105

To order books in bulk, phone 403-949-2039
To arrange a media interview phone 1-888-FABJOB-1 (1-888-322-5621)

www.FabJob.com

PRINTED IN CANADA

Contents

1. Introduction

As an image consultant you will have a dream career, getting paid to do what you love—helping people look and feel good about themselves.

You will discover how to get started and succeed in this fabulous job in this guide, the *FabJob Guide to Become an Image Consultant*. In the pages that follow, you will read about the importance of image in people's lives, see why there is increasing demand for professional image consultants, learn about the many benefits of this career, and discover the steps to take to get started.

1.1 The Importance of Image

Looking good is important to people throughout the world, and particularly in North America. According to a recent Gallup poll, seven out of 10 Americans said physical appearance is important "in terms of happiness, social life and the ability to get ahead."

And it's not just important for the young. *Parade* magazine published the results of a national survey of men and women aged 18 to 75 that found 84 percent disagreed with the statement, "When you become old, looks are no longer important." However, while physical appearance is a significant part of image, there is more to image than looks.

1.1.1   What Image Is

Merriam-Webster's Dictionary defines image as a "mental conception" of a person or organization. In other words, image is the beliefs that we have about someone or something. It may be the impressions we form when meeting someone new, or it may be an individual's or company's reputation that has developed over time.

Our impressions about other people may be based on how they look, talk, or behave. A person's overall "image" may consist of a variety of factors including their clothing, grooming, tone of voice, vocabulary, facial expressions, eye contact, gestures, and social behaviors (also known as etiquette).

Just as individuals have an image, so do companies. While public opinion about a corporation can be influenced by advertising, there are many other factors involved in developing a company's image. For example, we may form impressions of a company when visiting their retail outlets, speaking with a customer service representative on the phone, or seeing a company spokesperson interviewed in the news.

1.1.2   Why Image Matters

Image matters because people often make assumptions based on limited information. In their book *Social Psychology*, H. Andrew Michener, John D. DeLamater, and Daniel J. Myers explain that when we observe a single physical characteristic or behavior in someone, we tend to assume that person has a number of other qualities, too. For example, someone may be perceived as confident because they have a firm handshake. They may be seen as trustworthy because they make eye contact. They may be judged as capable, professional, successful – even wealthy or intelligent – because they are well dressed. The reverse is also true.

A Career by Any Other Name

A variety of different terms are sometimes used to describe image, image consultants, or image consulting. For example, you may hear image referred to as appearance, personal brand, or personal presentation. Or you may occasionally hear image consulting activities referred to as:

- Appearance Management

- Fashion Consulting

- Fashion Styling

- Image Management

- Makeover Consulting

- Perception Management

- Personal Branding

- Visual Branding

- Wardrobe Consulting

You could use some of these terms to describe yourself. For example, instead of calling yourself an image consultant, you might decide to call yourself a fashion stylist, makeover consultant, or wardrobe consultant.

Or you might decide to specialize in areas you'll read about later in this guide, such as: Closet Organizing, Color Consulting, Communication Consulting, Etiquette Consulting, or Personal Shopping.

Personal Image in Business

According to Brian Tracy, author of the bestselling *The Psychology of Achievement*, "many capable men and women are disqualified from job opportunities because they simply do not look the part." Caroline Dunn and Lucette Charette of the National Research Council of Canada found that "People are affected by your appearance whether or not they realize it, and whether or not they think appearance is important." Dunn and Charette summarized the research in this area and found that a first impression has significant, measurable effects on the observer:

"Your appearance strongly influences other people's perception of your:

- financial success

- authority

- trustworthiness

- intelligence

- suitability for hire or promotion

Your personal presentation [communication skills and appearance] influences people's behavior toward you, including:

- complying with your request

- trusting you with information

- giving you access to decision-makers

- paying you a certain salary or fee for contracted business

- hiring you or purchasing your product

These perceptions and behaviors are consistent among observers and persistent over time. In other words, most people will tend to form the same kinds of opinions about you based on your appearance."

Image in Personal Relationships

Image has an impact on people's private lives as well. You probably know from personal experience how much more respect you receive from store clerks when you are well dressed.

TIP: If you haven't yet experienced this, try an experiment. Go shopping at a fine store dressed in what you would normally wear to clean your basement or move furniture. Then visit the same store looking well-groomed and wearing your best suit. Observe how you are treated by the staff, as well as anyone else you encounter, in both situations.

Beyond how we are treated by strangers or service staff, our image can have a significant impact on our happiness by affecting the development of friendships and romantic relationships. Children learn that looking or acting "different" often results in teasing and bullying. Adults experience similarly painful consequences.

Thomas F. Cash, professor of clinical psychology at Old Dominion University in Norfolk, Virginia, has been studying the psychology of personal appearance for more than 30 years. In appearances on television shows such as *20/20*, and print media such as *Time Magazine*, he has shared his research findings that being physically unattractive results in discrimination against both men and women.

Corporate Image

For corporations and other organizations, image can affect the financial bottom line. *Fortune* magazine's annual rankings of most admired companies has found a correlation between a company's reputation and its profits. Not surprisingly, the most admired companies have higher financial returns than the least admired.

In a study for the Council of Public Relations Firms, Jeffries-Fox Associates researched the business literature, and identified the following benefits for companies that have a good reputation:

- Increasing market share

- Lowering market costs

- Lowering distribution costs

- Being able to charge a premium

- Avoiding over-regulation

- Being able to weather bad times

- Greater employee alignment and productivity

- Being able to attract and retain talent

- Being able to attract investors

- Gaining more favorable media coverage

If a company's reputation, or image, is not as good as it could be, the company may be losing out on all of these benefits.

1.2 Image Consulting as a Profession

As you can see from the previous section, a poor image can be costly as well as painful. Both individuals and companies can experience tremendous benefits by improving their image. That's why a growing number of people are turning to professional image consultants.

1.2.1 Overview of the Career

An image consultant is a professional who advises individuals and companies about their image. According to the Association of Image Consultants International (AICI), the world's leading professional organization for image consultants, "An image consultant specializes in visual appearance, verbal and nonverbal communication."

Types of Services

There are a wide variety of image consulting services you can offer to women, men, and companies. According to AICI:

> An image consultant counsels individual and corporate clients on appearance, behavior and communication skills through individual consultations, coaching, presentations, seminars and workshops.

While consultations and coaching are similar, the former typically involves giving advice about what to do, or actually doing something for the client (e.g. organizing their closet or shopping for new clothes), while coaching may involve teaching or working with the client as they learn a new skill. For example, during a makeup consultation, you might tell the client what makeup they should wear, while if you are coaching the client, you might show them how to actually apply makeup. Many image consultants provide both consulting and coaching. Examples of the specific types of services that you might offer during consultations or coaching sessions include:

- *Image Analysis or Makeover Consulting:* giving the client feedback on the overall image they are projecting and helping them develop a new image

- *Wardrobe Analysis or Fashion Styling:* reviewing the client's current wardrobe, determining what should be discarded or purchased, and coordinating outfits

- *Color Analysis:* advising the client which colors they should wear

- *Makeup Analysis:* you can also coach or consult on other specific aspects of physical appearance such as skin care, hairstyle, accessorizing, etc.

- *Vocal Communication:* coaching or consulting on voice, grammar, vocabulary, etc.

- *Non-Verbal Communication:* body language such as gestures, posture, eye contact, etc.

- *Etiquette Consulting:* business etiquette, social graces, dining

- *Closet Organizing:* may be part of a wardrobe analysis

- *Personal Shopping:* buying clothing or other items for the client

In addition to advising or coaching clients themselves, most image consultants have a network of strategic partners they can refer clients to, such as hair stylists, makeup artists, dieticians, dentists, personal trainers, plastic surgeons, and voice coaches.

Image consultants are also hired to offer presentations, seminars, workshops, or training programs (the terms are often used inter-changeably) on topics related to image. A company may hire you to give presentations on topics such as: dressing professionally (including dos and don'ts for casual Fridays), telephone etiquette for customer service staff, communication skills for new supervisors, and other business topics. Likewise, a college or government agency might hire you to present seminars for job-hunters on how to dress for interviews.

Types of Clients

People are most likely to want or need a new image when they are preparing to make a change in their life, such as applying for a job or seeking a promotion. And, of course, there are people who may simply feel it's time to change their image.

As an image consultant, you can give these people advice on physical appearance, communication skills, and behaviors that will help them achieve their goal — whether it is to get a new job, to make a good impression, or simply to feel good about themselves.

You may decide to work with a particular type of client, or choose to provide a variety of services to many different clients. While many individuals hire image consultants themselves, you may also be hired by corporations or organizations to consult with individual staff members. For example, a company might hire you to help a new supervisor learn how to command respect through effective verbal communication, or to coach a senior executive on how to make a good impression during television interviews. Many corporations also hire image consultants to provide training programs for groups of employees.

In addition to the types of clients described above, some image consultants specialize in working with particular types of individuals, like:

- Beauty pageant contestants

- Cancer survivors

- Lawyers and their clients

- Politicians

- Singles seeking a mate

- Spouses of recently promoted executives

- Television personalities

- Transvestites and transsexuals

As you can see, virtually anyone who wants help with their image is a prospective client for an image consultant. Anna Soo Wildermuth, AICI, CIM, principal of Personal Images Inc., served as President of the Association of Image Consultants International. She says:

"Today, image professionals are beginning to be on the same level as interior designers. Anyone who wants to look their best and be appropriate will now hire an image consultant."

But it hasn't always been this way. In the 1980s, image consultants were typically hired only by politicians, media personalities, and other high profile individuals in the public eye.

1.2.2   Growth of the Industry

While image has been important throughout much of human history (see the box on the next page for some milestones), image consulting is a relatively new industry.

John T. Molloy is believed to be America's pioneer image consultant. His bestselling 1975 book, *Dress for Success*, introduced to the public the idea that dressing professionally leads to greater success in the corporate world. Molloy and his book received widespread media coverage. Over the next few years, an increasing number of people with a knack for helping others look their best began to offer professional image consulting services.

For the past two decades, the industry has been strong. In *The Best Home Businesses for the 90s*, authors Paul and Sarah Edwards reported, "Image Consulting has grown from being virtually unknown 15 years ago to a $130 million-year business at the start of this decade." They accurately predicted, "In the nineties image consultants will undoubtedly expand still further."

Today the industry is booming. The exact number of image consultants is not known because most people working in the industry are self-employed and do not belong to a professional association. However, Marion Gellatly, President of the Association of Image Consultants International (AICI), estimates over 1,500 image consultants nationwide (compared with 1,000 in 2004) are reaping the benefits of helping people look their best while earning excellent incomes.

Why the Industry is Booming

In 1972, a study by Thomas Cash found that 23 percent of U.S. women were dissatisfied with their overall appearance. A generation later, the number of women dissatisfied with their appearance had more than doubled to 48 percent. What this means for you is a huge market of people who could use your services.

Some Image Milestones

1363   England issues a law restricting the amount of money the working class can spend on clothing, and prohibiting them from wearing silk and other precious textiles.

1431   Joan of Arc is executed in France. The charges against her include committing heresy by wearing men's clothing.

1895   *The Gentlewoman's Book of Dress*, written by Mrs. Douglas, is widely read by fashionable women of the time.

1963   Mary Kay Ash establishes Mary Kay Inc., paving the way for women to enter the workforce as beauty consultants.

1975   John T. Molloy's *Dress for Success* is published.

1983   Professional associations for image consultants (Association of Fashion & Image Consultants and Association of Image Consultants) are formed on the East and West coasts, respectively. In 1990 the two groups merge to form AICI.

2011   Millions of people tune in each week to watch reality TV shows featuring image makeovers such as *What Not to Wear*. Image consulting is hotter than ever before.

Much of this can be attributed to aging baby boomers. Ranging in age from about 42 to 61 (about 30 percent of the U.S. population), most are not content to grow old looking like their parents. Instead, many are taking action. Diet books continue to top bestseller lists, women's magazines are filled with fashion and beauty advice, and consumers are increasingly turning to experts who can help them look better.

According to the American Society of Plastic Surgeons, people between the ages of 40 and 54 had 47% of all cosmetic procedures in 2009, while those over 55 had 26%. From 2000 to 2009, total cosmetic procedures increased by 69%.

And it is not just women who want to improve their looks. About 9 percent of all procedures in 2009 were performed on men, with liposuction, nose reshaping, cosmetic eyelid surgery, male breast reduction and hair transplantation among the most popular procedures.

While baby boomers form the largest market for image services, they have set the standard for all generations. In the fast-paced 21st century, with the image-conscious baby boomers, stylish Generations X and Y and very active seniors, looking good is a growing phenomenon that is here to stay.

As an image consultant, you can help people look their best, while enjoying a career that offers you a tremendous number of benefits.

1.2.3   Benefits of an Image Consulting Career

There are many reasons why image consulting is a fabulous career choice. The advantages of an image consulting career include:

Booming Industry

Image is a multi-billion dollar a year industry. Opportunities for image consultants are increasing every year, with plenty of opportunities for newcomers. See section 1.2.2 to learn why this industry is so hot.

High Income Potential

Image consultants typically earn at least $50 per hour, while those who offer corporate training programs can earn up to thousands of dollars per day. Some of the image consultants you'll read about in this guide earn up to $200,000 per year due to their skills in corporate training and executive coaching.

Flexibility and Freedom

Image consultants can also enjoy the flexibility of working full-time or part-time — and even out of the comfort of their homes. True, they must be ready to go and tend to the busy people who use their customized services, but they often have quite a bit of leeway. While you may decide to sometimes work evening or weekend hours to accommodate clients, you can take time off whenever you want.

Exciting Job with Opportunities to Learn

Image consulting is a fun and exciting career that offers opportunities to learn and grow. Susan M. Fignar, President of Chicago-based image consulting firm Pur*Sue, started out providing overall appearance one-on-one consultations. Over the past two decades, she has experienced both personal and professional growth. She explains:

> "I have taken a lot of what I have learned and developed and turned it into an image management and executive coaching series focusing a lot on communication skills, leadership, team building, and interpersonal communication skills."

As an image consultant, the sky is the limit for you, too.

Opportunity to Build Great Relationships

If you love working with people, image consulting is an ideal career choice. Becoming an image consultant is a way to make lasting connections with clients, strategic partners, and other image consultants. Catherine Graham Bell, AICI, CIP, of Prime Impressions in Kingston, Ontario, describes meeting with other professional image consultants:

> "At the first AICI meeting that I attended, there was an immediate warmth and openness that I experienced. We call on each other for help with new questions and situations that arise, we share our research and refer clients to one another."

Making a Difference

Image consultants, like the ones you will read about in this guide, will tell you that one of the best rewards of being in the business is the positive change they make in their clients' lives. Bell says:

> "It is exciting to see people gaining confidence, realizing that they actually possess the skills necessary to move forward, and developing new techniques to open new doors in their careers and personal lives."

You Can Start Now

Unlike some other careers, image consulting is a profession you can get started in immediately, regardless of your educational history or current financial situation.

While many image consultants have various degrees, you can become an image consultant without a formal education. Of course, as Karen Brunger, of International Image Institute in Toronto, Ontario, points out, "Some advanced education is beneficial. The higher your education, the more marketable you can be as an image consultant." While no degree is necessary, in this guide you will learn ways to help you quickly acquire education and credentials.

If you have image consultant know-how but don't yet have a huge bank account, you can start your own image consulting business at home with little or no upfront expenses. If you have access to transportation and a telephone, you have the basics to get started. Add some marketing materials, such as a good website, and you will be ready to start selling your services.

If any of these benefits sound good to you, read on to discover the steps to start becoming an image consultant.

1.3 Inside This Guide

The *FabJob Guide to Become an Image Consultant* will take you step-by-step through getting started and succeeding as an image consultant. These steps, and the chapters they appear in, are as follows:

Chapter 2 ("Areas of Expertise") covers the major areas that image consultants work in. In this chapter you will get an introduction to visual appearance, communication, and behavior. This chapter also includes information about what image consultants need to know about corporate image.

In Chapter 3 ("How to Do Consultations") you will learn how image consultants apply their knowledge and expertise. This chapter has information about how to consult with individuals and corporations, and how to find and work with strategic partners.

Chapter 4 ("Developing Your Skills") describes how to prepare yourself to become an image consultant. Here you will discover the skills clients are looking for, and read about ways to learn image consulting through volunteer experience, educational programs, and work experience in the image industry.

Chapter 5 ("Starting an Image Consulting Business") gives practical information on what you need to do to get started, including how to set up your office, choose a business name, and set your fees.

In Chapter 6 ("Getting Clients") you will learn about the types of people that are most likely to hire image consultants. Then you will find practical advice on how to market yourself to get individuals and corporate clients to hire you.

The book concludes with stories of several successful image consultants, plus a list of helpful resources for learning more about all aspects of the career.

When you are finished with this guide you will know what steps to take next and where to go from there. By applying what you learn here, it's just a matter of time before you'll be where you want to be... in an exciting career as an Image Consultant!

2. Areas of Expertise

People hire image consultants because they want an expert to help them develop their image. In this chapter you will learn about major areas that many image consultants become experts in.

Of course, just reading this chapter alone will not make you an expert. That will come with further experience and knowledge. If you have no previous experience in the areas covered in this chapter, you might think of it as an introductory course in "Image Consulting 101." It is packed with helpful tips and knowledge generously shared by successful professional image consultants and covers three key areas:

1. visual appearance

2. communication and behavior

3. corporate image

While it is very helpful to have basic knowledge of each area, if you are like many image consultants, you will probably choose to specialize in working with particular types of clients and develop your expertise in specific areas further. Elsewhere in this guide you will find resources for learning more about the specific areas that interest you. In Chapter 3 you will learn how to apply your knowledge and expertise when working with clients.

> **TIP:** Different image consultants use different systems. For example, some identify a client's "season" to help them find the best colors to wear, while others don't use seasons. In this guide we present information on a variety of systems, along with resources for learning more, to help you develop your own unique approach to image consulting.

2.1 Visual Appearance

"You only get one chance to make a first impression."

As an image consultant, you will help clients make a great first impression. You will help them show the world who they really are, or convey the image they want the world to see. It begins with personal style and includes specific aspects of appearance from wardrobe to grooming.

2.1.1 Personal Style

Style is the expression of someone's personality through their appearance. There is no single "best" style. If there were, we could simply give you a list of dos and don'ts that would apply in all circumstances. Everyone would dress alike, and there would be no need for image consultants. But no single look is right for all people in all situations.

Even when people work in the same profession, they may express their unique personality through their style. We can most easily see this in the field of popular music. From Cher to Gwen Stefani, and from Elvis to Sean Jean Combs (also known as P. Diddy), we see celebrities with many unique fashion styles.

Most of your clients will probably not want to look so distinctive, but chances are they will have one or more styles that "fit" better than others. By helping your clients find their own style, you will help them express what's natural to them. What feels best often looks best. Someone who feels comfortable and confident in what they are wearing can create a better impression than someone who is well dressed, but feels uncomfortable and moves stiffly.

Women's Styles

Georgia Donovan, an author, speaker and fashion consultant known as The Clothes Doctor, describes a number of basic styles to help you identify your client's look. (Note that styles can overlap.) For each style we have included examples of celebrities (both legendary and current) that fit that style.

Classic

The classic look never goes out of style. A woman fitting this profile uses a neutral palette for makeup, but has defined cheekbones, eyes dressed with mascara, and defined brows. Hair is typically in a chignon or pulled back. Celebrities who fit this profile best include Sophia Loren and Gwyneth Paltrow.

Dramatic

Dramatic people are self-confident and flamboyant. They wear defined eye makeup, and use their face as a palette like an artist beautifies a canvas. The dramatic hairstyle, such as a chignon, is not typically worn every day. They typically wear black heels and black slacks. Celebrities that fit this profile best include Elizabeth Taylor, Beyonce, and Victoria Beckham.

Elegant

Elegant women fill the room with their presence. Their look is polished and classic, with makeup based on a neutral palette. Their lip color and eye makeup is soft, but their lashes are dramatic. An elegant woman may wear a black Armani suit, black turtleneck, and black slacks. Celebrities that fit this profile best include Grace Kelly and Katie Holmes.

Natural

Women with this style have a wholesome look. They wear minimal makeup, with maybe just a touch of lipstick or mascara. Their clothing is comfortable and cozy. They style their hair simply, maybe pulled back in a ponytail or loosely laying on their shoulders. Celebrities who fit this style best include Michelle Pfeiffer and Cameron Diaz.

Romantic

Romantics wear romantic frilly, feminine clothing, often with satin. They wear soft makeup, with pink and lavender colors. Celebrities like Jennifer Love Hewitt fit this profile.

Sporty

When a woman with sporty-chic style gets dressed, she doesn't invest much time or thought, but still manages to look fabulous. They may wear something such as a grey pair of trousers with loafers, a turtleneck sweater, and a jacket. Their hair is short or simply styled. Women who define this style include Katharine Hepburn and Jennifer Garner.

Men's Styles

According to Certified Image Professional Maureen Costello of Image Launch in Chicago, Illinois, the following different styles are good examples of personal styles for your male clients:

Classic

This is a man who dresses in a traditional and classic way and has the air of a gentleman. Celebrities with this style include George Clooney and former British Prime Minister Tony Blair.

Dramatic

This is a man who is confident, independent, and likes to get noticed. A peacock of a man. Celebrities with this style include Mick Jagger and Johnny Depp.

Elegant

This is a man of grace, mystery, and extremely fine taste — a man of discrimination and distinction. Celebrities with this style include NBC news anchor Brian Williams and fictional superspy James Bond.

Natural

This is a man who is at ease in many situations. He feels like a good friend, very genuine and sincere. Celebrities with this style include Matt Damon and Apple Computer CEO Steve Jobs.

Romantic/Alluring

This is a man with sex appeal. Fabio was legendary for this look. Current celebrities with this style include George Clooney, Brad Pitt and Leonardo DeCaprio.

Sporty/Rustic

This is a man close to the earth, who likes the outdoors and enjoys sports and nature. Famous personalities that reflect this style include the Marlboro Man and Indiana Jones.

2.1.2 Body

As an image consultant, you will learn to see body flaws as challenges, and help your clients either fix their flaws or hide them. To understand what can be fixed, it helps to know that people are born with one of three body types:

Ectomorph	Long and lean (such as Nicole Kidman and Johnny Depp)
Mesomorph	Muscular and athletic (such as Madonna and Arnold Schwarzenegger)
Endomorph	Round and prone to putting on weight (such as Rosie O'Donnell and Robin Williams)

If someone is an endomorph, no exercise plan will ever make them look like Nicole Kidman. However, almost any body can look better.

Fixing Body Flaws

If you are working with clients who are dissatisfied with their bodies, you may refer them to another professional. For example, if you are working with an overweight client who isn't getting promoted at work and feels their weight is contributing to the problem, you could refer them to a cosmetic surgeon, personal trainer, and dietician. You will find information on working with these and other types of professionals (also known as "strategic partners") in section 3.7.

However, in most cases, clients will want you to assist them in looking their best with the body they have now.

Know What You're Working With

To help your client choose the best clothing for their body, start by determining their size and shape. During a client consultation, you will take a variety of body measurements (see chapter 3 for tips on doing client consultations). Basic body shapes include the following:

Triangular	Hips are larger than shoulders
Inverted Triangular	Shoulders are larger than hips
Rectangular	Balanced hips and shoulders, lean
Apple-shaped	Balanced hips and shoulders, round
Hourglass	This body type on women is also called shapely (an example is Marilyn Monroe)

In addition to shape, height is also a consideration. Different clothing manufacturers have different height guidelines, but here is one you may want to use as a starting point for your female clients:

- Petite (Under 5'3")
- Medium height (5'3"–5'7")
- Tall (above 5'7")

For men, Tall may be defined as more than 6'2", while Big may be 6'2" or shorter with a waist measurement equal to or bigger than the chest.

From Flaws to Fabulous

"Once my client understands her figure type, how to balance her body, and hide figure challenges, shopping becomes easier. With the help of an image consultant, the client does not take items into the fitting room only to be discouraged by how they look and feel. Wardrobe choices are defined. The overwhelming feeling when walking into a department store is gone. Getting dressed for any occasion is no longer overwhelming, it is fun."

— *Lori B. Johnson,*
Your Best Image Personal Image Development

There are many ways to help clients look their best, no matter what their body type or shape. Here are a selection of tips from several image consultants.

According to Karen Brunger of the International Image Institute, the image consultant can consider the height of her client and then follow these guidelines:

Short	Choose the shortest, narrowest, smallest styles.
Average	Choose medium or classic styles.
Tall	Choose the longest, widest styles.

Other tips based on height include:

Short	Wear monochromatic colors to give the illusion of one long line.
Tall	Shop for clothes that fit your proportions. Buying an item of clothing whose hem just fits may emphasize how small that item really is.

Tips for Women

Here's how Catherine Graham Bell of Prime Impressions helps her female clients look better:

Big Bosom	*Good choices:* Use more detail on the lower part of the body — a print or fuller skirt. A minimizer bra under a soft silk sweater is a nice choice. V-necklines and shoulder pads slenderize the bust-line. *Bad choices:* Very tight T-shirts. Stay clear of pockets and details in the bust area.
Flabby Arms	*Good choices:* Bracelet length sleeves on sweaters and blouses. *Bad choices:* Sleeveless tops or sweaters.
Thick Waist	*Good choices:* Sweaters or T-shirts that come about 4" below the waist worn over a skirt or slacks. Loose fitting garments. *Bad choices:* Anything tucked in with a large wide belt.

Big Ankles	*Good choices:* Long skirts with a slit at the side. *Bad choices*: Cropped pants, especially the tight Capri style that ends just below the knee.
Big Buttocks	*Good choices:* Long, flowing skirts or slacks with a looser leg shape. *Bad choices:* Short skirts, long sweaters pulled over the buttocks.

Tips for Men

Maureen Costello of Image Launch provides these tips that you can recommend for helping men with body "flaws" look their personal best:

Short neck	Wear a V-neck shirt or a collared shirt with a shorter collar stand (where the collar is attached).
Long neck	Wear a turtleneck or a long pointed collared shirt.
Broad shoulders	Wear a softer shouldered (raglan) jacket that falls over the shoulder line.
Broad hips	Wear a pleated pant and cuffed pant hem.
Long arms	Wear French cuffs.
Small body frame	Wear a bow tie and a three-button jacket.
Large belly	Stay clear of knit shirts. Instead, stay with woven shirts and a longer tie to the belt buckle.
Wide feet	Wear a square box toe shoe with a side buckle (monk-strap shoe).

Knowing your client's body – as well as their personal style – will go a long way to helping you advise them on their wardrobe. But there are a number of other things to know about wardrobe.

2.1.3   Wardrobe

"Recognizing that each woman is unique, I help them enrich their lives and teach that while clothes are a necessity, fashion can be joyful and fun... and that what you wear speaks volumes about who you are."

— *Georgia Donovan,*
Fashion Consultant

When an image consultant provides a wardrobe service, the client can look forward to a new and improved organized closet, with less clothing but more outfits to wear. As Lori B. Johnson, certified image consultant and owner of Your Best Image Personal Image Development, notes, "Everything in the wardrobe matches. Coordinating wardrobe pieces and adding accessories and makeup are easy."

Before you offer this service to your clients, learn the basics below on creating an ideal wardrobe.

Key Elements

Like other areas of image consulting, different consultants have different opinions about which wardrobe items are essential. Below you will find sample lists for both men and women. Again, consider these lists to be a starting point for developing your own recommendations. Your client's exact needs will depend on a number of factors, including whether or not their workplace requires business dress or business casual (see section 2.3.3 for a discussion of business casual).

Wardrobe Basics for Women

Marjorie Brody, of Brody Communications, Inc., recommends the following basic business wardrobe for women:

- Black or gray suit
- Dark burgundy or navy suit
- Contrasting jacket and skirt
- Two-piece dress
- Several white, off-white blouses
- Solid color blouse; may be pastel
- One pair gold, one pair silver earrings
- Scarves that pick up colors from the suits
- Black pumps; navy or taupe pumps
- Neutral or taupe hosiery
- Black leather handbag

- All weather coat

- Black, brown, or burgundy briefcase

According to Constance C. R. White, author of *Style Noir*, every woman needs these key elements in her wardrobe:

- One trouser suit

- A jacket and skirt that work together

- A blouse

- A knit top

- A basic cotton man's T-shirt

- A pair of jeans

- A short black evening dress

- A glossy raincoat of water-repellent micro fiber

- A pair of black pumps — with medium or low heels

- Three pairs of stockings, one pair of trouser socks

- A large silk scarf

- A black leather or nylon handbag — medium size

- A small evening bag

Wardrobe Basics for Men

Louise Elerding, of Fashion Feng Shui International, recommends the following basics:

- Basic solid color suit

- Subtle pattern suit

- Blazer

- Two pairs of trousers

- Ten long-sleeved dress shirts

- Ten silk ties

- Two pairs of leather shoes

- Belt

- Twelve pairs of over-the-calf socks

- All-weather coat

- Briefcase

According to Brody, basic business wardrobe options for men are:

- Solid-color navy and gray suits (one each color)

- Five pairs black socks, two pairs navy socks

- Pinstriped navy suit, same in gray

- Four burgundy/red print or striped silk ties, two patterned silk ties

- Charcoal-gray suit

- Two navy/mauve ties

- Navy sport coat with gray trousers

- One black leather belt

- Six white cotton shirts

- A blue or pinstriped shirt

- Leather briefcase

- One pair black slip-on shoes, one pair black lace-up shoes

As mentioned, your clients' specific needs will vary based on a number of factors including their personal style and occupation. In section 3.3 you will learn how to do a wardrobe analysis for a client.

Accessories

Remember to include accessories when doing wardrobe consultations. Here are some tips to keep in mind.

- By adding a necklace or colorful scarf, you can change the entire look of an outfit.

- Switch your eyeglasses with your outfits. Not all eyeglasses are meant to be worn with all outfits. "It can either compete with or complement your overall look," points out image consultant Donna Panko, of Professional Skill Builders, Inc. Don't forget about sunglasses as an option.

- It doesn't have to cost a million dollars to make you look like a million. Buy costume jewelry if it is of good quality and not easily detected as faux. You can mix and match faux with the real deal.

- When you think accessories, sometimes less is more. Don't super size it. If the earrings are too big and if the necklace is too chunky, leave them at the store. Accessories should show off who you are, not hide you.

- Gold and silver can be worn together as long as the lines are similar. Too much matching can lead to overkill.

The Color of Clothes

Color has a psychological impact on the person viewing it. Catherine Graham Bell recommends following these color codes in the corporate world. (This information is also applicable for casual dress.)

- Red commands power and energy. If a client has a presentation to give, or works in sales, red is an excellent color to wear. If the client is shy, red is a good choice, unless the client is not comfortable wearing this energetic color.

- Yellow conveys youthfulness. An unseasoned or younger client looks more polished, professional, and credible in yellow.

- Green radiates harmony and calmness, and demonstrates credibility. Olive green is good for men in meetings, but women need to be careful when wearing it, as it can make them look drab.

- Blue expresses serenity, peace, and introspection, in a variety of shades. A navy blue suit is the most acceptable to wear. Different hues of blue can also work and can add trust and credibility to your client's image. It looks good on television, too.

- Purple expresses power and creativity. It's good for business meetings or presentations.

- Pink is a feminine color, not as powerful as red. Pink is not a good color for television presentations.

- Orange conveys a confident and outgoing nature. Depending on the client's skin color, orange may not work. People with reddish and auburn hair can usually wear orange or coral, while blondes typically cannot wear orange.

- Brown creates a comfortable and practical feeling in the onlooker and wearer. For the most part, this color is acceptable any time. However, although men often wear brown suits, blue creates a better impression and gets better results in business.

- Black denotes creativity. Many city people wear black as a fashion statement, but black clothing can create a washed-out look in a client with fair skin or hair. It's fine for retail, architectural firms and advertising agencies.

In addition to the color of clothing, image consultants work with their client's skin tones and hair colors.

2.1.4   Color Analysis

Color analysis is a procedure based on the theory that everyone has a dominant color in their skin that is either a cool color (blue tones) or a warm one (golden tones). By identifying that color, you can plan complementary colors for clothing that will flatter the client's skin tones. Image consultants may give clients color palettes or color keys to show them which colors look best.

"Knowing your clients' personal color key will enhance their facial features, maximize their wardrobe dollars, heighten their level of image confidence, and attract success," says personal appearance coach Louise Elerding.

Lori B. Johnson notes, "Many of my clients have expressed how much easier wardrobe, accessory and makeup coordination is now that they have had their color analysis done and are following the guidelines I leave with them." Before working with her, one of Johnson's clients had run for political office twice, losing both elections. She and the client worked together to improve his image, which included changing the colors he was wearing. He won the next election.

Warm and Cool Colors

According to Louise Elerding, cool and warm tones can be found in skin color, eye color, and hair color as listed below. Evaluate your client by seeing which colors dominate overall.

> **NOTE:** This section gives general information about colors. For step-by-step advice on how to do a color analysis for a client (including the tools you will need), see section 3.2.2.

Skin Tone

- If your client's skin tone is dominantly pink, white, neutral beige, olive or blue-black, it is a cool tone.

- If your client's skin tone is ivory, peachy, reddish, golden beige, golden-black, golden-bronze, it is a warm tone.

Eye Color

- Cool-colored eyes are cool dark brown, gray-blue, gray-green, blue, hazels (brown and green mixes with some gray effects), gray, soft brown, and taupe.

- Warm-colored eyes are golden-brown, rich dark brown, warm hazels (combinations of gold, moss greens, browns, yellows), greens, aqua, clear blue, and light golden brown.

Hair Color

- Cool hair has either a blue base or an ash base to it, including: blue-black, medium to dark brown, gray, salt and pepper, platinum, ash blonde, ash brown, cool dark brown.

- Warm hair colors include: red, auburn, chestnut, copper, golden brown, golden blonde, yellow-blonde, golden gray, strawberry blonde.

Seasons

Once you know if your client is a cool or warm color, you can determine their season. The descriptions below provide general guideslines for the seasons. Examples of qualities and colors were provided by Karen Brunger. Concepts for each season, additional colors, and comments in quotation marks are from the online encyclopedia *Wikipedia*. You can find more information about color analysis at sites such as **www.color mebeautiful.com**.

> **TIP:** A warm or cool personality can also provide clues to colors and seasons. Image consultant Teresa Lopuchin of Self Image notes that springs are usually bubbly people, unlike summers who are usually quieter and more to themselves.

Winter

"The concept is a bright winter day with snow on the ground, very stark and dramatic," notes *Wikipedia*. "Many African and Asian people are winters, as are most Caucasians with very pale skin, dark hair, and strongly colored eyes."

Appearance	Dark hair or grey hair, cool skin tone and eye color
Qualities	Striking, dramatic, sophisticated, distinctive, bold
Celebrities	Oprah Winfrey, Demi Moore, Eva Longoria, Richard Gere
Good colors	White, charcoal, black, true red, lemon yellow, hot pink, emerald

Spring

The concept is the bright colors of a sunny spring, such as you might see in a blossoming garden. Springs should wear bright colors and "avoid dark or muted colors, and high-contrast black and white."

Appearance	Light hair, warm skin tone and eye color
Qualities	Glowing, vivacious, cheerful, friendly, youthful
Celebrities	Kate Hudson, Cameron Diaz, Matt Damon
Good colors	Ivory, coral, bright turquoise, warm pink, coral red, teal

Summer

The concept is "flowers seen through a summer haze." Colors are soft, misty, and understated.

Appearance   Light hair, cool skin tone and eye color

Qualities   Soft, gentle, sincere, refined, peaceful

Celebrities   Reese Witherspoon, Gwyneth Paltrow, Leonardo Di-Caprio

Good colors   Soft white, taupe, mauve, rose, ocean green, powder blue, charcoal

Autumn

The concept is the colors of an autumn day in the woods. Autumns look best in rich, earthy tones.

Appearance   Dark hair, warm skin tone and eye color

Qualities   Natural, strong, decisive, elegant, mature

Celebrities   Julia Roberts, Jennifer Lopez, Jim Carrey

Good colors   Eggshell, oatmeal, cocoa, olive, khaki, golden brown, burnt orange

2.1.5   Makeup and Skin Care

Today's cosmetics take getting dressed to a whole new level. You'll show your clients how to reach these levels without overdoing it.

Some image consultants refer to a circle of makeup consultants for makeovers and advice. (See section 3.7 for information on finding these "strategic partners.") Karen Brunger prefers working with makeup artists that she has trained because she knows that they share the same vision. Another option, as mentioned during the introductory chapter, is to do the client's makeup yourself.

Advising Clients About Makeup

"The primary concern on applying makeup is color. You have to use colors that are going to work with your undertones. You don't want to put something on that's going to fight with those," explains certified color and image professional Charli Mace of Color Tools. How do you know what colors are best for your client? "I stay with neutrals for the base palette of makeup," she adds.

In addition, "Balance, proportion, eye shape and position, and bone structure are all considered," adds Lori B. Johnson. "We discuss facial contouring and how to minimize flaws and play up best features. I show simple techniques to make the most of the eyes, mouth, cheekbones, etc. I can give them a face-lift without any invasive procedure."

However, before you show your client how to apply makeup, you need to know what look you'll be aiming for. According to Mace, there are four basic images that you need to know. In section 3.1.3 you will find questions you can ask your client to help determine their makeup needs and the image they're looking for.

Corporate	Understated, a neutral palette, simple, no maintenance
Casual	Minimal, not a lot of eye makeup: a moisturizing foundation, a little eyeliner, and lip color
Creative/Trendy	Mostly for the younger set (under 30)
Nightlife	Shimmery and sultry

In addition to showing your client how to apply makeup, you can recommend products to help them achieve a particular look. There are at least ten makeup tools that every woman should have in her kit. In the pages that follow you will get advice on what you can say to your clients about these products:

1. Foundation

2. Concealer

3. Face powder

4. Eyeshadow

5. Eyeliner

6. Brow filler

7. Mascara

8. Blusher

9. Lip Color/Gloss

10. Bronzer/Highlighter

Foundation

Foundation gives you an even canvas for every other color to lie on. Foundation can be applied with a foundation brush, sponge, or fingertips. Unlike the foundations of yesteryear, which were cakey in feel and not the most flattering look for skin, today's foundations can give a sheer, luminous glow.

There are several different types of foundation on the market today so you can choose one that suits your skin type. Here's a brief overview:

- Sheer foundation is a natural-looking, liquid foundation that gives a barely there feel.

- Cream foundation is smooth. It gives enough coverage to fill in wrinkles. Stick foundation is a solid cream that comes packaged in a swivel stick for easy application.

- Matte foundation has the most coverage, but, if too much is applied, can look like powder sugar on top of a funnel cake.

- Tinted moisturizers are the sheerest foundations. They are a combination of sheer foundation and facial moisturizer. They are great for summer when you don't want to wear a lot of makeup.

- Oil-free foundation is great for skin that is oily and/or acne-prone.

- Light-reflecting foundation is a newer foundation that has tiny spheres that bounce light off of the face giving the face a dewy appearance.

- Skin-tone adapting foundation is the newest entry into the foundation category. It is said to match any skin tone so finding one to perfectly match your own is foolproof.

A color off the shelf may not match someone perfectly, so you can blend colors. Aim to match the color of the jaw line.

Concealer

Whether you have dark circles, blemishes, age spots, or another imperfection, the right concealer can cover it up. Concealer is available in a variety of skin tones (match the lightest color of your skin), as well as in pale yellow (for counterbalancing pinkish skin tones), pale lilac (for counterbalancing rosy skin tones), pale green (for counterbalancing reddish skin tones) and in white (for highlighting areas of the face).

Concealers come in liquid, stick, pot, cream, and wand form for various applications. Apply under foundation or, if used alone, set it with a powder.

Face Powder

Face powder is used to set makeup and hold it in place. During the day, it is typically used to touch up makeup.

Powder comes pressed in cakes, enclosed in small compacts, and loose in containers. Pressed powder is mainly useful for touch-ups during the day (it contains oil, so can contribute to the shine it is supposed to fix), while loose powder is used for setting a makeup application when it is complete. Loose powder is applied with a wide, fat brush.

Powder comes in a variety of colors to match foundations and in a translucent shade, which can be used with all colors of makeup. Translucent powder is best for people with more flawless skin.

Eye Shadow

Eye shadow is available in powder, cream, and wide pencil form. It is applied with an applicator (in the case of powders or creams) or directly from the tip of the pencil and comes in virtually every color and finish, from matte to frosted (shiny).

Eye shadow can either be worn as a bold color or a natural hue to bring attention to the eyes. To make an eye appear larger, put light colors on the lid, followed with a darker color by the crease up toward the brow. You can highlight the brow with a lighter color.

Eyeliner

Eyeliner makes eyes look more dramatic. A thin line of black or deep brown is best during the day. Save colored, thick, or smudged/smoked liner for nighttime affairs.

To make an eye look wider, start on the inside corner of the eye and bring the eyeliner around. To make an eye look larger, make the outside of the eyeliner line a little thicker than the inside line. Underneath the eye, stay thin, stay in the lashes, and don't bring it any closer to the center than the middle of the eye or it closes the eye up.

Mascara

Mascara is applied to the eyelashes to create thicker lashes and a more defined eye. It comes in a variety of colors, but black or brown is appropriate for most circumstances. If you have short lashes, opt for a lengthening or curling mascara. If you have thin, sparse lashes, look for thickening mascara.

> **TIP:** No matter how much you love it, toss your mascara after three months. Bacteria can form on the brush, causing an eye infection.

Brow Filler

If your client has over-plucked or sparse brows, introduce them to a brow pencil or brow putty. When using a pencil, you want to stay close to the natural color of the eyebrow. Use a sharp pencil to bring the line to the outside, and use a powder eye shadow to fill in the brow.

As a guideline, use a pencil: put it in front of your lip, across the side of your nose, straight up to your eye and that is about where the natural arch should be. Pluck only the most visible strays.

Blusher

Blusher is used to give a warm, healthy flush to cheeks and is available as a powder, cream, or gel. Powder blusher is brushed onto the cheeks with a wide brush and is usually applied after the foundation and powder are already in place. Cream and gel blusher (sometimes called rouge) is applied on top of the foundation but before the powder.

Dab it with the fingers in spots along the cheeks (following the line of the cheekbone) and blend it in with the fingertips or with a cosmetic sponge.

Generally speaking, pink blusher looks best on blondes, and rose or brownish blusher looks best on dark haired clients. Red-haired clients should use peach-toned blusher.

Lip Color and Lip Gloss

Lip color is available as lipstick, cream, or lip pencils and comes in a wide range of colors from palest whites and pinks to deepest reds and browns. It is applied following the natural contours of the lips or can be applied beyond the natural lips to emphasize or enhance the natural lip shape.

For a business meeting, opt for a lip color that will give just enough shine along with a healthy amount of color. Use a lip liner (in a tone slightly darker than your lipstick) before you put your lipstick on.

Lip gloss is a shiny, clear, or tinted product meant to add a sheen and sparkle to the lips after (or instead of) the application of lip color. It's also available with glitter.

Bronzer/Highlighter

A tanned look is not just for summer. Bronzers and bronze-toned blushers are used year round to give skin a healthy glow. Use a bronzer on cheeks, forehead, chin, and nose, alone or under your blusher, for healthy, warm toned skin.

Makeup For Men

Most of your male clients will probably not want to wear any kind of makeup. However, you may find that some of your male clients will consider a bronzer if they want to appear tanned, while others may need makeup for television appearances.

Here are some tips on makeup for men from the *FabJob Guide to Become a Television Reporter*, by Rebecca Coates Nee. This advice is also useful for your clients who will be interviewed on television, such as executives, speakers, authors, politicians, and celebrities.

"Yes, it's true: men wear makeup in TV news. The main reason is the lights, which can make your face shiny and pale. It's best to find a powdered foundation that's not too oily, so it doesn't clog up your pores. Be sure to pick a color that matches your skin tone. Use a make-up sponge to blend it in around your jaw. If it's the right color, you won't have a visible makeup line. You may need to take extra care to cover your beard.

TIP: The most popular brands used by on-air talent in television are MAC, Clinique and Merle Norman. Their foundations provide good coverage without being too oily."

Skin Care

Both your male and female clients can benefit from proper skin care. While you can refer clients with serious skin problems to a professional dermatologist or cosmetic surgeon (see section 3.7), in many cases, you can offer advice on how to enhance their skin.

Here are seven skin savers from dermatologist Dr. Kahlil Khatri, who provides his personal day-to-day strategies to avoid getting that sun-damaged "lizard" look in the book *Doctors' Orders: What 101 Doctors Do to Stay Healthy*, by Cal Orey. Give this list to both your male and female clients — and tell them these are golden rules to follow:

- Avoid sun exposure. Ultraviolet light (UV) rays can cause premature aging. Sunscreen 15 SPF for daily use is fine.

- Take warm, quick showers. Do not take a long, hot shower. It can dry your skin. Use lukewarm water instead.

- Avoid smoking, which causes aging around the mouth and eyes.

- Wear UV-protective eyeglasses. When there is bright light you will squint, and that will cause lines on your forehead and around your eyes.

- Exercise. Getting a move on – such as walking outdoors or on the indoor treadmill – can increase blood flow, which can give you that healthy glow.

- Eat right. The saying "You are what you eat" certainly can apply to skin.

- Moisturize. It can keep your skin from cracking and drying. Try using chamomile lotion daily, because it is a medicinal plant and can help prevent skin damage from sunburn and windburn.

2.1.6 Hair

Hair Color

"Hair has many variations in color. Each person has about seven different colors in the hair which harmonize to create a predominant color," explains Karen Brunger. Before advising your clients about their hair, consider some of the impressions created by different colors. You can also do an online search for photos of celebrities who have frequently changed hair color such as Cher and Jessica Alba.

Blonde

Famous manes: Katherine Heigl, Gwen Stefani, Owen Wilson

Soft and fun are two words that come to mind. "There is a certain cachet about being blonde. It is like a magnet," says Sharyn Hillyer, M.A., a relationship therapist who practices in Beverly Hills, California.

Nettie Giandomenico, a color specialist in Pasadena, California, categorizes the personalities of blondes in terms of hue. Gold blondes are youthful, with a warm sense of humor. Beige blondes are sophisticated and classy. Strawberry blondes are natural and fun-loving.

Light Brown

Famous manes: Jennifer Aniston, Sarah Jessica Parker, Brad Pitt

Light browns are seen as being grounded and dependable. They also can be seen as mousy or plain. While men used to hum along with the song *Jeanie with the Light Brown Hair*, a female brunette may not see herself as very exciting. "She wouldn't think of herself as gorgeous — but nice," says Hillyer.

Dark Brown/Black

Famous manes: Salma Hayek, Angelina Jolie, Johnny Depp

People with dark brown or black hair may be seen as exotic. Dark brunettes convey power. "They also see themselves as mysterious and dramatic and tend to wear dramatic colors," adds Hillyer.

Red

Famous manes: Nicole Kidman, Marcia Cross, Conan O'Brien

Reds are seen as fiery and emotional. There are different shades of red. "Others see a cool, darker red as sultry and a little more mysterious," says Giandomenico. "Warm reds (orange-red) are seen as wanting to be noticed and assertive. Warm reds see themselves as being energetic and natural, while cool reds see themselves as fun and sexy."

Seasonal Hair Tones

Although hair color may change during life, natural changes harmonize with the skin and eyes. Applying color that is not in harmony with the hair's natural undertone, value and intensity can destroy balance. The hair color can be too ash, too red, too light, or too dark.

For clients who need or desire hair dyeing, determining their seasonal hair tone will help you choose the right hair color for them. Here are a few things to beware of when recommending colors.

Summer

Red could create sallowness, or a sickly yellowish skin color, in the complexion. Straight ash can work, but colorists tend to be leery of using "green." Silver hair can act as a natural highlight, since the natural hair is already ash.

Winter

Dark, cool hair is the most difficult to color. If the hair is lightened too much, the person may appear washed-out. If the hair turns brassy, the client's skin may appear an unhealthy orange.

Spring

Ash colors may cause the skin to appear pasty. Light springs should avoid colors that are too red or too dark. Light hair may fade to a creamy gray. Dark hair may be dulled by the gray.

Autumn

Be careful about going too light and bright. Look at the natural coloring for guidance. Red hair may fade to a golden gray. Brown hair may clash with gray in a salt and pepper look.

Face Shape and Hair Style

There are four basic face shapes which can indicate what length and style of hair will look best on your client. Your job as an image consultant is to help a client identify their face shape, and then find a stylish haircut that flatters and frames the face. Hair expert Karen M. Shelton of HairBoutique.com shares her insight on face shapes:

Oval   Length equal to one and a half times the width. An oval face may change according to age or weight gain or loss. People with a classic oval face usually have small features.

Round   If your client has a round face it will be as wide or almost as wide (within 1/4 - 1/2 inches) as it is long.

Rectangle   Longer than it is wide. (Also known as *long*.)

Triangular   Wider forehead that narrows gradually to a slightly pointed or rounded chin.

Hairstyles are always changing, so you'll need to keep informed. Read fashion and hair magazines, go to hair shows in your community, and visit **www.hairboutique.com** for several interesting articles on hair.

2.1.7 Grooming

"Good grooming sends the message to people that your clients like themselves and take care of themselves," says Donna Panko of Professional Skill Builders.

Nail Care Tips

"Your hands are always on display," says Donna Panko. If your client is going to wear nail color, they must avoid chipped nail polish. "The message it sends is that you don't pay attention to details. It may not be your intention, but that's what it sends." Here are some tips that you, as the detail-oriented image consultant, can point out:

- Your nails need to be clean.

- Your nails need to be filed evenly.

- Your nails should be free of hangnails.

- Your nails should have a consistent shape.

- The shape of your nails needs to follow the shape where your nail meets your finger. So if it's square or oval, then that's the best nail shape for your client.

- Your nails should be neither too short nor too long.

- Red nail polish may not be appropriate for conservative companies or the health field. White, pink and creme nail polish are always in style.

- The more conservative the workplace, the more conservative nail jewelry, like rings or nail polish decals, should be.

Grooming can be defined simply as "to care for one's appearance." It involves ensuring that all aspects of personal appearance are neat, clean, polished, or otherwise cared for.

For example, rather than just telling a client what to wear, you would tell them how to care for their clothing to present a professional image. You might check to ensure that garments look professional and are not too tight, and provide a list of things to watch out for, such as fallen hems, missing buttons, wrinkles, and stains.

Don't your clients already know grooming basics? Not always, according to Donna Panko. Some of your clients will not give the same attention to their casual dress as they give to their corporate attire. "They think because something is business casual that they can drop the word business and focus on the casual. They think that they can take something out of the dryer and put it on," explains Panko.

As an image consultant, you will give your clients, in a delicate manner, grooming advice on any of the following:

- Clothing
- Hair
- Makeup
- Facial hair
- Personal hygiene
- Dental care
- Fragrance
- Nail care

In section 3.1.2 you will find a client questionnaire on grooming, along with additional tips you can give your clients to help them always appear well groomed.

2.2 Communication and Behavior

Physical appearance may be the most obvious area of expertise for an image consultant, but it is not the only one. What people say and how they say it, their body language, and their behavior all speak volumes about them. As an image consultant, you can address many areas of communication and behavior with your clients to help them project a positive image.

In this section you will learn the basic elements of communication and behavior, along with tips you can share with your clients.

2.2.1 Basics of Communication

A study of face-to-face communication conducted by Albert Mehrabian at the University of California, Los Angeles, found that the percentage of the meaning conveyed through each channel of communication was as follows:

Verbal (the actual words used) 7%

Vocal (tone of voice and other vocal qualities) 38%

Visual (gestures, facial expressions, etc.) 55%

While these figures do not apply in all communication situations, this now famous study helped make people aware of the importance of vocal and visual (non-verbal) communication. However, most of us intuitively know that tone of voice and body language communicate more than words alone.

Imagine asking someone "How are you?" If that person replies "Fine" in a curt manner, with a frown on their face, and their arms crossed, are they communicating that they really feel fine? As an image consultant, you can help show your clients the importance of each type of communication, and help them make an excellent impression.

Verbal Communication

Although the UCLA study found only seven percent of a message's meaning was conveyed through the words alone, that doesn't mean the words your client uses are unimportant. Quite often, judgments are made about a person's competence, education, and trustworthiness just by listening to them speak.

Words are particularly critical in a number of forms of communication, including e-mail, telephone calls, interviews, and speeches. Something said in a television interview, for example, can come back to haunt the speaker. An excellent example of this is the perception of former U.S. Vice President Dan Quayle as not very intelligent because of several misstatements attributed to him, such as "It's wonderful to be here in the great state of Chicago."

There are many areas of verbal communication that image consultants can address, evaluate in their clients, and improve upon to achieve more effective communication. Areas you may work with include:

Vocabulary

Words are power. A large vocabulary helps people express themselves effectively and gives them the air of being educated, credible speakers. However, speakers must use words properly. A safe rule of thumb is that if you don't know exactly what a word means or how to use it correctly in a sentence, don't use it at all. Using a word incorrectly can embarrass the speaker and confuse the listener.

Speakers also need to ensure they are speaking appropriately. Using large words unnecessarily can be perceived as pretentious. If someone wants to appear down to earth and likeable, it may be preferable to speak simply and directly — for example, "I drove across town in my car" instead of "I traversed the community in my automobile."

Pronunciation

In addition to ensuring words are used correctly, they also need to be pronounced correctly. When someone hears a speaker pronounce nuclear as "nucular," probably as "probly," or espresso as "expresso," they may assume the speaker is not well-educated.

Grammar

Hand in hand with proper word usage is correct grammar. Using proper grammar lends credence to a message. It also speaks to the intelligence and class of a speaker. Speakers may be judged harshly if they make grammatical errors such as using the word "none" instead of "any" (e.g. "I don't want none") or the word "seen" instead of "saw" (e.g. "I seen my friend yesterday"). The first step to overcoming grammatical errors is to become aware of them, then practice using correct English. Even replacing "yeah" with "yes" can help someone make a more positive impression.

However, following rigid rules of grammar can sound unnatural and pretentious. If you have seen the television show *Frasier*, you have heard overly formal English spoken by the Niles Crane character. This style of speaking can be inappropriate in particular situations. For example, a politician speaking to a blue collar crowd may not be well received if his speaking style rigidly follows all the rules of grammar.

Fillers

Conversation is often cluttered with unnecessary filler words and phrases. Good speakers minimize the use of fillers like "uhh," "um," "like," and "you know" in their conversations. These fillers (the technical term for them is "vocal disfluencies") can make people sound uncertain, nervous, or as if they do not know what they are talking about. Minimizing fillers can add to a person's credibility. It also keeps the focus on the content and prevents the message from being muffled.

Other Verbal Problems

There are a number of other words that people should avoid using in conversation:

- Profanity is best left out of business and social settings. Swearing reduces a speaker's credibility and distracts from the overall message.

- Slang should be eliminated or, at least, selectively used.

- Jargon or acronyms (abbreviations) should only be used if everyone present understands their meaning.

Vocal Communication

A person's voice quality is also important. This includes the volume, rate, and pitch used by an individual. These aspects of vocal communication can bring with them assumptions about the people using them.

Volume

A person with a naturally loud voice can appear insensitive and domineering. In truth, there may be insecurity issues at play, and the speaker feels they need to speak loudly to be listened to.

A naturally soft-spoken person may be thought self-effacing and shy. These people may feel they are not good enough or worth being heard. It is also stressful for listeners who are unable to hear their conversation partner or a presenter.

People need to pay attention to their volume when in public situations. When speaking in a crowd, people are encouraged to use a volume that will reach those at the back of the room. This also applies to small groups. Voice projection should depend on the size of the group and the topic being discussed. The smaller the group of people, the lower the volume should be. Also, if the topic being discussed is of a delicate nature, the volume should drop to match its gravity.

In business, some subjects should never leave the boardroom. In these cases, any discussion of such matters outside the office should be done in hushed tones to preserve confidentiality. Your client needs to be aware of the volume of their voice as well as who else may be able to hear them. This can prevent embarrassing slips and being labeled as someone who can't be trusted with private information.

Rate

A fast-talking person may appear to others to be shifty or untrust-worthy. Some people feel that fast talkers do not really know what they are saying, and their thoughts are not well reasoned out. Those who speak more slowly may be slower, more methodical thinkers. They may think carefully about what they say. The impression, however, can be that these people lack intelligence because they are "slow."

Other Vocal Qualities

People who inject energy and expression into their voices are thought to be more creative, confident, and credible. They can keep the attention of an audience with greater ease. When speakers don't pepper their speech with expression and emotion, they risk losing their audience. A monotone delivery – and a monotone speaker – can be seen as boring. It may be that a person is very interesting but nervous or inexperienced speaking in front of other people.

Other vocal qualities that can create a poor impression include breathiness, raspiness, and whininess (e.g. actress Fran Drescher's famous voice).

Diction

The manner in which people speak can shape a person's image and the perceptions others have about them. A lisp or stutter can affect a speaker's confidence. These problems can also distract listeners and cause the message to get lost. Likewise, an accent can cause people to make assumptions about the speaker. Southern drawls may be incorrectly associated with slow thinking, while other accents may make a person sound uneducated or "street."

With matters of diction, image consultants also call upon the expertise of voice coaches. These professionals work with clients to help correct speech impediments or tone down the strength of an accent. However, as with other vocal and verbal communication challenges, you may be able to assist clients yourself. Section 3.4 has advice and exercises for communication consultations.

Non-Verbal Communication

As the UCLA study found, non-verbal forms of communication can be particularly powerful in face-to-face communication. If there is conflict between the words being said and the message communicated by the body, the body is more likely to be believed.

If you've ever watched television without the sound, you'll know that you can tell much of what is going on without hearing a word. It is not only your own body language that is important. Reading other people's non-verbal cues can help you in your business and personal life.

The power of body language, then, is something image consultants will identify and interpret for their clients. Consultants counsel people in many areas of body language. Here are a few aspects of non-verbal communication to consider:

Posture

Body language is often a reflection of a person's state of mind. If a person is confident and happy, their body language reflects that. The opposite is also true. You can change your body language to match how you'd like to feel or appear to be feeling. Just as different clothing can make a person feel and look differently, a confident posture also helps make a person feel confident.

Sitting up straight and leaning forward in a chair can say a great deal about someone. It shows that they are interested, engaged, and involved in the conversation. People should sit toward the front half of their chair. This makes them appear alert and interested and makes getting up easier as well.

Standing up straight and walking purposefully can give even the smallest person presence and energy. Conversely, a slumped posture suggests low spirits and disinterest in a conversation or situation. Good posture does more than just give a person an authoritative presence. It is also good for the muscles and bones.

Gestures

Gestures often illustrate how you are feeling and what you are thinking. However, many gestures are culturally specific, and a gesture with a positive meaning in North America can have a very different meaning in other countries.

Using gestures when you talk helps make a conversation or business presentation more animated and interesting. Gestures stress the most important parts of what a person is trying to express.

Gestures can be misleading. They sometimes suggest feelings to other people that may not be accurate. For example, a person standing or sitting with their arms crossed may be seen as cold, aloof, or angry. The truth may be that they are chilly and are trying to stay warm.

Many gestures like crossed arms are unconscious, and it is up to image consultants to identify inaccurate gestures and help their client replace them with ones more indicative of the person's personality.

Gestures should also match the situation. In a small group, more controlled and subtle gestures are appropriate. In larger groups, people can use more open and exaggerated gestures.

Interpreting Gestures

In *How to Read a Person Like a Book*, Gerald I. Nierenberg and Henry H. Calero describe numerous gestures commonly used in business settings.

FabJob co-CEO Tag Goulet, a part-time university instructor of interpersonal communication, has been discussing these and other gestures with adult students for over ten years. She says, "A gesture may be nothing more than a habit, or a physical reaction to something. For example, someone may rub their eye because they are tired or having a problem with a contact lens. But the person seeing the gesture may not realize that. People need to be aware of what messages they are communicating — intentionally or not."

Following are just a few examples of gestures and the meanings they may convey. Others can be found in Neirenberg and Calero's book as well as other books on body language that are listed in the Resources chapter of this guide.

Gesture	What It Says
Arms crossed	"I'm afraid of you" OR "I disagree with you."
Head resting on hand	"I'm bored."

Head tilted	"I'm interested in what you are saying" *OR* "I don't understand."
Index finger along cheek, other fingers curled around chin	"I'm not impressed."
Pinching bridge of nose, closed eyes	"I'm concerned."
Touching nose	"I'm not sure" *OR* "I'm lying."
Showing palms of hand	"I'm open."
Clenched hands, thumbs rubbing	"I'm anxious."
Tugging at ear	"Stop talking. It's your turn to listen."
Rubbing eye	"I don't see it."
Steepling with fingers	"I'm confident."
Rubbing back of neck	"I'm frustrated."
Touching throat	"I'm anxious."
Touching chest	"I really mean it."
Unbuttoning jacket	"I'm open to what you're saying."
Fidgeting	"I'm bored."
Straddling chair or leg over arm of chair	"I don't have to follow the rules."
Seated with foot kicking	"I'm bored."
Leaning back, fingers laced behind head	"I'm the king of the castle."

Facial Expressions

There are seven basic emotions which humans express the same way, no matter what culture they are from. The emotions are happiness, sadness, surprise, fear, anger, disgust, and embarrassment. When one of these emotions shows clearly on someone's face, we instantly understand it.

People can learn to mask some of these feelings to keep from offending someone or expressing an emotion or opinion they would sooner keep to themselves. Sometimes showing anger or disgust in certain situations can work against you.

Some facial expressions are more difficult to hide. Tightening the jaw and lips is often unintentional and can signal feelings of anxiety, tension, nervousness, or anger. Furrowed eyebrows can show feelings of confusion or surprise. Image consultants assist people in becoming aware of and mastering their facial expressions.

Smiles are also an important part of a facial expression. It seems simple, but a smile can go a long way in business as well as personal relationships. While there are some situations where smiles are inappropriate, in most situations, a smile puts people at ease and tells those around you that you are enjoying being with them.

Eye Contact

Eye contact establishes rapport and trust. As a speaker, good eye contact helps exhibit confidence. As a listener, eye contact shows respect and interest in what is being said. A rule of thumb is to maintain eye contact until you can clearly see the color of the other person's eyes. However, 100 percent eye contact is intimidating. In a typical North American conversation, the speaker makes eye contact about 40 percent of the time, while the listener makes eye contact about 70 percent of the time. Depending on the situation, you may be able to convey interest by making more eye contact.

Other cultures have different preferences for eye contact. For example, some Asian cultures see direct eye contact as disrespectful, while some Arabic cultures consider it disrespectful not to make prolonged direct eye contact. It's important to consider these differences when doing business in or visiting other countries.

Proximity

Proximity, or personal space, is another aspect of non-verbal communication. While some people are comfortable having strangers close to them, others require much more empty space around them to feel comfortable. People should pay attention to how others react when they feel their space is being invaded. Such actions as stepping backward, leaning away from another person, or avoiding eye contact are all signals of a violation of personal space.

In North America, people feel most comfortable with three to six feet of personal space in interpersonal communication. Other cultures accept much less space and participate in hugs and cheek kissing when greeting people. Still other cultures find physical contact with strangers unacceptable. By watching another's reaction, you can gauge the comfort levels and avoid any uncomfortable or embarrassing faux pas.

Space plays a role in business meetings and personal encounters alike. Seating arrangements can dictate the mood of a gathering. If you sit behind a large desk while the other person perches on a chair, it can be seen as a play at power. This space can interfere with open communication. Conversely, sitting side-by-side can create a more equal, comfortable sharing environment.

Mirror, Mirror

A key to using non-verbal communication to your advantage is mirroring the other person. This involves discovering a person's personality and tailoring your behavior to complement it.

If the person is mellow, use smooth, slow gestures. If the other person is high-spirited, use enthusiastic gestures and ways of speaking. This creates a comfortable interaction and lays the foundation for a relationship. However, beware of trying to exactly duplicate another person's gestures, as this may come across as insincere or manipulative.

2.2.2   Conversation

Conversation is a true art and, for some, a lost one. Being a good conversationalist can draw people to you and enhance your overall image.

Image consultants spend a great deal of time advising in this area. As a consultant, you will counsel people on what to talk about, what not to talk about, how to keep a conversation moving along, and how to turn chance encounters into business or personal relationships. This section includes some tips you can share with your clients.

Introductions

The purpose behind conversation is to form and build upon relationships. It can be intimidating to enter a room and not know anyone. There are easy rules to follow when it comes to initiating social interaction with someone you don't know. These simple steps can make it easier and less stressful to get a conversation rolling.

- First, approach a person with a smile on your face. This friendly gesture puts people at ease and shows that you are interested if not eager to connect with them.

- Be sure to make eye contact as you approach a person. Eye contact helps establish a connection and rapport between people.

- When entering a room full of strangers, find a person or group of people who look receptive to newcomers. People who stand open to the rest of the room and who often look around the room are great targets for conversation. Finding a person or group of people who are carrying on a light and friendly conversation can make the transition easier.

- Always offer your name and ask for the other people's names.

Body Language

When meeting a person for the first time, a handshake and eye contact help establish chemistry between people. When you meet someone, always shake their hand. Regardless of the other person's gender or status, extend your hand and present a firm, but not bone-crushing, grip. You should try to match the other person's firmness. Squeeze once, pump once, and release the grip after about a three-count.

Don't wait for others to offer their hands. Initiate the handshake. A good handshake is accompanied by good eye contact and a genuine smile. This lets people know you are strong, confident, and friendly.

Names

It's key to remember the other person's name. One way to do this is to use the name immediately in conversation. If you happen to miss the name during an introduction or can't recall it, come clean and ask the other person to repeat it. Trying to wing it can be disastrous.

To avoid awkward encounters, always present your name when you run into people you've met only a few times before. This refreshes the other party's memory, ensures they know your name, and allows them to concentrate on the conversation rather than searching their minds for who you are. Adding where you met them so they can put your face into context is a good idea as well.

Introductions tell you what a person wants to be called. Respect that. If a person introduces himself as "Michael" or herself as "Rebecca," use the full form of the name. Wait until you are invited to call him "Mike" or her "Becky." After all, if your new friend wanted to be called Mike or Becky, they would have introduced themselves as such.

Some names, especially foreign ones, can be difficult to pronounce. Take the time to learn how to properly say someone's name. This shows that you care enough to put forth an effort.

Introducing Other People

When introducing other people, it is a good idea to include a piece of information about each person. This can present common ground for the people being introduced, which can then spark a conversation. It also places you in a "host" position. Considerate introductions take the stress out of meeting new people and make the situation enjoyable.

It is sometimes confusing as to which person to introduce or present first. A common and accepted introduction sequence is as follows:

- Mention the most honored or senior person in the group first; you can also introduce the least-known person first ("Ms. Important, I would like you to meet Mr. New").

- Introduce a person from your company to a potential client or customer.

- If you don't know anyone, introduce people from left to right.

- When two equally ranked people of both genders are introduced, name the woman first.

The 30-Second Commercial

In most business, networking, and even social situations, you do not have time to tell each person you encounter everything you do and why it may be of interest to them. Many image consultants suggest that their clients prepare a 30- or 60-second "commercial" to use during an introduction. This is sometimes referred to as an "elevator pitch."

Prepare a short description of yourself to take the pressure off in an interview or when introducing yourself to a group of people. Your pitch should be informative, succinct, and catch the interest of the group.

This self-introduction aims to fill another person in on what you do and possibly sell the other person on the benefits of working with you. In under a minute, you answer some basic questions another person may have about you and your profession. The commercial can include the following information:

- Your name and position

- The company you work for

- Who you serve

- What you do for them

- Your specific talents and skills

- The benefit of this service to your clients

You can see an example of a commercial for an image consultant in section 6.3.2 of this guide.

Mingle

It is definitely tempting to stay with a person you know when at a gathering. But this defeats the purpose of networking for business. It also eliminates the possibility of meeting interesting new people. When at a social event, mingling is the best way to practice your conversation skills. Spend only five to ten minutes with each person you talk with, then move on to meet someone else.

Making Small Talk

Conversation at cocktail parties, business seminars, the bus stop, and baby showers all follows the same basic principles. It may be called small talk, but it can be larger than life. You don't have to be extroverted and experienced to master the art of small talk. All you need is some simple instructions and practice.

Conversation is like a tennis match — you receive the ball, swing at it, and send it back over the net. The hope is that other people will then add something of their own and send the ball back to you. When the ball is in your court, provide some information and then turn it over to your conversation partner. Be warm and engaging so they can add their experiences to the conversation. Conversation is two-sided, and both parties should feel comfortable sharing ideas and anecdotes.

Icebreakers

The easiest conversation starter is to talk about what brings you both to the party, seminar, or gathering. Discussions about the lecture topic or host of the party can lead to other areas of conversation.

It's a good idea to be prepared when entering a situation in which you don't know anyone and will be meeting new people. Arrive armed with some possible topics for discussion and some questions to ask if there is a lull in the conversation. These questions should be open-ended to encourage expansion. Asking someone "How was your day?" can too easily be met with a simple "Fine." If you ask "What did you do today?" more information can be drawn from the other person.

The following icebreakers are an opportunity to share information about yourself and discover something about the other person, too:

- Have you always lived here?
- What's the best vacation spot you've ever visited?
- What do you like to do with your leisure time?
- Tell me about your family.
- What would you do if you won the lottery?
- What is your favorite part of your job?

Complimenting a person is also a great icebreaker. A person's appearance can present the opportunity for a conversation. They may be wearing a "conversation piece" that begs explanation or comment. These are also safe topics, as the other person is obviously proud of and open about the article or else they would not be wearing it.

A unique piece of jewelry or article of clothing can spark a discussion. Jewelry and clothing can also indicate a person's affiliations and hobbies — for instance, a person wearing a lapel pin may be advertising their membership in the Rotary Club. A team or business logo on a shirt or hat can tip you off to a person's occupation or sports loyalty. Don't let these opportunities pass you by. Use your powers of observation to make conversation easier.

Topics of Conversation

Some basic small talk topics are safe and universal. Here are a few subjects that can give a conversation a kick-start:

- current movies

- popular books

- local cultural events

- hot restaurants

- unique and exciting vacation spots and travel

- what you do for a living

- weather

- gardening

The more information offered in a conversation, the more likely it is that you will find common ground. It's amazing how many hobbies, experiences, or even people you'll share in common with strangers — you just have to dig a little deeper to find out what they are.

It's important to let a conversation evolve and flow naturally. If a conversation is going well, do not change the subject. Once a topic is spent, ease into another subject to boost the energy level and recharge the conversation.

What Not to Say

The old adage remains true today — when it comes to conversation, don't talk about religion and politics. These days, those aren't the only taboo subjects to avoid in conversations. Some topics can bring a conversation to a screeching halt. Here are some areas that are best avoided when getting to know new people:

- Avoid passing on rumors or gossip.

- Don't tell questionable stories or jokes.

- Do not dwell on personal misfortunes, especially those that are just occurring.

- Discussion about the costs of items can be uncomfortable.

- Don't ask how much a person earns or discuss your own salary.

- Don't delve into your health problems and concerns or the other person's health (unless the other person is suffering from something obvious and temporary, such as a cast).

- Avoid discussing religious and political affiliations, as these often create heated debate.

- Avoid discussing controversial subjects, especially when you don't know where the other person stands on them. If these topics do come up, try to take a neutral stance when you are with clients, business associates, or people you do not know well — even if you hold strong opinions on the subject.

- It is best to avoid talk about negative items in the news (for example, divorce or bankruptcy), as you don't know what the other person is experiencing or has gone through in the past.

Listening

Good conversationalists are good listeners. You should not only listen well but also show that you are listening. Lean toward the speaker to express your interest in what they are saying.

A key to listening and absorbing what you hear is repeating in your head what the other person is saying. Then paraphrase (restate in your own words) what was said to confirm your understanding.

Keeping eye contact and facing the speaker can also help you become a better listener. Ask questions if you missed something that was said — the act of questioning forces you to process the information. These tips help you show proper respect to the other person in your conversation and encourage the sharing of ideas. Additional tips on effective listening can be found in section 4.2.2.

Conversation Killers

There is always a risk of conversation casualties. Writer, trainer, and speaker Debra Fine of the Fine Art of Conversation (**www.debrafine. com**) identifies definite conversation killers to be aware of. Fine's book, *The Fine Art of Small Talk,* has additional tips and tricks to becoming a great conversationalist.

The Interrogator

There is a fine line between engaging in conversation and interrogating another person. It is often done out of nervousness — a person has questions in mind but doesn't know how to let a conversation evolve from the answers.

This style of conversation draws information out but does not explore it. It is rapid-fire questioning that can feel like you should be behind a double-sided mirror. Avoid being an interrogator. If you are on the other side of the conversation, ask an open-ended question to slow the pace.

The Bragger

Braggers are people who fill the conversation with stories about themselves, boasting about their accomplishments and experiences. They hope to be the envy of everyone but end up discouraging open and genuine conversation. Be on the lookout for these conversation killers.

The One-Upper

No matter what has been done, the one-upper has done it bigger, better, faster, or sooner. These conversationalists turn every story into a competition. Avoid being a one-upper. Share your experiences but don't feel compelled to do one better. It will only destroy the rapport as well as the flow of conversation.

Monopolizers

Monopolizers take hold of the conversation and never let go. They tell stories about themselves without opening the conversation up for an exchange of experiences with someone else. It can be uncomfortable for other people to speak with monopolizers, as they tend to disclose too much information about themselves without knowing how it will affect others. Monopolizers need to pass the ball to others and invite them to participate more actively in the discourse.

The Interrupter

These people feel the need to make their point and will do so whether you're finished making yours or not. They think they know what you're going to say and are too impatient to wait for you to say it. This habit can kill a conversation, as the other person no longer sees the point in discussing anything.

2.2.3   Business Communication and Etiquette

The world of business is very image oriented. A good impression can mean the difference between making the deal and walking out of a meeting empty-handed. Good business etiquette can help boost your confidence, competence, and likeability with colleagues as well as clients.

As an image consultant, you will advise clients on the myriad of business responsibilities, from making telephone calls to how to conduct yourself at business functions.

Phone Etiquette

A great deal of business is done over the phone. A pleasant and strong telephone manner can help seal the deal. Here are some basic tips to help your clients make a good impression on the phone:

- Smile. The other person can't see you, but they can hear the smile in your voice. This puts the person on the other end of the line at ease and makes the caller seem more likeable as well.

- Stand when making business calls. This injects more energy into the voice because the diaphragm is expanded.

- Be polite and personable with the receptionist, the assistant of the person you are calling, or anyone else you speak with.

- Always identify yourself both to the receptionist and the person you are calling.

- Unless you have a relationship with the individual, don't call them by a first name. This familiarity is earned.

- If you are offering information over the telephone that you've said countless times before, try to keep it fresh and different. It keeps the other person engaged in the conversation rather than feeling as though they are listening to an impersonal recording.

- If you become disconnected from a person you called, it is your responsibility to call back. You have the number accessible and know how to reach them.

Leaving a Message

Only about 30 percent of telephone calls placed ever reach a live person. The rest result in hang-ups or voice mail messages. So, voice mail is an important business tool. That being said, it should not replace face-to-face conversation or two-sided telephone conversations.

When leaving a voice mail message, keep it short, clear, and simple. Leave your name, company, and telephone number along with a short reference as to why you are calling. Try not to leave detailed messages or ramble — these messages often get deleted.

If the reason for the call is to discuss a conflict or problem, do not go into detail or become emotional on a person's voice mail. A negative message can be saved, replayed, and used against you later. There is also a chance that the issue will be resolved before the person checks their messages, and harsh or emotional words will reflect poorly on you after the fact.

A good idea when leaving voice mail messages is to review them if given the option. That way if you have gone into too much detail or do not like the sound of the message, you can record it again.

Your Voice Mail Message

It is a good idea to update your outgoing voice mail message often. Leaving a daily status on your message can exhibit professionalism and presence. It is also a commitment. You have to remember to change it each day. There is nothing worse than leaving a message on a voice mail that says it's Tuesday when it's really Friday.

As well, return all messages the same day, even if it is returned after hours via another voice mail message. This shows that the call and caller are important to you.

Call Waiting

If you have call waiting, be careful when you use it. If you have placed a call and then hear that beep in your ear, don't put the person on hold to take the other call. If you must pick up, ask for permission first and wait for them to answer you before switching to the other line. Never put someone on hold more than once in a conversation. This tries the patience of the phone partner and can lead to resentment.

Cell Phone Consideration

Cell phones can be great for convenience but they can also be inconsiderate. Considerate cell users are those who turn their phones to vibrate or turn them off altogether during important meetings. If a call comes through, it's best to ask if those around you mind if you take it.

Excuse yourself if you need to make a call and find a quiet place to use the phone. There is no such thing as privacy, so a cell phone conversation should not cover confidential or sensitive issues. It is especially important to speak clearly when on a cell phone. If there is a bad connection, don't try to yell through it. Instead, hang up and redial.

Speaker Phones

Conference calls are common in today's workplace. This means most telephones have a speaker phone option. If using speaker phone, be sure to alert the other person that this is the case. That way, the other person knows that it is not a private conversation and that others may be present, and allows them to choose their comments accordingly.

When on a conference call, each speaker should identify themselves before contributing. That way the person on the other end of the phone knows who is saying what. You can't count on others to recognize each voice and properly attribute the comments.

E-mail

USA Today reported that many business problems are caused by e-mail. There is no facial expression or tone of voice accompanying an e-mail message, so its content is easy to misunderstand. E-mail should therefore be used carefully and thoughtfully. Business e-mails follow some different rules than personal e-mails.

Although e-mail is more informal than other business correspondence, it still needs to be professional. These messages are often saved, printed, and can be circulated. Unless you know the other person well, keep the style serious and professional. An inappropriate style can affect how the recipient perceives you.

The greatest advantage to e-mail technology is that it is quick. The greatest disadvantage can be said to be the same. Many people write an e-mail message and send it without giving it much thought. Unfortunately, there is no way to get the message back once the "send" button is pressed. Before sending, always reread an e-mail and make sure you are comfortable sending it as is. Also double-check the recipient's address to ensure you are sending it to the correct person.

Here are some other tips on successful e-mail communication to share with your clients:

- It is considerate to keep everyone's e-mail address confidential. If you are sending an e-mail message to a number of people, enter the recipients in the "blind carbon copy" (bcc:) section.

- Business e-mail messages should be concise. The writer should always use proper grammar, spelling, punctuation, and sentence structure in every business e-mail message. Some people type in all capital letters because it is easier and faster to do so. This comes off as shouting and can lead to misunderstandings.

- Avoid forwarding jokes or other "junk" e-mail to business associates, as this creates a poor impression of your professionalism.

- There is no such thing as absolute privacy. E-mail can be monitored by a corporate server or intercepted by skilled hackers. To be safe, don't use e-mail to discuss confidential matters.

- Don't send attachments unless they are necessary. Large attachments can fill up a person's in-box quickly and, given the number of destructive viruses passed from computer to computer, people are generally wary about opening attachments.

- An easy way to connect with recipients is to attach a signature to the bottom of an e-mail message. Including your phone and fax numbers, address, e-mail address, name and position in each message makes it convenient for people to reach you.

- It is good practice to reply to each e-mail message as soon as possible — within the first 24 hours, if not the same working day. Consider using an automated reply to let people know their message has been received and when you expect to reply personally. If the original message requires extra attention or research, send a quick note back explaining the situation and promising to respond as soon as you can. This lets the sender know you received the e-mail and shows that you are giving the issue or question the time it deserves.

- E-mailers should also be cautious when using priority markings for their messages. Unless a message is time-sensitive or urgent, avoid using those settings. Overusing the "high priority" tag will annoy recipients and cause them to ignore this rating on all your messages.

Other Written Communication

Fax Etiquette

Faxing gives a sense of presence even when the sender is far away. This is a valuable tool. However, the technology should be used carefully. Never transmit confidential or sensitive material over the fax unless the receiver has arranged to be standing by to pick it up.

Also, a cover sheet identifying the recipient's name is a must unless the fax is going to a one-person office. Fax cover letters should be professional and basic — no cute cartoons or busy designs.

Business Documents

Most businesses rely on computers and word processors for daily affairs. For letters, reports, proposals, and internal memos, spell check should be used every time a document is created.

But spell checks are not foolproof. Some typos form legitimate words, but not the appropriate ones. Grammar checks are not always correct either. Nothing replaces a keen, careful eye reading over a document before sending it to the next stage. A few extra minutes can save the embarrassment of a misspelled word, incorrect grammar, or wrong word usage. These types of errors can make people question the strength and validity of the rest of the work.

Personal Notes

Sending a handwritten thank you note after receiving a gift is a thoughtful and polite gesture. It shows you appreciate the thought and acknowledge its receipt. These cards should mention the gift received and include a personal note of thanks. Most thank you cards should be sent within two days of receiving the gift. In the case of a wedding, cards should be sent within a few weeks to give time for the couple to return from the honeymoon.

In the age of computer processors and the Internet, letter writing and penmanship are fading out. A handwritten note gives a card or letter a personal touch. It tells the recipients that they mean enough to you to warrant a bit of extra time writing a note. Again, it is not only what you write but also how it is written. Even short notes or letters should be read over to make sure the grammar and spelling is correct. Good penmanship is another consideration. Clear, neat handwriting gives the impression of an organized, competent person.

When it comes to networking, many people also send cards after meeting with someone at a function or seminar. These cards will include a note reminding the individual about the circumstances of the meeting and a reference to something specific that was discussed to help the person place the name. You may also write a few lines expressing what a pleasure it was to meet them and perhaps include an invitation to develop a business relationship in the future. Just sending a card can make a person stand out from the competition in business.

Writing for Publication

Many of your clients may be able to enhance their image by getting published. Writing an article for an industry magazine can help them develop a reputation as an expert in their industry. Corporate newsletters are often eager for writers to contribute columns or articles. Your client may even want to write a book about their area of expertise, or hire someone to ghostwrite it for them. Section 6.3.5 describes other ways to get published.

Remind your client to carefully proofread and edit their work. Writing should reflect the writer's skills and personality, and poor grammar and typos can interfere with that goal.

Business Meetings

To show bosses that you are involved and an asset to the company, come to meetings prepared. Proper protocol at meetings can give you a powerful presence. When attending a meeting, you should:

- Sit as close to the meeting leader as you can. This implies common ideas and values.

- Match the energy level and general speech style of the meeting leader.

- Discuss issues without arguing about them.

- Sit up straight with your feet under your side of the table.

- Be aware of your non-verbal cues.

- Contribute to the content of the meeting.

- Stand to shake hands with new people at the meeting or to greet colleagues when they enter before a meeting.

The person leading a meeting should take the time to plan and prepare it. Employees who lead organized and thorough meetings are remembered. Those with chaotic meetings are remembered as well, but not in a positive way. To project a positive image when chairing a meeting, here are some tips:

- Arrive early to make sure the room is clean and ready.

- Start and end the meeting on time.

- Pass out an agenda and stick to it.

- Reserve an appropriate, comfortable conference room that meets all your needs.

- Provide refreshments.

- Don't summarize the meeting for latecomers — it implies acceptance of the behavior.

- Stand as you present information from boards or charts to keep energy in the meeting (and it makes you a large presence in a room full of seated people).

- Don't rush through the information.

- Invite input from attendees.

- Be aware of your body language and the cues of others — don't play with a pen or fuss with your clothing. Watch for signs of confusion or boredom in the attendees' faces.

- If the meeting is long, provide breaks to allow people to replenish their coffee, use the washroom, or stretch their legs.

- End with what should happen next to implement the decisions made or presented at the meeting.

Business Functions

The company picnic and client cocktail party are all part of the job. They are meant to personalize the workplace and allow people to loosen up and let their personalities shine through. However, there is an expected code of conduct at these functions. Dress appropriately, eat and drink modestly, and don't do or say anything you would have to apologize for later.

A huge mistake is not attending a business event at all. If you are invited to a corporate function, it is good form to accept. Even if you leave early, be sure to make an appearance. While you are there, make the most of the situation by introducing yourself to senior employees.

Business functions can be stressful events. Although these are events away from the office and taking place outside office time, poor judgment and behavior at a company party can cost you your job. Be yourself, but err on the side of caution and behave conservatively.

2.2.4   Dining Etiquette

Dining etiquette is a valuable skill, both professionally and personally. Having knowledge of proper table manners and settings can make formal situations more comfortable and allow a person to shine. Here are tips from the *FabJob Guide to Become an Etiquette Consultant*:

Place Settings

Deciphering the map of the table can help you ease into formal or informal dining situations. To eliminate the confusion of which plate to use or which glass is yours, remember this rule of thumb: Anything to do with food is located on your left and anything involved with beverages is found on the right.

The bread plate, then, is to the left of the dinner plate, whereas the wine glasses are to the right. The napkin is placed either on the dinner plate or tucked to the left of the plate. The next page has illustrations of both informal and formal place settings.

An easy rule to remember is that you work from the outside of the setting inward. The left of the plate can have up to three forks — a seafood fork, a standard fork, and a salad fork. To the right can be a spoon, a fish knife, and a dinner knife. A spoon or fork can also be placed above the plate for dessert. If salad is being served at the table, a bowl may be placed to the left of the dinner plate. It should be left there unless the service staff moves it to the center of the dinner plate.

When in doubt, watch the host. They are the first to pick up their napkin, the first to pick up a glass, and the first to pick up their utensils. They are, however, the last person served. Everyone at the table should be served before anyone begins to eat. The exception is in a restaurant if one meal is taking longer to prepare than the rest. That guest should encourage the others to eat before their meals get cold.

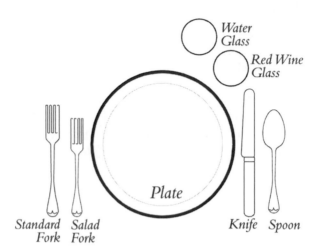

Informal Place-Setting

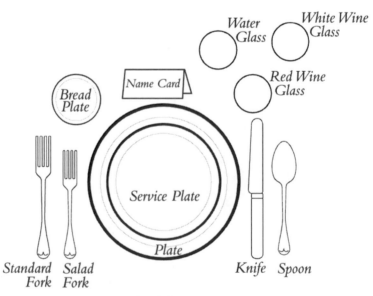

Formal Place-Setting

The host should also pace their meal so they don't finish eating before the last person at the table. None of their guests should eat alone.

Rules of Etiquette

The host invites the dinner guest to be seated. They sit only once everyone is beside their chairs. Guests sit from their left (and the chair's right) to avoid collisions when taking their seats.

Posture is as important at the table as it is at any other place. Sit up straight with your back several inches from the chair. Elbows should be kept away from the tabletop until the meal is over and all dishes have been cleared. Even then, you should not lean heavily on them.

During the meal, you can rest your wrists on the edge of the table. In Europe, it is considered poor table manners to place your hands in your lap during a meal — hands should always be above the table.

We have all used utensils since we were children, but we don't necessarily know how to use them properly. Once the knife has been used, it should never touch the tablecloth. While many people rest the blade on the plate and the handle on the table, it is proper manners to rest the entire knife on the edge of the plate when not in use. Once you have finished eating, the fork and knife should be placed parallel to one another at the ten o'clock/four o'clock position on the plate.

If you would like something from the table, it is polite to ask for it to be handed down. Never reach across the table to pick it up. If you need to leave the table, you should excuse yourself and place your napkin on your chair.

If you are the host, and you offer more food to your guests, avoid asking if they would like "another" serving. This suggests that they have already eaten enough. Instead, offer additional helpings in the same manner that you did the first time around.

The host will often take the responsibility of filling wine glasses as well. These glasses should be filled only half full. At times, other guests will take on this role. If serving yourself wine, you should always refill the rest of the glasses first before filling your own.

If a guest asks for the salt, place both the salt and pepper shakers on the table in front of them. They should not be handed from guest to guest, and other guests should not intercept the shakers and use them. They should be passed to the original guest first. While this may not be the most efficient method, it is the polite one.

Meals and Meetings

A great deal of business is done over meals. Breakfast meetings allow you to get a lot accomplished while leaving the rest of your day uninterrupted. Lunch meetings are most common. Make reservations when possible, and try to meet before or after the usual lunch rush. Dinner meetings are more social than lunches. They can also take longer.

Discuss important issues before the entrees are served so you have the rest of the meal to get to know the other person better. Check out a restaurant beforehand to ensure it is consistent with the image you want to portray. Becoming a recognized regular at a good restaurant can reflect well on you when entertaining clients or colleagues.

There are basic principles to follow when at business meals. They will help you remain poised, respectable, and clean throughout the dining experience:

- Be careful with liquor consumption. A drink after dinner is acceptable, but you still need to maintain professionalism.

- Avoid ordering meals that you eat with your hands.

- Be careful when eating messy meals like pastas or burgers.

- If you invite someone for a meal, you should pick up the check.

- At buffets, do not overload your plate.

- Hold your drink in your left hand so your right is not cold and moist for handshakes.

Food Tips

Soup can be a tricky appetizer to eat gracefully. The trick is to dip the spoon into the soup and scoop away from your body. When the spoon is about two-thirds full, sip the soup from the side of the spoon. Avoid putting the entire spoon in your mouth or slurping the soup. It is acceptable to tip the bowl slightly to make it easier to spoon the last bit of soup from the bottom of the bowl. You should not, however, lift the bowl off the table or sip from the bowl.

If you happen to have a bone or pit in your mouth, be discreet. Return it to the bread plate using a fork. Use your napkin to remove inedible items from your mouth that will look unappealing any other way, such as fat or gristle from a piece of meat. An exception to this rule is fish. It is acceptable to use your fingers to remove tiny fish bones and place them on the plate.

There are some food items that can be eaten with your hands. Here are some that do not require utensils:

- artichokes
- asparagus (if not covered in sauce or cooked until quite soft)
- crispy bacon
- bread
- cookies
- corn on the cob
- fried chicken
- french fries
- hamburgers
- canapés
- hors d'oeuvres
- sandwiches
- berries on the stem and small fruits

Don'ts of Dining

Your mother drilled many rules of table manners into your head as a child. There are other rules she may have forgotten to mention. Image consultant Gloria Starr of Global Success Strategies clears the air on table manners and offers clients the following valuable don'ts when dining:

- Don't put liquid in your mouth while you are still chewing.

- Don't chew with your mouth open.

- Don't talk with food in your mouth.

- Don't mash your food together on a plate.

- Don't use a napkin or tablecloth to clean cutlery (ask for another set instead).

- Don't tuck your napkin into your clothing.

- Don't fiddle with cutlery or you'll appear nervous.

- Don't leave the spoon in your coffee cup or lick it after stirring.

- Don't lean back on the legs of your chair.

- Don't reapply cosmetics at the table.

2.2.5   Other Aspects of Personal Image

Habits

It can seem uncomfortable to discuss certain areas that clients need to work on. Some topics have traditionally been better left untouched. But as an image consultant, you are paid to discuss these matters.

Nervous habits are often unconscious. Pointing these habits out as they are exhibited allows clients to identify them and work toward stopping them. If they discover that they tug at their sleeves, bite their lip, shake their feet, or play with their hair when speaking in public, they can notice when it happens and immediately correct the behavior. Clients may also use specific gestures or say certain phrases too often. By drawing attention to these actions as they are being performed, clients can choose alternate words and gestures as replacements.

Consultants counsel clients about conscious habits as well. These habits can influence how others perceive you. Gum chewing is unprofessional at work and can be distracting when speaking with someone at any time. Sucking on candies should be minimized as well. This practice looks bad and can get in the way of clear communication.

Smoking is another habit that can detract from a person's overall image. It is a hot issue about which people have strong opinions. The best advice is not to smoke when meeting with clients. Smoking in the car or before a meeting isn't advisable either. Smoke clings to clothing and lingers on breath, so you can carry it with you into the meeting. If you need to have a cigarette, do so only once the meeting is over.

Social Activities

Image consultants do not try to make a person into someone else. Instead, they take the person as they are, accentuate the positives and help eliminate the negatives. When it comes to hobbies, most consultants encourage clients to pursue activities that already interest them. These hobbies can translate into great social opportunities.

Many businesspeople close deals on the golf course, so it may be advantageous to pick up the clubs and rekindle an interest in the links. Attending local sporting events also presents networking opportunities. Offering to take clients to professional sporting events is a great way to build rapport and have an enjoyable time outside of work.

Other hobbies, from reading to horseback riding to rebuilding cars, help make you a well-rounded person. It also provides you with possible areas of commonality as well as conversation topics to introduce when meeting new people. However, advise your clients if any hobbies might be perceived as "odd" by other people.

Memberships

Membership at a private club can be a solid career move. It provides people with a sophisticated place to conduct meetings and have business lunches. It also offers people with similar backgrounds and interests a place to get together, socialize, and network. These clubs can make your personal and business life richer and more rewarding.

Many image consultants encourage membership in professional associations and organizations. These affiliations offer business contacts and exposure in a given industry. There are organizations and associations for nearly every profession. Joining these groups shows others that you take your profession seriously and want to take an active role in the industry. Organizations also allow you to promote yourself, your talents, and your products to interested people.

People tend to do business with people they know. If other members of a social club or industry association need a lawyer or accountant or mechanic, they are more inclined to hire a person with whom they are familiar or have a relationship. In turn, you will likely be given better rates and special consideration if you do business with a fellow member. Membership really does have its privileges.

Do advise your clients that membership in some organizations may not be perceived positively by everyone. For example, some people see exclusive clubs as elitist or snobbish. By extension, there is a risk that members will also be viewed this way. It is also not wise to discuss memberships in controversial organizations if there is a possibility that someone may have a strong dislike for the organization.

Community Involvement

Some of your clients may want or need to be involved with community activities as a way of enhancing the image they need to achieve a goal. For example, if you work with beauty pageant contestants, politicians, or television anchors, they will be expected to be involved in charitable and community activities.

You may be able to find appropriate organizations for your clients to get involved with through the links below. Before getting involved with any organizations, they should be investigated thoroughly to ensure they are something your client wants to be associated with. If your client is on the Board of a Directors of a local charity that has a scandal, your client may be associated with it.

GuideStar is a searchable online database of over 1.8 million non-profit organizations in the United States. Visit **www2.guidestar.org/Advanced Search.aspx** to search by your city, state, and non-profit category (e.g. Arts, Environment, Health). CharityVillage offers a similar directory of Canadian organizations at **www.charityvillage.com/cv/nonpr/index. asp**.

What Else We're Judged On

People make judgments about others based on virtually any information they have about someone, including:

- Where you live

- What vehicle you drive

- Your business card

- Your name

- Your website

- Your office

- Your associates

In most cases, your clients will not ask for your assistance in these areas. However, it may help someone who wants a promotion to know that they are not conveying a positive image when they drive up to the office in a rusty station wagon spewing black smoke from the exhaust pipe. If you think you might be asked to consult in areas such as these, an excellent resource to refer to is *Reading People*, by Jo-Ellan Dimitrius, Ph.D., and Wendy Patrick Mazzarella.

2.3 Corporate Image

Corporate executives understand that a positive image affects the financial bottom line. As Anna Soo Wildermuth of Personal Images Inc. explains, successful businesses spend a tremendous amount of money creating a high-value image for their products and services. The most successful and respected companies in America take it one step further. They invest in the image of their most important asset: their employees.

Different companies reach the public (including customers, clients and shareholders) in diverse ways. Each interaction, whether it's speaking with a customer during a sales transaction or an executive being interviewed on television, puts the company's reputation on the line.

As a consultant in a corporate setting, you need to identify the image the corporation is trying to portray. You would then consult with individual employees or present training programs to groups of employees to help them put forth the right image on behalf of their employer. You might advise them on dressing for work, grooming, communication, etiquette, or any other areas described earlier in this chapter.

In this part of the guide you will be introduced to the basic principles involved in corporate image. In section 3.6, you will learn how to do image consulting in a corporate setting.

2.3.1   Brand and Culture

Brand

In order to ensure employees are presenting the right corporate image, you first need to know what that image is. To do this, you'll need to learn about the company's "brand." A brand is the "core meaning" or "essence" of a corporation. According to business publisher Thomson Derwent:

> "A brand distinguishes the product or service of one company from that of another. Through careful management, widespread use, and promotion, a brand will stand for a set of values and attributes in the minds of consumers. Pepsi is widely associated with fashion and youth culture; BMW stands for superior quality and reliability."

The increasing popularity of "branding" has changed the face of advertising. No longer do companies simply sell products or services; they sell a way of life or a set of values. For example, IBM doesn't sell computers — it sells "business solutions." As Virgin Group CEO Richard Branson describes it, the idea is to "build brands not around products, but around reputation."

As an image consultant, corporations will hire you to develop training programs that help employees project the brand image in every aspect of their work. When you are hired as an image consultant, many companies will brief you on the existing brand and how the company wants to be perceived by the public and its shareholders.

If you're still unclear about your client's brand, which makes it hard to develop a training program, try this exercise. Consider the products and services offered by the company and think of words associated with human characteristics, such as stable, exciting, interesting, or creative. Doing this will help to put a "human" face on the corporation.

You can find out more information on branding at **www.brand.com/ branding.htm**.

Corporate Culture

In addition to knowing the company's brand, you will also want to know the general "culture" of the company you're working with. While brands are fairly obvious in many companies, culture is more subtle. And whether or not a corporation has set out to develop a corporate culture, every corporation has one. According to Randall S. Hansen, Ph.D., of Quintessential Careers:

> "At its most basic, it's described as the personality of an organization, or simply as 'how things are done around here.' ... the culture sets norms (rules of conduct) that define acceptable behavior of employees of the organization."

One method used by those who study corporate culture, like Yale School of Management Professor Jeffrey Sommenfield, is to use "culture models." Summerfield's model breaks corporate cultures down like this:

- *Academies:* For steady climb through the organization; IBM is the classic "academy" where employees think of themselves as "IBMers" for life; constant training to reinforce the culture.

- *Clubs:* Group consensus and the good of the organization comes first; employees tend to have substantial equity in their company and expect to stay throughout their career.

- *Baseball teams:* Entrepreneurial style; people are rewarded for their individual contributions; great emphasis on personal freedom and flexibility.

- *Fortresses:* Concerned with survival; many are struggling to reverse their fortunes; no promise of job security or reward; often turn-around or crisis situations.

You should be able to get a sense of a company's culture during your first meetings with company representatives. Observe how employees behave during your interactions with them, and ask questions to learn more about how the company operates.

Learning about the company's culture can give you valuable insight into how senior executives and employees will respond to your programs. For example, if you are dealing with a "fortress," employees are likely to be most concerned with learning practical techniques that will help them keep their jobs. Employees working in a "club" culture may have little patience for training programs involving team games.

2.3.2 Communication on the Job

An employee should, of course, provide great customer service with each customer interaction, but they should also be communicating the corporate brand. Helping employees to effectively communicate a company's brand when they interact with a customer or client will be one of your primary tasks as an image consultant.

What employees say can enhance or detract from the corporation's overall image. One way companies help ensure that employees enhance brand image is to develop a corporate lexicon. *The American Heritage Dictionary of the English Language* defines lexicon as "a stock of terms or a vocabulary used in a particular profession or subject."

For example, many companies have unique terms for generic products that they sell (for instance, they may call a doorstopper a "miracle wedge"). Or management may have created titles for their employees to help reflect the corporate brand (such as Wal-Mart's "associates," Starbucks' "partners" or Disney's "cast members").

Corporations create lexicons to use in employee scripts (e.g. for customer service staff to use when speaking with customers) and to continually reinforce the corporate image with employees and the public. Image consultants can use the corporate lexicons in role-playing exercises to help reinforce these terms and ensure that employees become accustomed to using them in everyday customer transactions.

If the client you're working with doesn't have a lexicon in place, you might suggest that you work on building one. Building a corporate lexicon could be a chance to shine, as you can bring new and unique brand-building terms to the company.

Some good online resources for business terminology include **http://articles.bplans.com/business-term-glossary** and **www.nytimes.com/library/financial/glossary/bfglosa.htm**.

2.3.3 Corporate Dress

Clothing and corporate image are intricately entwined. When you walk into a company, the first thing you notice is the way employees are dressed. If all the men are wearing jackets and ties and all the women are wearing power suits, you may suspect this place is running a serious operation dealing with high dollars and important clients. On the other hand, a company whose employees are dressed in business casual attire might conjure up notions of an employer who takes its employees' comfort into consideration, or that it's a hub of creativity.

Appropriate dress for a company depends on a number of factors, including the industry. For example, financial companies often reflect a professional dress policy and the creative industry usually adopts a more casual policy. In any industry, salespeople often have the pressure of consistently meeting with clients, so there's more of a need for them to dress according to professional standards as opposed to someone who spends most of their working hours in an office. Location also comes into consideration; for example, the corporate environment in a city such as Honolulu isn't as aggressive as in New York City.

Uniforms

Some companies adopt a strict uniform policy where everyone must wear exactly the same clothing as an image-enhancing branding tool. In recent years, more companies have turned to the golf-shirt "uniform" (a golf shirt with the company logo and color-coordinated pants). Examples of the types of people we see in this uniform include restaurant servers, cable and telephone service people, and even franchised plumbers. A uniform ensures that employees show up to clients' doors appropriately dressed, and also causes them to become traveling advertisements.

According to a recent study completed by Personal Images, Inc. (**www.personalimagesinc.com**), a front-line employee image uniform program for 365 retail stores had over 90 percent of employees agreeing or strongly agreeing that their new, professional appearance fostered positive customer reaction, promoted pride within themselves and show-cased the company.

Choosing Appropriate Business Clothes

Employees who don't wear uniforms must decide for themselves – sometimes with the assistance of a company dress code – what to wear to work. This is a challenge for many workers.

According to a 2003 study by California State University marketing professor Dennis Tootelian, nearly two-thirds of Americans have felt inappropriately dressed at a business or a social function and more than two-thirds are uncertain about the differences among business attire, business casual and casual dress in the workplace. What's more, nearly 40 percent of people polled find it more difficult to decide what is acceptable at work today than ten years ago.

With so many people unsure about what to wear to work, it's no wonder that corporations hire image consultants to address style and image in the work place. For many, the biggest challenge is knowing how to dress appropriately in a workplace that allows casual dress.

Business Casual

Casual dress is what one might typically wear on the weekend or in the hours spent away from the office. Many companies allow casual dress one day per week (on "casual Fridays"). Other companies allow employees to wear "business casual" throughout the summer or every day of the week year-round. A July 2000 study by Bright Horizons Family Solutions and William M. Mercer Inc. found that 90 percent of companies surveyed allowed some form of casual dress.

Despite the shift to business casual wear in the last ten years, a recent survey by Dr. Jeffrey Magee, a consulting research psychologist based in Tulsa, Oklahoma, suggests that it might not be suited for business success. His survey results revealed that 50 percent of executives and 70 percent of employees feel that how one dresses influences their daily behaviours.

"The more casual and more relaxed the dress policy is, the more work productivity declines," says Magee. "People are more inclined to socialize in this atmosphere ... the workplace becomes less valuable as employees take its legitimacy less seriously." The result of studies such as Magee's has been a return to business formal wear for many companies. Or, at the very least, business casual is becoming dressier.

Magee sees the back-to-business-formal trend more often in people-jobs, such as doctors, lawyers and keynote speakers. In "introvert occupations," such as research assistant or a programmer, says Magee, the trend back to business formal is less apparent.

Marjorie Brody says that "instituting dress policies that are business casual without defining what this term means is the main problem." Her tips for business casual dress appear below.

Proper Wardrobe Options for Business Casual

by Marjorie Brody
BRODY Professional Development

A neat, clean, conservative and well-groomed businesslike appearance applies when a business casual standard is in place. When you have a client meeting scheduled, clients come first.

When meeting with clients out of the office, regular business attire is appropriate (e.g. suits, ties, tailored dresses), unless the client has a business casual policy and invites you to participate in their policy.

For meetings in the office with clients, dress should be appropriate to the client's expectations (i.e. if a client dresses in business attire, so should you.)

Women have the following options for business casual:

- Casual skirts, slacks or "skorts"

- Neatly pressed chinos or corduroys are acceptable

- Cotton shirts in solids, prints, or muted plaids

- Sweaters (not too tight)

- Blazers look good over slacks or casual skirt

- Low-heeled shoes or boots — wear stockings or socks

Men can wear the following as acceptable business casual:

- Chinos or "Dockers"-type trousers

- Sport shirts with collars or banded necks

- Polo shirts (with collars)

- Sweater or sport jacket

- Casual loafers or lace-up shoes

Appropriate business casual attire never includes:

- Jeans (of any color)

- Athletic wear (e.g. sweat suits)

- Leggings

- T-shirts

- Bare midriffs (low-cut garments, front or back)

- Any kind of workout clothes, running or gym shoes, sneakers or sandals

- Hats, caps

- Ripped or tattered clothing

- Extremely tight-fitting blouses, short skirts or other suggestive clothing

3. How to Do Consultations

In this chapter you will learn how to provide image consulting services to both individual and corporate clients. The chapter begins by explaining what to do during a "preliminary consultation" (your first meeting with a prospective client), then gives step-by-step instructions for doing specific types of image consultations, including: makeover consultations, wardrobe consultations, and corporate consultations. The chapter concludes with detailed advice on finding and working with strategic partners.

3.1 Preliminary Consultations

One of the most gratifying aspects of working as an image consultant is helping people reach their full potential. But in order to accomplish this, you must first identify areas in which they need improvement. This process begins during a preliminary consultation.

A preliminary consultation is your first meeting with a prospective client. Your purpose during the preliminary consultation is to turn that prospective client into a paying client. The way to do this is by identifying what your client needs and wants so you can communicate how your services will benefit them.

3.1.1 Getting Off to a Good Start

While you may already have spoken to the client on the telephone or met them at a networking event (Chapter 6 explains how to attract clients), your preliminary meeting may be the first opportunity to meet your client in person in a professional setting.

It is important to remember that the client will be judging your appearance and behavior during this meeting. Make sure your clothing and grooming are impeccable, arrive on time (or a few minutes early) at the client's office or home, and make sure you have everything you need for the consultation.

Over time you will develop your own checklist of what to bring to a client consultation. In the meantime, here is a list of items to bring:

- Your business cards

- A notepad and two pens

- Optional: a laptop computer

- Questionnaires

- A planning calendar

- Optional: a brochure about your services (see section 6.2.1)

- Optional: a price list (see section 5.4.4)

- Blank contracts (see section 5.5)

You can begin the consultation with some small talk, taking your cue from the client. As part of your preliminary conversation, ask the client how they heard about your company. This should be noted later in a marketing file so you can gauge the effectiveness of your advertising.

Once the talk has turned to business, offer them a business card, brochure or other printed material that describes your services in detail. You can give a quick overview of your services; however, during your meeting you should mostly ask and listen. Aim to have your client do about 80 percent of the talking. Of course, take your cue from them. If they prefer not to do a lot of talking, don't try to force it.

When a client contacts an image consultant, they usually have a specific reason. For an individual, the reason may be professional — perhaps they want to advance in their company and looking the part will help. Or they may have personal considerations, such as having recently gone through a divorce or hitting middle age.

Knowing why the client feels they need an image consultant's services can help you tailor your services to those needs. The sections that follow give you a variety of ways to determine an individual client's needs. (Section 3.6 covers corporate clients.)

3.1.2 Client Questionnaires

First give your client a general questionnaire and allow them time to fill it out. The following sample new client questionnaire was created by image consultant Marsha Miller. Your own questionnaire can include questions based on your own specializations.

Sample New Client Questionnaire

Basic Information

Name: _____

Address: _____

Phone: _____ Fax: _____

Email: _____

Employer: _____

Job Title: _____

Length of Employment: _____ Age: _____

Marital Status: ❑ Single ❑ Married ❑ Divorced

Children: ❑ Y ❑ N # of Children (if applicable): _____

Measurements

Height: _____ Weight: _____

Dress Size: _____ Pant Size: _____

Jacket Size: _____ Shoe Size: _____

Other Questions

1. How did you hear about this company?

_____

_____

2. Why do you feel the need to employ an image consultant? Please include information on life changes, such as re-entering the job market, divorce, etc. *(All information is kept absolutely confidential and used solely to provide you better service.)*

_____

_____

_____

3. What do you want to achieve from an image update? *(Check all that apply.)*

- ❏ A more professional image
- ❏ Greater confidence for personal satisfaction
- ❏ Want to look younger/slimmer
- ❏ How to put together wardrobe to save time
- ❏ Other (please specify): _____

4. In which areas do you feel you need advice? *(Check all that apply.)*

- ❏ Hair/makeup
- ❏ Clothing selection
- ❏ Putting together a whole wardrobe
- ❏ Accessorizing
- ❏ Speaking in social situations
- ❏ Speaking to groups
- ❏ Appearing in the media
- ❏ Dining etiquette
- ❏ Business etiquette
- ❏ Other (please specify): _____

In addition to a general new client questionnaire, you may also decide to give the client additional questionnaires during your preliminary meeting. Two sample questionnaires are shown on this page and the next. In section 3.2 you will find questionnaires you can use to evaluate various aspects of a client's image (makeup, grooming, wardrobe.)

Creative Fashion Profile

by Georgia Donovan
www.georgiadonovan.com

1. How would you describe your current fashion style?

2. Who is your style icon?

3. What is the biggest fashion mistake you have ever made?

4. What was your best fashion moment?

5. If you could only have two things in fashion what would they be?

6. How would someone describe you in terms of your clothes?

7. What is the best fashion advice you have ever received?

8. Do you have a signature piece you wear all of the time? What is it?

9. What would you never be caught wearing?

10. If you had unlimited store credit, where would you shop?

11. What do you wish you could wear but can't?

12. What was your most extravagant fashion purchase?

13. What fashion magazines do you read?

14. What would you change about your current style?

15. What's the one thing about yourself you'd like to change?

Sample Personal Style Questionnaire

Karen Brunger of International Image Institute includes the following questions on her personal style questionnaire:

- How will your life be different five years from now?

- How would you describe your current image?

- How would you describe your ideal image?

- How would you describe your personality?

- Whose personal style do you admire?

- What does a typical week involve for you?

How do you feel about your...

Personal style?	❑ Excellent	❑ Fair	❑ Below Average
Fashion awareness?	❑ Excellent	❑ Fair	❑ Below Average
Knowledge of colors that flatter you?	❑ Excellent	❑ Fair	❑ Below Average
Knowledge of styles that flatter you?	❑ Excellent	❑ Fair	❑ Below Average
Your image at work, play, and home?	❑ Excellent	❑ Fair	❑ Below Average

Karen's questionnaire also asks clients to answer the following for each category of clothing (Business, Business Casual, Casual, Active Wear, Formal Eveningwear, etc.):

Clothing Worn: _____

Occasions: _____

Frequency: _____
(in days per month)

3.1.3   Questions to Ask

Once the new client questionnaire has been filled out, go over it together, gathering more information as you talk and making notes for the client's file.

Here are examples of questions you can ask clients. Any of these questions can be included on a questionnaire, but asking them directly gives you an opportunity to discuss the answers.

General Questions

- What are your personal and professional ambitions?

- Do you travel frequently?

- Do you deal directly with the public in the course of your job?

- Do you meet with clients like CEOs or small business owners?

- Do you have small children?

- How would you describe your social life?

- Do you go to many parties? Are they job-related?

- Do you play a lot of sports?

- Have you recently had a dramatic weight loss or gain?

- Are you actively engaged in a body improvement program?

Shopping Preferences

- Do you consider shopping to be a chore or a delight?

- Do you buy clothes based on impulse, or do you methodically plan your purchases?

- In the past, have you typically chosen clothes based on (check no more than three):
  ❑ Color   ❑ Fabric   ❑ Price   ❑ Brand   ❑ Style

Personal Style

Most likely, the minute you have a face-to-face consultation you'll know what style your client is currently portraying. You can also ask your client questions such as the following to help determine their style or create another questionnaire, like the one in the previous section.

- What words would you use to describe your personality?

- What kind of clothes are you most comfortable in?

- Which of the following terms best describe you (rank in order):

    ❑ Classic

    ❑ Dramatic

    ❑ Elegant

    ❑ Natural

    ❑ Sporty

    ❑ Other

How Can I Help?

- Did someone else suggest you seek my services, or did you choose to come on your own?

- What area of your image needs updating (personal, professional, or both)?

- Do you need strictly wardrobe help or help with hairstyles and cosmetics? How about communication skills and etiquette?

- Why do you want these services now? (Try to get them to open up and be as honest as possible. If they have had a painful divorce and are trying to recover, that will help you determine what their ultimate goal is. Their goal may be greater self-confidence in their personal life. Do they want to move up the corporate ladder? Together, write down what they would like to achieve. It should be measurable, if possible, and practical.)

3.1.4   Observing and Evaluating Your Client

You may have a client who knows they need some help with their over-all image but isn't sure what to change. In addition to asking your client what they think needs to be changed, you can make your own observations as you speak to the client, using a form like this one. It includes sample questions you can ask yourself.

Sample Evaluation Form (Female Client)

Appearance

Clothing

- Do her clothes fit her well?
- Does she have a particular style?
- Does it suit her personality?
- Is her style age-appropriate?
- Is it appropriate for her job?
- Does she look drab?
- Are there any stains or wrinkles?
- Is there anything visible that shouldn't be such as slip, bra straps, panty lines, etc.?
- Is anything ripped or are any buttons missing?
- Is the length of skirt or slacks too short or too long?

_____

_____

Shoes

- What color and style of shoes is she wearing?
- Do her shoes work with the rest of her outfit?
- Is the style appropriate for her job?
- Are her shoes scuffed or do they need polish?
- Is the heel height appropriate?
- Are the heels run down?

_____

_____

Accessories

- What accessories is she wearing?
- Do her accessories fit with her outfit?
- Is she wearing too much noisy jewelry?
- Does she wear eyeglasses?
- Do they suit her and flatter her face shape?
- Is she wearing hosiery?
- Is the color right?
- Are there runs?

_____

_____

Hair

- Does her hairstyle suit her face and personality?
- Is the color vibrant?
- Does the color suit her?
- Is there a clear style to her hair or is it just "there"?
- Does it look severe?
- Does it fall in her face?
- Are there visible roots?
- Does she have dandruff?

_____

_____

Physical Flaws

- Does she have any skin problems like blemishes or age spots?
- Do her teeth need some work such as braces, whitening, veneers, etc.?
- Is she overweight?
- Does she have figure flaws?

_____

_____

Makeup and Nails

- Is she wearing an appropriate amount of makeup?
- Does it make her skin look fresh or dull?
- Is her lipstick smudged?
- Can you see lip liner?
- Does she have mascara flakes or raccoon eyes?
- Are her nails polished?
- Is the polish chipped?
- Is the nail length appropriate?
- Does she have ragged cuticles?

_____

_____

Other Observations

_____

_____

_____

Communication Skills

Verbal and Vocal

- Does she use proper grammar?
- Is she articulate?
- Does she fumble for words?
- Does she speak too quickly or slowly?
- Does she whine or drone?
- Does she speak too softly or loudly?
- Does she use slang or jargon?
- Does she swear?
- Does she sound educated?
- Does she sound confident?

_____

_____

Non-verbal

- Does she walk confidently?
- Did she extend her hand with a firm handshake to introduce herself?
- Does she make appropriate eye contact or appear distracted?
- Does she sit upright or slouch?
- Does she have nervous gestures?
- What is she communicating with her body language?

_____

_____

Other Observations

_____

_____

_____

_____

For male clients you will revise the questions accordingly (e.g. remove questions about makeup and add a section about facial hair). You can also add questions to suit your own specialization, such as conversation skills or etiquette.

3.1.5   Creating an Action Plan and Budget

Once your client has told you what they think they need, and you have made your own observations, the next step is to create an action plan. An action plan is simply a written statement that identifies what you want to accomplish (your goals) and how you plan to accomplish it.

While you could create an action plan on your own, then present it to the client, to get the client's agreement, it's more effective to first sit down with your client to discuss goals for improvement then create an action plan together.

Before you share your observations, be sure to compliment your client on the positive things you see in them. No one wants to be bombarded with everything that's wrong with them so be tactful when letting the client know which areas are the most glaring. Then describe the services that you offer to correct those areas.

Remember, you are the expert here. Your client may think they are good at selecting clothes, but you may disagree. If they need some convincing about a certain service, you need to gently but firmly state your opinion.

If they agree with your assessment, then you can proceed. However, you can't help those who aren't convinced they need it. If they are resistant, provide only the services they want. Stay professional and pleasant at all times. Perhaps by the time you have finished they will have changed their mind. In some cases the client may need time to decide how they want to proceed.

Once you and the client have determined the overall goals, list the actions that need to be taken to reach each goal. For instance, if they want a promotion, their actions might look like this:

Sample Action Plan

Step #1: Evaluate Areas That Need Improvement

- Clothing/style

- Makeup/skin care

- Hairstyle

- Accessories

- Hygiene, dental repair

- Posture/movements

- Voice quality

- Vocabulary, grammar, telephone manner

- Etiquette

Step #2: Plan to Correct Weak Areas

- Update wardrobe

- New hairstyle that fits in with corporate image

- Practice vocal exercises and study grammar

Step #3: Determine Priorities

- First priority — wardrobe

- Second priority — hairstyle

- Third priority — vocal exercises

Develop a timeline for accomplishing each priority. You can review your progress every week and adjust it as necessary. This is just an example. Every client's action plan is going to be unique but it should include the basic elements shown above.

Budget

If a client has many areas that need improvement, consultations can quickly become expensive. You certainly don't want them to utilize your services and be presented with a bill that shocks them. In your initial discussion you need to adequately and clearly explain what your rates are and give them some kind of estimate for the services you have in mind for them.

Before you begin performing any service, you need to have an idea of approximately how much your client has to spend. If their budget is very tight, you may need to determine which services they want or need the most and put others off for another time. A budget worksheet can help you both decide how to proceed.

See section 5.4.4 (Setting Fees) for advice on how much to charge for each service you provide.

Sample Budget Worksheet

Rank the services needed in order of priority, with number one being the most needed and so forth. Continue for all the services you wish to receive.

Appearance   Fee

WARDROBE CONSULTATION   *RANK:* ___

Individual coaching in consultant's office $_____
(minimum of 30 minutes)

Brief critique of clothing, taking measurements, $_____
determining body type, and discussion of appropriate
styles

HAIR/FACE CONSULTATION   *RANK:* ___

Individual consultation *(minimum of one hour)* $_____

Hairstyle/color critique, discussion of face/skin care and $_____
cosmetics, assessing new styles and color

Color analysis of client $_____

Evaluation of skin type, sampling products and $_____
instruction in makeup application

Digital photo taken for records $_____

ACCESSORIZING POINTERS   *RANK:* ___

Individual consultation *(minimum of 30 minutes)* $_____

Advice for putting it all together, including discussion $_____
of jewelry, scarves, handbags, briefcases, hose and shoes

CLOSET ORGANIZATION   *RANK:* ___

Individual consultation *(minimum of 30 minutes in office $_____
or one hour in client's home)*

Recommendations for closet system/organization $_____

Optional help evaluating present wardrobe $_____

SHOPPING ASSISTANCE   RANK: ___

Individual consultation *(minimum of one hour)* $_____

Estimate of purchases $_____

Client and consultant meet at agreed-upon retail $_____
location

Evaluation of clothing choices and recommendation for $_____
purchases

Speaking   Fee

VOICE/CONVERSATION CONSULTATION   RANK: ___

Individual consultation (minimum of one hour) $_____

Evaluation and discussion of quality of voice $_____

Demonstration of vocal exercises $_____

Audio taping $_____

Grammar and vocabulary review $_____

Client presented with written exercises to practice at $_____
home

NON-VERBAL COMMUNICATION CONSULTATION   RANK: ___

Individual consultation *(minimum of 30 minutes)* $_____

Video taping of client $_____

Evaluation of gestures, nervous habits, etc. $_____

Tips on posture, walking, shaking hands, eye contact $_____

MEDIA COACHING   RANK: ___

Individual consultation *(minimum of 30 minutes)* $_____

Video taping $_____

Evaluation of client's performance $_____

Pointers for gestures, clothing, etc. $_____

Practice interviewing sessions $_____

3.2   How to Do a Total Image Consultation

3.2.1   Body Analysis

For a total image consultation, start with the body. Your client may be losing weight and exercising, which will mean they are getting smaller, but your appointment is with them now. Deal with the figure they have at this moment.

Even if they lose weight, their basic bone structure and shape will not change. Discourage unrealistic body expectations — the average person isn't built like a supermodel. The primary purpose of image consulting is to make the best of what you've been given, although some clients may want referrals to specialists such as a cosmetic surgeon or personal trainer.

Catherine Graham Bell of Prime Impressions prefers to use the following tools during a client consultation:

- A tape measure

- A scale

- Rulers (to measure neck length, shoulders and hips)

- A wall chart (to measure height, the distance from the chest, hips, and knees from the floor)

- A computer program on body analysis

To do a body analysis, Bell uses a program she ordered and recommends called Your Personal Style Solutions from The Australian Image Company (see below). It includes a body measurement chart and allows you to key information into the computer. You can see a sample body analysis online at **www.fashion-411.com/Body_Type_Analysis.htm**. Here are some suppliers of products used by consultants:

- *The Australian Image Company*
  www.taic.com.au/09_Intl.html

- *Color Me Beautiful*
  www.colormebeautiful.com

- *Color Quest*
  www.color-quest.com

- *Direct Colour International*
  www.styleandimage.co.uk

- *Flying Colors Image Studio*
  www.susanrainey.com/analysis.htm

- *Improvability*
  www.improvability.co.uk/products/swatches.html

- *International Image Institute*
  www.imageinstitute.com/store

Begin by taking full measurements. Measure the inseam (length of the legs), arm length, waist, hips and bust as well as height and weight. Record all this in the client's file — they may be needed for alterations and they help determine what type of proportions your client has. Once you have determined your client's body characteristics, discuss what bearing it has on their clothing choices. As you saw in chapter two, there are rules for dressing that will minimize a client's flaws. Help your client select styles that will play up their assets and minimize their flaws.

If you have a female client, you can show her illustrations of the different body types and point out what style she has. Then, from the neckline to the shoulder pads, sleeve length, waistline, and hem length, go over what styles she should be looking for. Discuss dresses, skirts, sweaters, blouses, tops, slacks, even styles in swimsuits. This eliminates any guesswork for her. Your goal is to create the illusion of perfect proportion. You should have drawings or photographs of the correct styles to give her for shopping purposes.

Discuss fabrics — which ones wear well and hug the body, which ones are not flattering for less-than-perfect figures. You might have fabric samples on hand which you can let her touch and familiarize herself with. Also, discuss accessories — scarves, necklaces, shoes, color of hose, even the style and shape of handbags. It is the details that make or break an outfit. Show her pictures of the accessories she should be looking for. See section 3.3 for more information on Wardrobe Consulting.

3.2.2   Color Analysis

After completing the style and fabric part of the session, it's time to deal with color. Color is probably the area of clothes selection that most of us either neglect or ignore. "If it fits and the price is right, I can live with the color," is many people's attitude. But it shouldn't be so. The right color enhances and energizes our face. The wrong one drains our complexion and our eyes.

Here's how to help your clients surround themselves with vibrant, flattering color. First, here's a checklist of color analysis tools to bring to an initial client consultation. The first item, a portable full spectrum light, can be found at local stores or online at **www.naturallighting.com** and other sites. To find the other tools listed below, see section 3.2.1 for a list of companies that supply products.

- Portable full spectrum light

- Portable mirror with true reflection

- White cape and scarf

- Seasonal "flags" or charts (each flag shows a range of colors for the season); it's a way to demonstrate the seasonal colors all at once

- Metallic "drapes" for determining best jewelry (a drape is a large piece of fabric for putting below the client's face to view the change in appearance)

- Undertone drapes (for determining cool or warm)

- Seasonal drapes (for determining season)

- Flow drapes (for determining flow)

- Extendor drapes (to show full range of colors)

Begin by having your client remove any existing makeup and clip any hair off their face. Have them sit in front of a lighted makeup mirror. Place various colored drapes, one at a time, across their neckline and chest. The drapes will represent selected warm and cool colors.

As you work, observe changes to their complexion when the colors change. Colors that are flattering to their complexion will make their face and eyes brighter, while other shades will make their skin look washed out or muddy. Once you have determined if their color palette should be cool or warm, continue the process to find their best shades. These are recorded in their profile.

You should have booklets with swatches of fabric or blocks of color that illustrate the colors the client should look for when shopping to give them. (These can be obtained from the suppliers in section 3.2.1.)

What do you say to a client who laments that their whole wardrobe is in the wrong colors? Do they have to rush out and spend a fortune on all new clothes? Not necessarily. What is vital is having the right color around their face. Scarves or ties with several shades can brighten up the wrong color blouse or shirt. If the blazer isn't the right color, then make sure the top underneath is. At least your client can salvage some things with this method. Then when they shop for new things, they need to make sure they are in the right palette.

While your knowledge of colors will improve your client's look, it's also important to find out their preferred colors. Don't count on your clients wearing a garment if they don't like the colors.

"I ask what their favorite colors are, and what colors they get compliments about when wearing," says Lori B. Johnson of Your Best Image. Ask your clients to pull out from their closet their favorite items of clothing, clothes that they have received the most compliments on and that feel good to wear. Maybe it's their rainy day sweater or their Saturday night dress. Look at the colors in their choices. Whatever makes them feel good and brightens up their day should be considered for their personal color chart.

3.2.3   Skin Care and Makeup

The next logical step in the consultation is skin care and makeup, since your client is already bare faced in front of the mirror.

Ask your client questions about how their skin reacts and determine what type of skin they have. Offer some suggestions for basic skin care and refer them to specialists if needed. Your client needs to know how to nourish and protect their skin because a healthy complexion is one of the most important assets to an all-around polished image.

Some image consultants have cosmetics on hand to do makeovers. Go over products with your client, using their personal color analysis as a guide for lipstick, blush and eye shadow shades. Show them the correct application and then let them try it on their face. They need to learn how to do this for themselves. Keep trying until they get the knack of it. Record every product, brand and color you used. Your client may decide to buy everything they try.

How do you determine what makeup style is best for your client? You'll want to consider the following six essential things:

- facial shape

- career

- lifestyle

- makeup preferences

- budget

- time the client wants to spend doing application

Some questions you can ask your client before making recommendations are as follows:

- Do you have any allergies?

- Where do you feel your problem skin areas are?

- What is your basic skin care regimen?

- Can you be faithful to a morning and evening skin care regimen?

- Do you have to reapply makeup in the middle of the day?

- Do you use a lot of glamour products? If so, what are they?

- Do you remove your makeup at night before going to bed?

- Do you feel you use too much or too little makeup?

- What type of makeup products are you currently using?

- How do you feel your makeup is reacting with your skin?

- If you were stranded on an island, what two makeup products would be a must-have?

- What do you feel are your best and worst facial features?

While you are dealing with makeup, give your client suggestions for a daytime face and an evening look, explaining the difference. Consider recording this part of the session on a camcorder and giving them a copy of these personalized cosmetic application tips. Remind the client that the colors you chose were in keeping with their color palette.

If you are giving them information in writing, you will need to create a form with space to record their skin type, what type of products you used on them and their makeup colors. You can even give directions for how and in what order to apply everything. Your client will definitely appreciate your attention to detail.

Also give your client grooming tips to ensure their makeup looks good. According to Donna Panko of Professional Skill Builders, Inc., the number one mistake women make is using too much makeup, while the number two mistake is not wearing any makeup. So why is too much or too little a big grooming mistake? "Makeup needs to complement your client's overall look," says Panko. She offers these recommendations:

- Be current. Encourage your client to know what up-to-date makeup looks like and, if they are behind the times, to schedule a makeup session with a good makeup artist.

- Blend, blend, blend. Make sure your client knows the importance of having the right makeup brushes and techniques.

- Teach your client how to put on the right amount of makeup in a ten-minute time frame.

- Convince your all-natural clients that makeup can provide a more polished look. It doesn't take much, just some concealer, powder, mascara, blush, and lip gloss.

- Encourage your client to go to a makeup professional once per year and bring their own makeup products, allowing the expert to show them new techniques.

- Don't forget about eyebrows. Go to a professional to get the right eyebrow shape, pluck any straggling hairs, and find out how to maintain the shape.

3.2.4 Hair

While you'll determine what type of hair cut, style, and color will best suit your client, a hairstylist will carry out your suggestions. It's not your job to bring out the brush and blow dryer, but it is definitely your job to have an objective eye and creative vision.

Here are questions to consider:

- Does your client have a good haircut with style? How much are they willing to spend for a stylist?

- Does your client need a conditioning hair treatment?

- Is your client's hair color the best choice?

- Is your client's hair the right length for their face shape?

- Is your client using the right hair care products (volumizers, styling gels, etc.)?

- Does your client need highlights with bolder tones and hues?

Take a digital photograph of your client's face and, using a computer program, show them how they would look with various hairstyles. While programs used by beauty salons can be pricey (around $1,000), you can find other, less expensive programs online at websites like **www.thehairstyler.com** and **www.sollab.net/maggi**.

Show the client a variety of hairstyles so they can see what works and what doesn't. As with the makeup, some hairstyles are appropriate for the office and some for dining out. You can also show them different hair colors, highlights, etc. Once you have chosen at least a couple of possibilities, print out color copies for them to take to a stylist. They will probably want to know your recommendations for good hairstylists, so have a list ready. Make copies of the photos for their file as well.

Here are some quick tips from hair expert Karen M. Shelton of Hair-Boutique.com on finding the right style:

- The best styles will frame your client's face, enhancing and balancing their natural body shape.

- When choosing a style for your client's face type, remember to reduce hair where the face is wide and add hair where the face is thin or narrow.

- Suggest that your client accept their hair for what it is. If their hair is thin, wavy, curly, or straight, encourage them to not torture their mane with strong chemicals, which over time leads to damaged, unhealthy hair.

- When counseling your clients on what type of hairstyle is best for them, look for something that is kept off their face so that they can be seen.

- Flip through beauty and hair magazines together and search for hairstyles that appeal to your client.

- Take the photos you have chosen to the stylist for consultation and discuss the pros and cons with the hair professional.

- Encourage your client to find a stylist they can trust and who treats them with respect.

Hair Care

Recommend that your client invest in the best products for their hair. If they can't buy salon-quality products, insist that they buy the best they can afford. Advise your clients to keep their hair healthy with deep conditioning treatments as needed and be sure to have their ends trimmed every six to eight weeks.

Panko explains that when most people get their hair done, the professional styles it and they love it — but they can't maintain that look on their own. Encourage clients to make a styling appointment where they bring their own products and style their hair in front of the hairdresser, who will teach them techniques to get the look they loved.

Next, it's time to discuss the upkeep of their hair color. "You can't let your client have roots showing," explains Panko. "Also, color tends to wash out after about five or six weeks. Make sure their color matches their skin tone and eye tone."

3.2.5   Grooming

As mentioned in section 2.1.7, grooming can be defined simply as "to care for one's appearance." It involves ensuring that all aspects of personal appearance are neat, clean, polished, or otherwise cared for.

To assist you in advising your clients on grooming, you can ask them questions, have them complete a questionnaire, and share your observations from your preliminary consultation.

Specific areas you can cover include:

Personal Hygiene

A good way to begin discussing this delicate area is by giving your client a questionnaire. You can include questions such as:

❑ Do you bathe daily?

❑ Do you brush your teeth, floss regularly, and visit a dentist twice a year?

❑ Do you wear deodorant?

❑ Do you wear too much perfume? Your scent should not enter or stay in a room after you leave.

The next step is to discuss hygiene with your client. This is an opportunity to share valuable information with your client that can help them in their career and personal life. For example, clothing made of synthetic fabrics can retain body odor. Another example of a fact that your client may not be aware of is that some people have allergies to specific scents so fragrance is frowned on for the office. Review the tips in section 2.1.7 for more ideas of advice to share.

Nails

If your client neglects their nails, you should discuss general nail health, share tips on how to make them look better (section 2.1.7), and suggest products and specialists for problems. Show them how good buffed and manicured nails look instead of ragged cuticles and uneven nail length. List products they should have at home and at the office, and show them colors that you would suggest for polish.

Nails on the feet are not to be neglected either. "If a woman wears open-toe shoes, she needs to get a pedicure," says Panko. Of course, not everyone has perfect toes, but everyone can make sure that their toenails are clean and well-maintained.

Teeth

Depending on the client, you may need to discuss their teeth as part of their total image consultation. Many people have attractive faces that

Sample Client Grooming Questionnaire

by Donna Panko
Professional Skill Builders

1. Have you changed your hairstyle and color in the last year? ☐ Yes ☐ No

2. Do you wear eyeglasses? If so, have you changed the frame in the last year or two? ☐ Yes ☐ No

3. Do you ever wear clothes that have spots, falling hemlines or missing buttons? ☐ Yes ☐ No

4. Do you always put your clothes back in the closet in ready-to-wear condition? ☐ Yes ☐ No

5. Are your clothes pressed? ☐ Yes ☐ No

6. Do you own an iron? ☐ Yes ☐ No

7. Do you pay attention to the fact that casual does not mean sloppy? ☐ Yes ☐ No

8. When you're wearing Business Casual dress, are your clothes tucked in? ☐ Yes ☐ No

9. Do you have a belt-looped garment where a belt is required, but ignore it? ☐ Yes ☐ No

10. Do you polish your shoes on a regular basis? ☐ Yes ☐ No

11. Do you shave on a regular basis? ☐ Yes ☐ No

12. Has anyone ever told you that you have body odor? ☐ Yes ☐ No

13. Are your undergarments appropriate? ☐ Yes ☐ No

14. Do you have visible panty lines? Runs in pantyhose? ☐ Yes ☐ No

15. Have you been fitted for a bra in the past six months? ☐ Yes ☐ No

are spoiled because of uneven, crooked or discolored teeth. Make suggestions for improving their smile if necessary, and offer referrals for cosmetic dentists and at-home whitening kits.

Glasses

Another often overlooked part of a face is eyeglasses. They should be contemporary and suit the shape of the client's face as well as the style of their wardrobe. Someone who has a round face, curly hair, round earrings, and round glasses is off base. They will look better having eye wear with a frame that complements their face shape — a style a little more horizontal.

Many image consultants take their clients to see a vision specialist to help them find the right frames. Another option may be to use the computer program you use for hairstyles. Use the digital photo of the client's face to add various styles and colors of glasses. Once you have narrowed the selection down to a couple of good ones, print out color photos which can be taken to an optometrist or vision store.

Clothing

Good grooming also extends to clothing and ensuring there are no stains, wrinkles, rips, etc. Give feedback on your observations and do a complete wardrobe consultation if necessary.

Ending the Consultation

At the end of the consultation, you should review everything you covered and make sure the client has copies of everything. Give the client ample time to ask questions — you have given them a great deal of information to absorb in one sitting. Stress that you will be available for further sessions if they feel the need.

Tabulate how much they owe you and provide a written statement. Make a note in your calendar to contact them in two to three weeks to see what progress has been made and to see if they need any additional consultations. (See section 3.5 for other suggestions.)

3.3 Wardrobe Consultations

3.3.1 Deciding What to Keep, Fix, or Discard

The easiest way to deal with a client's wardrobe is to separate items in their closet into three piles on the floor: what to keep, what to fix, and what to discard. Start by having your clients take this quiz:

Wardrobe Questionnaire

1. Have you worn this garment in the past year? ❑ Yes ❑ No

2. Does this item fit you properly? ❑ Yes ❑ No

3. Is the fabric comfortable? ❑ Yes ❑ No

4. Is the fabric in good shape? ❑ Yes ❑ No

5. Do the lines flatter your body type? ❑ Yes ❑ No

6. Is this your style? ❑ Yes ❑ No

7. Is this the best color for your skin tones? ❑ Yes ❑ No

8. Will this garment make it another year? ❑ Yes ❑ No

9. Is this garment clean? ❑ Yes ❑ No

10. Does this garment fit into your current lifestyle? ❑ Yes ❑ No

11. Do you own too many of the same thing? ❑ Yes ❑ No

Interpreting the Results

Question #1: Have you worn this garment in the past year?

Chances are if you haven't worn an article of clothing in a year, you won't wear it this year. So why hold on to it?

Question #2: Does this item fit you properly?

If the answer is no, it may be time to toss it. For a second opinion, take it to your tailor. They will let you know if it is savable by taking off an inch or loosening up a seam. But if it's not, make way for new threads.

Question #3: Is the fabric comfortable?

It might have looked good in the store but, once at home, it turned into that itchy mohair sweater that gives you a week-long rash. Get rid of it!

Question #4: Is the fabric in good shape?

If your client's favorite pair of jeans has holes in them beyond any fashion statement, or if their once favorite pair of Manolo Blahnik heels have lost their soles, it may be time to say goodbye to them.

Question #5: Do the lines flatter your body?

If your client is five feet tall and wearing an ankle-length skirt that she practically swims in, put it in the toss pile. A piece of clothing that doesn't look good on the body has no place in the closet.

Question #6: Is this your style?

Maybe your client bought it on a whim. Maybe it was a birthday gift from Aunt Sally. Whatever the reason, it's still a canary yellow boa that's never going to be worn and is taking up space where a beautiful silk scarf can go. If a garment does not enhance your image, let it go.

Question #7: Is this the best color for your skin tone?

A good way to separate clothes is to take a good look at them and weed out anything that is not in your client's color scheme.

Question #8: Will this garment make it another year?

Whether it's a down jacket that has lost too many feathers or a sequined tube top that is now "so last year," all clothes have an expiration date on them. Sometimes, no matter how much your client loves them, it may be time to face the music that this item isn't in shape now and won't be worn next year. So help them to part ways.

Question #9: Is this garment clean?

Your client went to a party and somebody spilled sauce on their silk shirt. After a few days at the dry cleaner's, the shirt came back with the "Sorry, we tried everything but still couldn't get your stain out" tag. Yet, instead of getting rid of that shirt, they stuck it back in the closet for the magic stain lifter to fix. Reality check: there are no magic stain lifters that aren't sold in your local grocery store's cleaning aisle.

Question #10: Does this garment fit into your current lifestyle?

We all go through different stages of life and some of us have a clothing scrapbook in our closet to prove it. We keep clothes from our first job (even though we're at an executive level and wouldn't be caught dead wearing them right now) or maternity clothes long after there's any possibility they'll be needed again. If your client owns a piece of clothing that doesn't reflect who they are in their current life roles, make some room in their closet for items that do. Out-of-style clothing implies to onlookers that your client's job skills may not be up to date.

Question #11: Do you own too many of the same thing?

In life, there can be too much of a good thing. Too many calories, too many t-shirts, and too many decal sweaters are three things that can kill anyone's perfect wardrobe. It's fine to stick to things that work, but if your client already owns one or two of the same piece, there's no need for a third, fourth, or tenth. The only exception to this rule is when it comes to undergarment essentials. But while you are weeding out what to save and what to pass on, examine bras, underpants, socks, and pantyhose. If they are too big or too small, or have holes or runs, it's time to get rid of them.

Have a box or garbage bag for discards, and another one to hold items that need altering or cleaning. You may want to encourage your client to donate their discarded clothing to a charity such as the Salvation Army (**www.salvationarmy.org**), a battered women's shelter, or My Sister's Closet (**www.mysisterscloset.com**).

3.3.2   Closet Organizing

The closet is more than a dark hole where you dump your shoes and stand waiting for inspiration every morning. It is the place where outfits are built and where the proper organization can set the tone for a productive day. On mornings when you're running late you can reach into an orderly closet and find everything you need to put together a professional and impeccable outfit.

So what are the secrets you can share with your client for closet organization? First, they need to invest in some tools that will maximize the space and efficiency of the area (read the rest of this section for product ideas). There are many closet organizers available today in home improvement stores that will stack, hang and literally double the space in a closet. Recommend that your client take a Saturday afternoon and browse through the closet displays and select a system.

Once the closet organizers have been purchased, the real work can begin. Have your client dress in old jeans and comfortable shoes — there's a lot to be done. Empty out every single item from the closet and vacuum the floor. Remove any nails or hooks so you're starting from scratch. Now is the time to install whatever new goodies were purchased. Recommend that there be:

- Adequate space for hanging dresses or other items that reach to the floor. It's preferable to hang slacks full length rather than folded, but in small closets that's not always possible.

- Space for shoes — either in clear boxes on a shelf, shoeboxes with snapshots of the shoe on the front of the box, or a bag that hangs over the closet door. Try to keep them off the bottom of the closet floor where it's dark and difficult to identify the shoes.

- Shelving for folded knits and casual shirts; hooks or hanging space for belts.

- Depending on space, you may also have boxes for jewelry and a place for hats and handbags.

- Some kind of light source. If the closet doesn't have its own fixture, pick up a light that doesn't need electricity. Your client can't find outfits in the dark.

- A full length mirror either on the door, in the bedroom near the closet, or in the closet.

One important but often overlooked item in the closet is the hanger. Padded hangers are wonderful but can be pricey. Your client should have all the same kind of hanger so clothes will hang smoothly. If they don't want to invest in all padded hangers, have them buy the smooth plastic kind. Pull out all the wire hangers from dry cleaners and recycle them.

There are several methods for aligning clothes into the closet. One of the best ways is by building outfits (see the next page for tips on how to put together outfits).

For example: a gray suit is worn with a burgundy silk blouse, so the jacket and skirt go side-by-side into the closet and the blouse hangs beside them. Then build another outfit and keep hanging outfits until you have single items. They are then grouped together (all blouses, all slacks, etc.) by color — dark to light. Then when the client needs to pick a suit for the morning, there's no fumbling for a top to put under a suit. It's all right there.

Another option is to hang all jackets, all skirts, all blouses, etc., together by colors. Have the client choose whatever method will be more efficient for them. As they place the wardrobe back in, have them note what needs to be purchased. For example: "I need a white long-sleeved blouse, new lightweight black slacks, and brown leather flat shoes." This will make shopping more productive and help your client avoid impulse buys which won't work with the rest of the wardrobe.

Accessories are given the same treatment as the clothes — discard what doesn't pass the checklist test. Hang all belts together. Purses can either be hung or placed in an open basket. Scarves can be hung with clothespins from a coat hanger or clipped from a pants hanger. Shirts and knits are carefully folded and then placed by color on a shelf above the hanging rack.

TIP: A small sachet hanging in the closet gives clothes a subtle fragrance that won't overwhelm.

Congratulate your client! They have an orderly closet that will practically dress them every morning.

Putting Together Outfits

According to Karen Brunger, a wardrobe "module" equals one jacket, two bottoms, three tops, shoes, two hose for each bottom, and a bag. (She says that five wardrobe modules are a good number for each season.)

When putting together a wardrobe module, you…

1. Lay the third layer (for example, the jacket) on the bed as if it's on the body.

2. Find the best two bottoms (skirt or pants) that work with that jacket by laying them on the bed with the jacket.

3. Find the best three tops that work with the jacket and either bottom.

4. For each shirt that requires a tie, find at least one or two ties that work.

5. Find the shoes, belt, and bag that work with these combinations.

6. Find at least two pairs of hose/socks that match each bottom.

7. Find jewelry or accessories.

8. Find appropriate underwear for this module.

9. Find appropriate outerwear for this module.

3.3.3 Wardrobe Shopping

Shopping is many peoples' favorite pastime. But for many others the challenge of schlepping through store after store, looking through crowded racks to find something that fits both their size and price range, is anything but fun. They need help. That's where you come in. You have the skill and expertise to help your clients find flattering clothes that fit their lifestyle. You've already had an initial consultation with this client in which you have discussed their body type, recommended styles and selected a color palette. You have brought along a color swatch book and illustrations of the styles they need to look for to help you both with the selections. Your client has made a list of items that need to be purchased.

To carry out the shopping, arrange to meet at an agreed-upon location such as a mall with numerous women's or men's clothing stores. (See section 3.7.1 for detailed advice on finding and working with clothing retailers.)

Advise your client to wear comfortable, easy to remove clothing with good foundation garments and pantyhose. Have them style their hair and apply makeup so they can face the mirror all day and be positive. Comfortable shoes are a must!

Consult the client's list and review what you're shopping for. Beginning with the most important items, head for the appropriate department. For instance, your client may need a two-piece suit for interviews and special occasions. Suits are sold separately or as a single piece; buying separately allows you to purchase different sizes for each piece.

With your client following you, begin inspecting the racks of jackets and skirts or pants. As you pull out items to look at, make judgments about the fabrics, color and details, showing your client why you are choosing some things over others. Create a stack of items for the client to try on. Then test the client's knowledge and let them choose, asking them to explain their choices. Praise them for good choices and let them take unsuitable choices into the dressing room so they can see why it's not a good choice.

Have the client try on the items in front of a mirror while you point out the positive and negative details. If the outfits need to be accessorized, then select jewelry, scarves and shoes while the client is still dressing.

Drop off items for purchase at the cash register and mark them off your list. Make suggestions about prices and sales so your client can learn the difference between value and price. Have them keep all receipts and ask at every store for their return policy. Continue this process for as long as necessary or until all the items on the list have been purchased.

Beware of overshopping. If your client has exhausted themselves or their resources, continue your adventure another day. No one makes good decisions when they're worn out. At the end of the consultation, help the client with their purchases and bill them for your time.

For Clients Shopping Alone

If your client has not engaged you for a shopping session, compose a "wish list" for future shopping or to ask for as gifts. Don't forget big items like outerwear and boots, depending on your climate.

After a wardrobe consultation, your client should have a very good idea of the style and fabrics that suit them as well as what they need to purchase right away. Note the items on the "wish list" in their file and give them the original list to take with them.

Also give the client the materials described in section 3.2.1 on total image consultations, such as an illustration of their body type and examples of clothing styles that suit their body. Clear, color photographs on card stock are ideal. The client also needs a color swatch book or card that pictures the correct color palette for their complexion — something small that can be carried in a purse or briefcase. Including a list on the back of the card of suggested colors for accessories like shoes, hose and jewelry would be helpful as well.

Also consider printing a small card with a list of items to shop for, a list of local retailers that are good sources of items, and tips for finding bargains. Tuck a copy in with the materials your client is to take home.

3.4 Communication and Etiquette

Assessing how a client speaks and behaves can be a delicate issue. Choose your words carefully and make suggestions, don't issue commands. Remember that part of your job is to encourage and motivate your client like a coach or a teacher.

Much of your consulting work with individuals may involve teaching them basic skills. Section 2.2 has a wealth of information on communication and etiquette which you can share with your clients. However, because most people learn best by doing, this section includes a number of exercises you can use with your clients to supplement the information you give them.

Vocal Exercises

Have your client read and answer some casual questions while you film them with a camcorder. Play the tape and point out what you think needs improvement. How is the client's voice quality? Do they speak too softly? Many women have a difficult time conveying authority with their voices because they feel uncomfortable speaking up. On the other extreme, some people are too loud and appear domineering. There is a happy medium that you're shooting for — assertive, confident and self-assured, but not obnoxious or overbearing.

Go over elements of vocal control such as pitch, tone and volume, and practice these with the client. Emphasize the importance of deep breathing and speaking from the diaphragm rather than from the nose or upper chest.

Karen Brunger videotapes her clients in a mock presentation or job interview that would require normal speech. First she asks them to act out the scripted situation as they would ordinarily do. Then she asks that they replay the same situation but be as boring as possible. Lastly, they are asked to act out the situation with exaggerated and extreme expression and gestures.

She finds that most often, the first two scenarios are surprisingly similar. The level of emotion the clients exhibit is essentially the same in the boring and the normal portrayals. The over-the-top portrayal turns out to contain the level of expression and emotion one would expect in a normal situation. The clients view the tape and compare what they look like compared to how they think they look when using different levels of expression.

Image consultants can also help clients learn to enunciate well for clearer communication. Here are a few examples:

- With a pencil in your mouth, read a number of sentences. This helps to strengthen the mouth muscles. Reading tongue twisters can also help improve diction.

- Reading childrens' stories aloud is a great exercise. While doing so, exaggerate the inflection and enunciation of the consonants.

- Read the nursery rhyme "How Now, Brown Cow" while exaggerating the movement of the mouth and jaw.

Such exercises can help improve problems clients may be experiencing with diction. Serious speech problems will likely require a voice coach to resolve.

Improving Vocabulary

If you want to work with clients on vocabulary, consider developing a quick vocabulary test or using an online test like the customizable one at **www.vocaboly.com/vocabulary-test**. If your client wants to improve in this area, you can suggest a number of exercises to help them add new words to their vocabulary daily. They can either actively seek out unknown words using a dictionary or take note of words in the newspaper or books that they may not be familiar with.

Non-Verbal Communication

Not all communication is verbal. Show the client a series of body positions and what each one communicates. Have them practice simple movements like walking across the room, sitting down, and listening to a conversation. Focus on eliminating nervous gestures. An excellent way to make your client aware of their gestures is to videotape a conversation. Encourage them to take notice of their movements while participating in a meeting, attending a social event, or during dinner.

Conversation Skills

Let your clients know that developing conversation skills isn't an immediate process. Clients can start small — begin by saying hello or starting a brief conversation with people in the grocery store or at the bank. They can work themselves up to chatting with people at parties and other gatherings. Practice makes perfect, and image consultants can help their clients master this art.

Etiquette

An excellent way to get hands-on training in dining etiquette is to go out for dinner or lunch and practice the behaviors described in section 2.2.4. Likewise, you can have your clients practice business etiquette by taking opportunities to introduce people at social functions.

Image consultant Gloria Starr of Global Success Strategies videotapes her clients in meetings and other interactions. Then she reviews the tape to show clients what they are doing right. It is important to note the positive as well, as many clients feel vulnerable and ashamed for not already knowing these rules of conduct. Then she makes suggestions about different approaches her clients may take and different gestures that will be more effective in a situation. By using videotapes and exercises, you will help clients identify strengths, work on weaknesses, and develop a professional image.

3.5 Follow Up

Every good business owner understands the importance of customer follow-up. It is an opportunity to learn how your company performed and met the client's expectations and what needs to be improved for the future. It also can mean additional revenue because you can educate clients about additional services.

It's a good policy to send everyone a quick note thanking them for their business after providing your services. It can be a form letter, but make sure that you sign it and add a quick personal note. This should be mailed two to three days after the completion of the consultation.

Another idea is to mail a short survey about a week after their service. Ask the client to rate the quality and value of your services. Leave a blank spot for additional comments. This accomplishes two things: you get an idea of how you can improve, and you have another opportunity to remind your client that you provide other services. Offer a discount or small gift for completing the survey.

If the client has any concerns, you can follow up immediately. Otherwise, about a month and a half later, a short phone call is effective. Ask your client how they are doing, and if the service has been beneficial to their life. If they respond positively you can mention another service that they might need now or in the future. Keep the conversation light and friendly.

If they aren't interested in further consultations, keep their name and contact information in a computer database and, every season, send some kind of marketing tool — a postcard or short letter that reminds them of your company and lets them know of new services.

Sample Client Follow-Up Survey

Name: _____

Address: _____

_____

_____

Phone: _____   **E m a i l :** _____

Questions:

1. Overall, were my services helpful?   ❑ Yes   ❑ No

2. Did we achieve the goals of our session?   ❑ Yes   ❑ No

3. Did I use appropriate materials or   ❑ Yes   ❑ No
   presentations?

4. Was I easy to understand?   ❑ Yes   ❑ No

5. Did you feel comfortable asking me questions?   ❑ Yes   ❑ No

6. Would you recommend my services to your   ❑ Yes   ❑ No
   friends or family?

7. Were you comfortable with other service   ❑ Yes   ❑ No
   providers (i.e. hairstylists, makeup artists, etc.)
   you met?

8. If you could change anything about our session to help me
   better serve you, what would you change?

   _____

   _____

9. Would you like to subscribe to my newsletter?   ❑ Yes   ❑ No

10. May I contact you in the future to inquire if you   ❑ Yes   ❑ No
    have further goals you would like to work on?

Other Comments:

_____

_____

_____

Teresa Lopuchin of Self Image meets with her clients twice a year to reevaluate the colors. She also evaluates new hair coloring to make sure what they choose on their own is the right color for them. According to Lopuchin, simple changes like a new hair color can twist your color chart a tinge.

3.6 Corporate Consultations

As discussed in section 2.3, businesses hire image consultants for the same reason individual clients do — they are concerned about the image they project.

3.6.1 Conducting a Needs Analysis

When preparing for a meeting, executive coach Timi Gleason, a former human resources director who is currently a consultant with Executive Goals, recommends you find out who is going to be there, and what the expectations for the meeting will be. Make sure you bring enough business cards and brochures (see section 6.2.1 for information on marketing materials) to give to everyone there, and prepare a list of references to send at a future date, depending on the outcome.

When a corporate client contacts an image consultant, they usually have a specific reason. One way to start determining the needs of a client is by overall visual impression. An initial look at the company or department, form of dress and level of interaction with clients are all part of the initial assessment. Anna Soo Wildermuth of Personal Images Inc. relies on her years of experience and good instincts, combined with a series of questions, to draw an overall picture of her clients when they have that first meeting.

During the initial client meeting, you can begin with a quick overview of your services. However, as mentioned in the section on individual consultations, you should mostly ask and listen. Aim to have your client do about 80 percent of the talking.

Of course, take your cue from the client. If they prefer to ask the questions, then you should certainly answer. However, your purpose during this meeting is to turn a prospective client into a client. Identify what your client needs and wants so you can communicate how your services will benefit them.

Sample Questions for a Training Needs Analysis

- Who is this training for?

- What kind of training programs have they had in the past? Were those programs effective or not? Why?

- Why do you want to hold the current training?

- What are the specific problems you want solved?

- What specific topics do you want to be covered?

- What are the results you expect from this training?

- What do you need to be satisfied with the training?

- What do the participants want from attending this program?

- Is there anything else you think I need to know?

- Do company practices support this training?

Prepare a list of questions to ask the decision makers. You want to find out what kind of image they want to portray, whether they want you to work with individual employees or present training programs to groups, and what issues they want to address.

The final question can help give realistic expectations for the training. For example, if you are being asked to train customer service representatives to give more personal attention to customers, but the company awards bonuses based on how quickly customer calls are handled, the training is unlikely to achieve its objective. Here are a few examples of questions that Juanita Ecker of Professional Image Management asks prospective clients:

- Do your employees project a sloppy appearance?

- Are you concerned about the impact of image in today's market?

- Do any employees need to refine their business etiquette skills?

During this needs analysis you may have to adjust your line of questioning as you find out more about the organization's needs or current challenges. Do they want you to address increasing customer service complaints? Do they have a new manager who could use etiquette training? Do they need to develop a corporate dress code policy?

Based on the information you receive from the needs analysis, you can explain how hiring you will meet those needs. Don't forget to close — that is, ask for their business. Say that you'll send a letter of agreement or proposal for the prospect's review and that once it's signed you can start scheduling consulting sessions. You can follow up with a brief proposal that includes a cover letter, a summary of what the consulting will involve, and your fee.

> **TIP:** If you are contacted by a company you haven't approached, and are invited to submit a written proposal to do image consulting, ask questions to ensure that the process is actually open. In some cases, the consultant has already been selected, and companies solicit proposals only to confirm the decision or show someone higher up in the organization that the decision maker has "shopped around." In such cases, writing a proposal will be a waste of your time.

If for some reason the meeting doesn't result in a commitment, you still need to send a follow-up letter thanking the prospect for the opportunity to make a presentation and wishing them the best of everything. The prospect may turn into a client after all. If you have already agreed on what needs to be done, you might simply submit a contract covering the agreed-upon points (see section 5.5 for sample contracts).

3.6.2   Individual Coaching

When corporations hire someone to provide coaching to individuals, it is usually a key person in the organization. In many organizations, it's no longer enough for senior employees to have excellent credentials on their resumes. They are expected to have an image that fits with the standards of the corporate environment. In the *FabJob Guide to Become a Life Coach*, Allan M. Heller says:

> A coach may be hired to work with managers, department heads, or executives (the latter is referred to as executive coaching). In these cases, the coach is usually hired to groom a recently-promoted executive for his or her new role, or to assist one who may be having difficulty

adjusting. Sessions between executives and their coaches are often intense, and can last up to two hours once or twice a week.

Although the image consultant is working directly with an individual, as Heller notes, "the company is officially the client, not the person or people being coached. Therefore, the outcome of the coaching is whatever the company's goals and missions are, not the employees'."

Based on what the company needs, you may provide coaching on professional appearance, communication skills, or etiquette. Refer to sections 3.2 to 3.4 for more information about these areas. Following is an example of coaching you can provide in an area that many businesspeople find challenging – media interviews.

Media Coaching

For many people, facing an interview on camera or on the radio is one of the most nerve-wracking ordeals they have ever experienced. They want to appear intelligent and articulate, but instead fumble for words and display distracting gestures. As an image consultant, you can help your client learn the skills necessary to make an impressive media appearance. You can teach them to answer questions with ease and look like a media professional. Here's how.

Start out with a general interview as you would in any consultation. Initiate a conversation about the client's job. What kind of image is important in their profession? Have they ever been on television or the radio before? If so, how did it go? What were the areas they needed to improve on? Make thorough notes of all this information in their file.

Then do a casual evaluation yourself. Has the client had an image consultation? Do they need one? Before you proceed to media coaching, they may need to learn the basics of overall appearance and speaking ability. How is their voice and vocabulary? If a voice coach is in order, now is the time to make a referral for an in-depth consultation.

The next step requires a camcorder and an assistant. Give your client something short and easy to read and have your assistant record the client. Then conduct a mock interview in your office. You pose as the interviewer, while the client sits and responds just as if it were a genuine interview. Play the recording and point out areas that need to be worked on. Make notes in their file and give them a copy of suggestions for improvement. Then without the camera running, practice the session again until you feel the client is making progress.

Record the client responding to the same questions and show where they're improving. Here's a quick checklist to help you evaluate your client's performance:

- ❏ Is the client's voice too soft? Too loud? Strident, strained or nasal? Help them relax and breathe from the diaphragm. Practice with them.

- ❏ Does the client use slang or street expressions?

- ❏ Does the client look stiff and uncomfortable? Have them keep practicing. Deep breathing reduces visible nervousness.

- ❏ Is the client speaking in technical jargon? Eliminate it and substitute with a normal vocabulary.

- ❏ Is their pronunciation correct? How about enunciation? The client should speak clearly in a strong voice.

- ❏ Where are the client's hands? Do they distract from the message?

- ❏ Rate the overall performance.

The key to relaxing and performing well in an interview is to learn the skills and practice them until they become second nature. Give your client homework and make another appointment to come in for a final evaluation.

Tips for Successful Media Interviews

- Remind yourself that everyone gets nervous. Take a deep breath and let it out slowly just before you go on air. If possible, take a few sips of water to moisten your mouth or tuck a small mint discreetly in your cheek.

- Don't sit too far back in a chair. You'll look defensive, like you're ready to bolt out of the studio.

- Try not to bite or lick your lips. You'll look scared.

- Don't slouch or lean too close to the interviewer. Your voice will come across weak and you'll look sloppy.

- Keep control of your hands. Don't wrench or wring them or drum your fingers nervously.

- Don't jangle jewelry.

- When asked a question, take a few seconds to compose yourself and think of an answer. Then respond.

- Look at the interviewer, not the camera. Try to imagine that you're both in your office at work having a casual conversation.

- Don't wear small patterns or the color red — it vibrates on camera. Also avoid bright white, as it makes your teeth look dingy.

- Don't exaggerate your makeup. Consider applying extra powder.

- Don't wear anything too tight, trendy or flashy. Go for a classic look. Navy blue is generally a good choice for the camera. Make sure everything is well pressed and neat.

- Remember, unless a show is live, it will be edited. Hopefully they will remove any obvious faux pas.

3.6.3   Presenting Training Programs

A typical training program is a workshop or presentation that may range from 45 minutes to a full day or longer, depending on how much information the company wants you to present.

The people attending your presentation may be customer service staff, supervisors, or any other group of employees. If the company or department is small, all employees may be required to attend.

Usually the human resources director is in charge of coordinating the meeting with the employees. The human resources director will arrange for a room and light refreshments and make sure you have access to a podium, loudspeaker, electrical outlets and extension cords. You might also bring a slide show or PowerPoint presentation.

When conducting your needs analysis, you should advise the people you're meeting with about the many topics you can present training programs on.

As mentioned in the introduction to this book, you could give presentations on topics such as:

- Dressing professionally (including dos and don'ts for casual Fridays)
- Telephone etiquette for customer service staff
- Communication skills for new supervisors

One program offered by Professional Image Management is "The Art of Dining," which explains the intricacies of formal dining and how to entertain business clients.

Often the management has specific concerns they want you to address in the seminar. For example, they may have concerns with their employees' appearance — problems with casual dress, inappropriate clothing, etc. When they do give you specific areas to cover, they should be kept in confidence and handled with tact in the consultation. Saying something like, "I understand from the management that there is a problem with..." will only alienate the staff. Instead, make sure you cover the problem area, but mention it along with other information.

Employees can be wary of mandatory meetings and be resistant to anything you have to say. Your job is to make this time fun, interesting and informative.

One principle of training is that lecturing alone is not an effective way of working with most groups. Instead, consultants who lead training programs typically have trainees take part in a variety of activities such as group discussions, role plays, brainstorming, games, and so on.

A Sample Workshop

Begin by introducing yourself, including a brief summary of your experience related to the topic of the workshop. Next, you want to explain to the participants why image matters. This is especially important if they are required to attend, and your session lasts for several hours or longer. Tell them "what's in it for you."

Marsha Miller says a good tag line to offer them is: "Dress for the job you want." This should help the group see that focusing on a professional appearance benefits the employee and not just the company.

Give Real-Life Examples

A good way to open this session is to offer specific examples of image "makeovers" that are routinely conducted in the business world. Here are some examples you can use:

- Attorneys who advise clients facing criminal charges what to wear and how to behave during a trial.

- Movie stars who hire stylists to help them present a particular "image."

- Politicians who have "makeovers" in order to get elected.

- Average people who want to be successful in their careers and attractive for themselves and their families.

Dressing for Court

by Marsha Miller

When Eric and Lyle Menendez, the now infamous California brothers convicted of killing their parents, first stood in a courtroom to face charges, they were dressed to kill (pardon the pun). Both wore dark, elegantly cut suits, expensive watches, stylish silk ties and soft Italian leather shoes. Both looked like young men with trust funds who knew their way around Rodeo Drive.

Enter prominent criminal attorney Leslie Abramson. The next court appearance was quite a different scene. Gone were the designer labels, the edgy dark looks. Instead the brothers wore button-down oxford shirts, pastel crew neck sweaters and khaki pants — a look that declared that these were harmless college boys who belonged in a chemistry lab or study group but certainly not at the defendant's table of a criminal court room.

The lesson we can learn from savvy attorneys is that our total image – clothing, hair style, accessories, how we walk, etc. – sends a message. In our professional lives we ignore these messages at our own peril.

Or you might start off with a mini-lecture that gives real-life examples:

> Why should the average person be concerned about an image? Isn't that a feature of being famous — something that involves Hollywood stars and other celebrities?

> Certainly celebrities are preoccupied with their "image." They pay tons of money to publicists to help them create a persona with the public. But an image isn't something that only famous people have. Every one of us leaves an impression of who we are, how much education we have, and what our occupation is, simply by how we dress, speak and carry ourselves.

> Suppose you were sending your three-year-old to a preschool. You walk in to deliver your toddler to the teacher and there stands a man in rumpled clothing, sunglasses and a trench coat. He mumbles out that he's your child's teacher, avoiding eye contact with you as he talks. Do you feel good about leaving your precious little Susie with him for the day?

> Or perhaps you're opening a savings account at the local bank. You walk in and ask for help and the teller directs you to the bank president. A man with a dark Armani suit, sporting a $30,000 watch and Italian leather loafers shakes your hand. You notice he has diamond rings and a gold chain around his neck. Do you find yourself wondering just what he's going to be doing with your money?

> Like it or not, we all pre-judge people. We shouldn't, but we do. It's basic human nature. A wise person understands this and makes it work in their favor.

Group Discussion

After giving the examples above, have the group discuss other examples of how they expect people in certain professions to look and behave. Your discussion might include clergy/church leaders, government officials, artists, lawyers and doctors.

> Discuss the expectations we have. Are they created by clothing, make-up, jewelry, speech, grammar, vocabulary, etc?

Then turn the discussion to the people attending your presentation:

What impression do you think the public has of people in your field? How is it created?

Depending on your audience, you might also have them discuss the following question in small groups or among the entire group:

What qualities do you want to portray? Pick out three and discuss how you might be able to communicate those by your clothing, speech or body language.

Honest	Creative	Innovative
Successful	Intelligent	Resourceful
Consistent	Capable	Reliable

Once you have established that there are valid reasons for average people paying attention to their "image," you can move on to ways to improve image. Depending on the time allotted for your presentation, you might do any of the following activities.

Slide Show or PowerPoint Presentation

Before your program, you could create a presentation. You can use clip art or photos you take yourself, or purchase photos to use. (Try an online search for "royalty free photos" if you want to purchase them.)

Show the slides, explaining in full what they are illustrating and how it applies to your listeners. Point out details and take the time to answer questions as they come up. In the presentation, you should discuss:

- The various body types and how to dress for each one.

- Color analysis and how it can help you select flattering shades for your complexion.

- Image busters that ruin an otherwise professional look.

- The importance of details like hair, makeup and nails.

- Accessorizing.

- How to put together a wardrobe from a basic suit.

- How to dress professionally on a tight budget.

By looking at examples on the slides, the employees will see for themselves what makes a polished look and what doesn't. Special emphasis should be placed on business casual attire or casual Fridays, whatever the company calls it. This is the most misunderstood policy in the business world today. Offer some specific outfits that are acceptable for business casual, and list what isn't.

Mock Fashion Show

Engage a couple of employees in a mock "fashion show." With the help of a local clothing outlet shop that you have a relationship with, take a couple of people from the audience and put them in pre-selected business outfits.

Point out details that make these outfits spectacular. Mention fabrics, cut, color, heel height, hem length — anything else that will help them pick something similar for themselves. Mention the source of the outfit and the total price so they can see how affordable it is. Show how the outfit can be dressed up or down depending on the accessories.

Mentioning price is a good time to discuss the difference between investment dressing and impulse buying. Purchasing a good, classic suit in a year-round material that fits well is an investment that will last your client for years. The pieces can be worn alone and paired with various separates to make new looks. It can be dressed up for interviews and funerals or dressed down for more casual days.

Educate them on how to look for good construction and a good fit. A suit like this may cost more initially, but it will pay for itself in the long run. Impulse purchases, on the other hand, are costly. You get home with a totally impractical item that doesn't go with anything else and will probably hang in the closet unworn.

Also instruct them about where to put the most money in their clothing. For instance, if your client works for a symphony or professional theatre, then they will attend many galas and opening night parties. This calls for a good selection of very dressy outfits.

But for most people the bulk of their wardrobe needs to go into basic work clothes like suits and separates. If you telecommute you probably need only a couple of nice outfits for meetings; otherwise you want clothes that will be attractive but still comfortable for sitting in front of a computer or dashing out to the post office. Lifestyle determines what a wardrobe should consist of.

Other price considerations need to be made when shopping by evaluating the cost of alterations and cleaning. A beautiful snow-white wool suit that looks stunning but has to be dry cleaned every time it's worn is not a good investment, no matter how reasonable the price tag is.

Color Analysis

Take a volunteer from the group and perform a color analysis on them. They need to be seated in front, preferably on a platform. Clip back long hair and remove any lipstick and eye makeup. Allow the group to see as you take them through the various colored drapes and instruct them what to look for. They will quickly become skilled at seeing the difference the right color makes in your volunteer's face.

Determine whether the volunteer has cool or warm undertones and then continue until you have their color palette. If appropriate, apply blush, eye makeup and lipstick in the correct colors. Once you have your volunteer made up, put the drapes up again — only this time, use the volunteer's own color palette. The difference is dramatic.

Wardrobe Makeover

Take the same volunteer and do a quick wardrobe makeover on them. (Pre-selecting the volunteer will help you ensure you have the right size clothing with you). Have them leave the audience and change into a suit that you have brought with you. Then bring them back out and, with shoes and other accessories, build a business outfit. Mention other colors, styles, and accessories that would work with the look. Take a digital photograph of your volunteer for your marketing files.

Ending the Session

If the group is still engaged and interested in learning more, you can suggest that the company bring you back for another session or schedule appointments for individual consultations. The beauty of owning your own business is that you can be creative and flexible in how you see clients. Remind them to take some of your written materials and thank them for coming. Be available after you close the session to talk with people. Also, thank the management for having you.

Handouts

Participants appreciate having material to take away with them. You can give handouts listing tips, resources, or questions. Following are examples of the types of questions you could include on a handout for participants to take away. If you have time, you could hand it out during the session and give the participants a few minutes to work through the questions. (Allow participants to keep their answers confidential.)

- Critique your image. Do you think you are doing everything you can to effectively communicate the qualities you chose?

- How can you improve?

- Do you feel services of a professional are needed to help you in this effort? What kind?

- Name three goals for the coming year that you have in improving your overall professional image. How do you plan to achieve these goals, and how can this company assist you in future workshops?

Communication and Etiquette Training

You can do variations on the exercises described above, using the information in section 2.2 of this guide. For example, for a communications training you could demonstrate different gestures and ask participants to write down what they think they mean. Once you have gone through all the gestures, discuss what participants answered and give them the actual meanings. Make sure you give them "disclaimers" as well, by explaining that gestures may be caused by something else such as habits or physical conditions.

Here are a few samples of etiquette training activities from the *FabJob Guide to Become an Etiquette Consultant*.

- Show a video or DVD of social situations and the correct way to meet people, shake hands, etc. You can show the video all the way through or stop the tape and, using various volunteers, act out the same actions. You could create your own videos or buy one from a company such as Protocol Consultants International at **www.protocolconsultants.com**.

- Have an assistant who can help you role play and act out various situations to illustrate proper manners, gestures, posture, etc. Using an employee who's well liked and a good sport can help remove any resistance you encounter in a group.

- Give them a handout with tips (e.g. one that explains in detail the basic rules of etiquette), resources, or questions.

3.6.4   Developing a Dress Code Policy

If a company wants your help writing a dress code policy, begin with questions such as:

- **What is the work environment?**
  Is the work environment a shared office building with many other professional businesses? If so, maybe it's best to follow their lead, either by adopting a more traditional dress code or, if it is an office in an industrial part of town, a business casual dress code.

- **Do clients or investors frequently visit the company's site?**
  If clients or investors visit the site frequently, often it's best to adopt traditional attire. This helps ease clients' and investors' concerns. But if all the clients run their business as a casual environment, it might be best to do the same.

- **What image is the company trying to portray?**
  If a company wants to portray an image of success, traditional business attire is probably the way to go. However, business casual will better suit a company trying to portray an image of "new business" or being youth-oriented.

- **What type of business is the company in?**
  Any business that has to deal with banks face-to-face on a regular basis should stick to traditional attire. Also, there's little room for business casual in a profession with a long history and public profile such as law. However, if a company is trying to send a message of creativity, permitting employees to wear their own styles to work could enhance this perception.

Seek Employees' Input

Although management will make the final decision on dress code, it's a good idea to poll employees and see how they feel about the topic.

They may not always answer, "We want a more casual office." Many employees feel that the office is more productive and work is more seriously approached when the attire suits a business-oriented mood.

Check Legislation

Although employers have the right to institute whatever dress code they desire, banning certain clothes and styles could lead to calls of gender discrimination and religious discrimination. Gender-issue examples include banning earrings on men and forcing women to wear nylons. Religious-issue examples include things like banning facial hair and religious headwear. The company's human resources department should be up-to-date on, or at least have access to, all the necessary state/provincial and federal legislation.

Making the Change

Once you have drafted a new dress code, it will have to be approved by the appropriate company personnel. In some companies this can be a time-consuming process involving several different departments. Once the dress code has been accepted, recommend that you present a training program to assist employees with adopting it.

3.7 Working with Strategic Partners

Strategic partners are the businesses and people you will use to help shape your client's image. Also known as image resources, strategic alliances or service providers, these people have knowledge in areas that might not fall within your expertise. They are also the businesses that will provide the merchandise to help you transform your client.

These strategic partners can include clothing retailers, hair stylists, makeup artists, dermatologists, dietitians, plastic surgeons, voice coaches, personal trainers, and etiquette and communication experts. Depending on the scope of the work your client wants done, you may use one or two of these partners, or a host of such experts.

Many image consultants specialize in some of these areas. If your strength is etiquette and communication training, offer that service yourself. If you have a background in makeup, work with your client to choose the right look for them through color combinations and product lines. You may be able to offer advice when it comes to body language and non-verbal communication but need to use an outside coach to bring your client up to speed on their public speaking skills.

Your background will determine which image resources you will need to use. You need to know your strengths and weaknesses. What services you will offer and what strategic partnerships you will choose are important for your business to run smoothly and successfully.

3.7.1   Strategic Partners and How to Find Them

Clothing Retailers

We've all heard that saying: "Clothes make the man." They can also drastically change the look of your client from frumpy to chic or from casual to ultra-professional. Arguably the most important of the strategic partners you will use are clothing retailers, which often carry shoes and other accessories you will need in your quest for the perfect makeover for your client.

Businesses who sell directly to the public include retailers known to be frequented by the rich and famous, to large chain department stores that are popular with the masses, to small individually-owned boutiques that only a few treasure. You need to familiarize yourself with the whole range of these retailers.

Are you going for high-end designer brands like Dolce & Gabbana, Gucci, Jimmy Choo, Marc Jacobs, and Prada? Then Saks Fifth Avenue would be a good choice. Will your client need a wide range of top fashion designers with the possibility of a lesser price tag? Nordstrom, which carries some 150 brands, could be the solution. Filene's and J.C. Penney might fit into your client's budget a little better while offering a variety of quality designers as well. From J.Crew and J. Jill to LL Bean and Land's End, each retailer has something to offer. Don't rule out local designers and boutiques, either. You can find some unique yet fabulous clothes and accessories that best suit your client at these lesser-known shops.

Before you can give your client advice on how to improve their appearance through wardrobe, you have to be knowledgeable about all your options.

Questions to consider include:

- Do the stores, shops, and boutiques carry a wide range of sizes?

- Are the clerks and owners helpful in meeting your needs, or are they intrusive with their own agenda?

- Will they special order merchandise for you? If so, how dependable are they in delivering the goods in a timely fashion?

When it comes to clothing retailers, the more thorough your research, the more confident you will appear, and that will set you apart from your competition.

Some image consultants decide what styles they will focus on and work with retailers who specialize in lines that flatter these looks. A new image consultant who comes into the market will have their own personal style they are comfortable with, says Michelle T. Sterling, AICI, principal of Global Image Group.

"Mine happens to be classically elegant," Sterling says. "I focus on basics in the classics, and work with some specific large department stores and boutiques." Some people are a little more creative, she adds, and should work with stores that reflect that style. "They should find alliances that resonate with them, that they can trust, and who they know are out for their best interest, and then establish a relationship with them. That is really the most important part — to establish relationships. I have great relationships with the stores I use in terms of their managers."

Most stores have an online presence where you can not only order merchandise but find out a national chain's local store locations and hours of business. There are a number of good links that will help you in your search. The following are a good place to start.

At Retailers on the Internet (**www.ecr.ryerson.ca/retailers.html**), look under the Fashion/Accessories section and a plethora of United States and Canadian retailers are highlighted.

Canada's Lou Lou Magazine has a list of online fashion retailers and links to their web pages (many of which have a store locator page) at their website (**www.louloumagazine.com/english/fashion/retailer**).

Hair Stylists

Another strategic partner, hair stylists offer your client the chance for a transformation that will be seen daily – hopefully without too much work on your client's part – yet can be changed in a few months if another look is desired. From cuts to color and perms to straightening, there is a lot that can be done to the tresses that frame a person's face. Hair weaves, extensions, and wigs may be a sought-after commodity. A male client may need some help sculpting his sideburns, mustache, or beard. A hair stylist can provide all of these services.

Hair salons can offer other services as well, like waxing eyebrows or giving manicures and pedicures. These professionals also offer products that your clients may need to keep their optimum look, including shampoos, conditioners, styling gels and hair sprays.

It is best to have a few salons and stylists in your repertoire. Some may work well with the masses, but your client may be more comfortable with a stylist that caters either to just men or just women. Other stylists may specialize in offering services to African-American men and women. Some salons lean toward the funky. Educate yourself about what is available in your area. Forge alliances with stylists who share your ideas about what is in style and what is outdated.

Ask family, friends, and business associates for recommendations. Sometimes your information may come from unlikely sources. If you see a stranger with a chic haircut, don't be afraid to ask them who provided the service. You never know where you may get a great tip.

The Internet also can help you in your search. There are several sites that list salons nationwide. *Essence Magazine* recommends the website Hair Stylist Locator for African American Hair. Located at **www. afrohair.com/haircare/hair.html**, it covers both the United States and Canada and even has an international salon finder. It has a wide selection, especially in the larger metropolitan cities.

Hair News Magazine has a website at **www.hair-news.com** that lists salons across the United States. Not every state is represented, but most of the major cities have a nice selection of listings. Beware: Pop-up ads run amuck here.

There are also some organizations serving salons and hair stylists that may be able to help you locate an appropriate professional for your client. They include:

- *American Board of Certified Haircolorists*
  www.haircolorist.com

- *The National Cosmetology Association*
  www.ncacares.org

- *The Professional Beauty Federation*
  www.probeautyfederation.org

It is extremely important to screen the stylists you send your client to for a new look. When you are using a new salon, you should follow up with your client. It even may be appropriate to go with your client to a stylist you haven't used often. Why? Because they may have their own ideas that conflict with yours. Remember: You are the one who has met with the client, analyzed the situation, and come up with a plan of action.

"You don't want to go to a hairdresser that keeps on putting down all the things you think would work well for the client," says Jon-Michail, AICI, CIP, founder and CEO of Image Group International. "It is not uncommon that this will happen. This is very simple. You have to be very clear who you are working with."

Makeup Artists

These beauty professionals provide your client with a new look through the use of makeup and education on how to maximize their best features with cosmetics.

These artists do more than apply makeup for daytime, evening, or special occasion looks. They know what product line is best suited for each type of job. They understand what products work best on different skin types. They know the best color combinations for your client. They are aware of the current techniques and hot new trends.

There are some specialties within this field. Some makeup artists cater to television and film personalities or work with models. Some specialize in corrective beauty makeup for those who have damaged skin or disfigurements.

Remember: Every makeup artist has their own style. Find one that suits you and your client. If possible, watch them perform makeovers on their customers — not only to see their technique, but also to see how they treat and interact with their customers.

The Makeup Artist Network (**www.makeupart.net/search002.html**) features resumes and portfolios of makeup artists. The pickings are a bit slim, but they offer a start. Another website, **www.weddingmakeup. com**, lists artists in and outside the USA, a short description of what they do, and a link to their website and e-mail address.

Dermatologists

If beauty is skin deep, then a good dermatologist is worth their weight in gold. These health care professionals are medical doctors who specialize in the treatment of skin disorders. They facilitate optimal skin care, whether your client has acne problems or is showing the impact of the aging process.

Dermatologists treat patients with more serious and unsightly skin conditions as well, like eczema, rosacea, and psoriasis. Before a makeup artist can do their job, these medical conditions may need to be taken care of first. A dermatologist may write out a necessary prescription or suggest skin care products that can help with some of the symptoms of skin disorders.

Your best bet is to go through professional organizations to find a dermatologist in your area. The American Academy of Dermatologists represents over 16,000 practicing dermatologists in the United States. The Canadian Dermatology Association can also help you in your search.

- *American Academy of Dermatologists*
  www.aad.org

- *Canadian Dermatology Association*
  www.dermatology.ca

Dietitians

Dietitians are healthcare professionals with a specific education and certification. Depending on their level, dietitians may study a variety of subjects such as food and nutrition sciences, business, culinary arts, sociology, and communication. They may take general science courses or study the more advanced sciences such as biochemistry, physiology, microbiology, anatomy, and chemistry.

In Canada, if someone advertises as a "dietitian," it means that they have a degree specializing in foods and nutrition from an accredited, four-year university program. In the United States, there are distinctions as well. A registered dietitian (RD) has completed a four-year bachelor's program, and the dietetic technician registered (DTR) holds an associate's degree from a two-year degree program.

If your client wants to change their body shape naturally, these professionals offer the appropriate expertise. They will help your client make informed decisions about food choices and nutritional needs. They identify nutrition problems and develop care plans. They can specialize in different areas such as weight control or may work with a special population group like senior citizens.

There are professional organizations that certify dietitians who can help you in your search. They include the American Dietitian Association and Dietitians of Canada.

- *American Dietetic Association*
  www.eatright.org

- *Dietitians of Canada*
  www.dietitians.ca

Dentists

Dentists are trained, educated and licensed medical professionals who do a lot more than fillings and root canals. There are cosmetic dentists and dental surgeons whose services your client may need to achieve that picture-perfect smile.

These professionals provide services like simple tooth whitening – which most dentists offer today – to more complicated procedures that cosmetic dentists perform, like reshaping and resizing teeth by bonding custom-crafted, ceramic veneers into place. Dental surgery can provide more drastic changes, with dental implants used to replace missing teeth or removable bridges or dentures. Cosmetic dentistry can also include gum-line contouring, laser therapy to clean the gums, and other procedures that will make your client smile with pride.

The dental profession also has associations that can assist you in selecting a professional in the area where you are practicing. Check out the websites for the American Dental Association and the Canadian Dental Association.

- *American Dental Association*
  www.ada.org

- *Canadian Dental Association*
  www.cda-adc.ca/en

Plastic Surgeons

Plastic surgeons are medical doctors who train in general surgery and then specialize in all aspects of plastic surgery, which is the branch of surgery concerned with restoration, reconstruction, or improvement of the shape and appearance of body structures. In both the United States and Canada, there are boards that certify plastic surgeons. Each country uses slightly different criteria.

Clients that go the route of plastic surgery will likely be seeking cosmetic procedures. These can range from facelifts, cheek implants, and nasal surgery, to tummy tucks, breast enlargement or reduction, and liposuction. Non-surgical procedures they can provide include laser hair removal, laser skin resurfacing, chemical peels, and injections such as Botox or collagen. Some of your clients may be seeking reconstructive procedures, which can include breast reconstruction after cancer treatments and scar revision after accidents.

The type of surgeon you need will determine what association you should go through. Visit the following websites for more information:

- *American Academy of Facial Plastic and Reconstructive Surgery*
  www.aafprs.org

- *American Society of Plastic Surgeons*
  www.plasticsurgery.org

- *Canadian Academy of Facial Plastic and Reconstructive Surgery*
  www.cafprs.com

- *Canadian Society for Aesthetic Plastic Surgery*
  www.csaps.ca

- *Canadian Society of Plastic Surgeons*
  www.plasticsurgery.ca

Voice Coaches

Sounding good can be as important as looking good, so a speech coach or voice coach can be a key alliance for your business. These professionals can help your client minimize a regional accent or dialect and work on incorrect speech habits. They can help your client speak with confidence and authority in personal and professional communication. These professionals can provide one-on-one training and help your client with a specific project, like an upcoming presentation.

One website that can help you find voice coaches in the United States and Canada is A2Z Vocal Coaches Directory (**http://vocal-coaches.com**). Just type in your city, state, or province to get a list of choices.

Personal Trainers

Getting into shape can mean working out with a personal trainer, preferably a certified one who has the education to help your clients meet their fitness and health goals. Personal trainers provide fitness testing and assessment and then put together an individualized program for your clients. A good personal trainer can provide your client with the motivation to make changes, whether that means losing weight or firming up specific areas of their body.

Several organizations certify personal trainers and can help you choose an appropriate professional in your area. They include:

- *American Fitness Professionals & Associates*
  www.afpafitness.com

- *International Fitness Professionals Association*
  www.ifpa-fitness.com

- *International Sports Sciences Association*
  www.issaonline.com

Educational Programs

Sometimes a client may need an educational program to change their image. Training programs can include sessions on business and personal etiquette or international protocol. Proper dining skills, from ordering the right bottle of wine to using the correct fork, can be learned at a seminar or workshop. A quick etiquette brush-up may be the difference between your client coming across as an inexperienced lummox or a polished professional. If etiquette consulting is one of your specialties, you might consider finding educational programs for other areas, such as public speaking.

Finding educational programs will take a bit of work. You need to define what category of learning you are seeking for your client. Local business and trade magazines may be your best bet, as well as the Yellow Pages.

These may seem like small details, but some of your clients may want big changes and a major overhaul may mean that some training or re-training is in order. Getting to the substance of a person may require coaching that may not fall into your field of expertise. Get to know local and regional professionals who can coach your client to stardom.

Other Service Providers

While the above list includes the commonly used partners, here are other professionals and places you may want to work with.

Color Analysis Consultants

Most image consultants do color analysis themselves, but there are professionals you can use if this skill isn't in your repertoire yet. Color analysis enhances a person's look with colors that flatter their hair, skin, and eye colors. Some of these consultants provide the client with a customized color palette that fits in a purse, thus making shopping for makeup, clothes, and accessories a snap.

Day Spas

Day spas offer such services as facials, massages, and other body therapies. They can also help your client de-stress, which can be an important element in changing their image.

Career Coaches

Career coaches assess a person's career options and help develop goals. Career coaches can also help someone handle the challenges of mergers, acquisitions and layoffs.

Speaking Coaches

Speaking coaches can help your clients prepare to give presentations.

3.7.2 Other Ways to Find Strategic Partners

Do your own personal research. Hit the streets to scout out the businesses that are in your region. Your local chamber of commerce should have a listing or booklet of your city or region's businesses with contact information. You can also get recommendations from other local professionals, family members, and friends.

Obvious places include the Yellow Pages, local newspapers, and local magazines. Scour these resources to see what is available in your area or the places you plan to set up shop.

The Internet offers a wide range of ways to search for the providers you are seeking. Most businesses have a presence on the Internet. Go to a search engine, type in key words (like "clothing retailer," "dentist," or "personal trainer") along with the city and state where you need the service, and a list of resources will pop up.

Familiarize yourself with a few good search engines such as Google and Yahoo. You want to use your time wisely to find up-to-date directories that are broken down by categories and have Yellow Pages to make your search a bit easier. They not only offer you current information but also often have help centers that assist you in narrowing down your search or using the site to the best of its capabilities.

Another way to research businesses on the Internet is by using sites that provide reviews of retailers and other service providers. An example of a site like this is Citysearch (**www.citysearch.com**).

At Citysearch, you can pick the state where you will be looking for image resources. Once you click on the state, you will be given a choice of cities or prominent city areas. From there you can navigate to service providers such as spas, clothing retailers, etc. This site generally provides up-to-date information and reliable reviews.

Each city has a "Best Of" page where users vote, for example, on the best store on chic and upscale Newbury Street in Boston. These "Best Of" pages also include sections with the editor's choices. This service offers valuable research already done for you. Citysearch also provides Yellow Pages for each city it highlights.

Your Internet travels should eventually lead you out of cyberspace. You should double-check your computer work by calling and making sure these businesses still exist and have not changed locations.

Professional organizations and associations are a good place to find reliable and quality providers. If you can't find them via the Internet, your local chamber of commerce will have a listing of local associations.

3.7.3 Choosing Strategic Partners

The top experts will tell you: You can't do enough research. There are several ways you can decide on which businesses you will use. Call and ask for a meeting with the manager of the store, suggests Michelle T. Sterling, AICI, of Global Image Group. Explain your credentials and why you would like to work with that store.

Then set up an interview process to see if the relationship is mutually beneficial. Sterling suggests that before you go in for an interview, you ask yourself:

- What type of clientele or niche does this potential partner serve?

- Does it match my clientele?

- What is the reputation of the company?

- Is the management team efficient and reliable?

- Is this an establishment that I want to work with?

Once you go in for the interview, some questions you may want to ask include:

- How long have you been in business?

- Have you always been in this location?

- What is your clientele like?

- Will I be working with the same personnel?

- Will you do special orders?

- What is the turnaround time on special orders?

- What is the turnaround on scheduling an appointment?

- Why do you think we would make a good partnership?

Some places you partner with may decide on an arrangement that includes commission or a referral fee. In that case, you will want to find out what the turnaround time is for payment. When you create an alliance with a clothing store, for example, you can sometimes act as a personal shopper there as well.

An option here is to set up a relationship which allows for commissions on the items that your clients buy, thereby adding to your bottom line. Not all image consultants do this practice, but Sterling says it is a good option for those image consultants with a retail sales background.

Evangelia D. Souris, of OPTIMUM, International Center for Image Management, says she chooses providers based on her prior experiences with them and the value they offer to customers. "I usually try to find stores that offer high-quality merchandise at a bargain price," she says. "That way the client is buying higher-end clothes at prices they normally pay and are getting a higher-end image as a result."

Gloria Starr says she takes the "mystery shopper approach" and goes into a store alone to check out the operation. "I am very aware of the clerk's knowledge of their inventory, their eye for color, ability to co-ordinate a look, etc.," she says. "Then when I am shopping for clients I will work with them again." If she is in a new store where she is not known, Starr will give the sales representative her card and explain that she is shopping with or for her client. "They can best assist me by bringing the correct sizes and letting me do all of the selling, as I have an established rapport with my client," she says.

For people-focused services like dermatologists, plastic surgeons, fitness consultants, or dietitians, Souris suggests asking:

- Where did you receive your training?

- How do you deal with a specific need (i.e. for a dentist, perhaps the use of veneers)? Have you ever dealt with such a need? What were the results?

- Can I contact any of your patients for references?

Starr says she usually selects people that she has personally used, such as her own hairdresser. She says this personal experience is useful, as is a solid referral from several people she knows well. "I asked my friend – who is a doctor – who the nurses are using for cosmetic surgery procedures," she says. "The nurses are in the know."

For all medical providers, verify certifications and licenses. You can check on board certification online by using the doctor's name at the American Board of Medical Specialties' (ABMS) Certified Doctor Verification Site (**www.abms.org**). You may want to check to see if the healthcare provider you are considering has any medical malpractice suits pending. Such legal documents are filed with the clerk of the county or circuit court in your area.

When it comes to plastic surgery, keep in mind that there is a difference between plastic surgeons, who have had extensive training, and cosmetic surgeons, who may have less experience and education.

Don't be afraid to ask how many years of experience a plastic surgeon, dental surgeon, or cosmetic dentist has under their belt. Find out their areas of expertise. You probably don't want to have a client get a facelift from a plastic surgeon who specializes in liposuction. Ask the surgeon how many facelifts they have performed in the last year, or what areas of specialty are covered by the cosmetic dentist you are assessing.

Personal trainers can be certified as well. Ask them about their certifications, background, education, and training. Find out how long they have been in the business. Do they specialize in any one area? Do they travel, or will your client have to go to them?

Ask any of the providers you are screening if they have past clients who can offer a recommendation. If they can't, that may be a tip-off to avoid making an alliance with this business or service provider.

Doing such background checks may seem intrusive. It also can require many hours of your time, but it is well worth the effort. You don't want to find out the hard way that the provider you chose didn't offer a quality experience or, worse, is incompetent.

Remember, these providers are a reflection of your business as well. One unhappy client can put a dark cloud over your business and it is completely avoidable. The flip side of that is reaping the rewards of a job well done by a provider who you recommended, which for your business could mean repeat clients or referrals from glowing recommendations.

Building strong alliances also has an added bonus. The strategic partners you send your clients to may be inclined to send clients to you. For example, the hair stylists you use in your business dealings have access to many clients who may benefit from an image consultant.

What do you do when you sit in a salon and are having your hair cut, colored, or highlighted? Most likely, you chat with your stylist. Salon owners and stylists often know their clientele's ambitions and life goals. They may be in the perfect position to suggest a session with an image consultant. This reciprocal system can work well with service providers who share your philosophy about style and substance.

Some people opt for formal agreements in this area, so you also need to decide what type of system you will have with the provider. Will you exchange referral fees or work on a honor system? These questions need to be answered before you begin your alliance with a partner.

3.7.4 Negotiating an Agreement

Many image consultants opt for verbal agreements with strategic partners and allow the client to pay for services as they use them. For example, you may accompany your client to a retailer and offer your advice, but then let the client pay when it's time to check out.

An increasingly common practice in business is the payment of "referral fees." For example, if you refer a client to a makeup artist or personal trainer, that strategic partner pays you a fee as a thank you for referring business to them that they otherwise would not have. Likewise, you could pay them a referral fee for any image consulting business they send your way.

There are no firm guidelines for the amount of a referral fee. It can be whatever you negotiate with a particular strategic partner, and might be a percentage of what they earn from the referral (e.g. five percent to 20 percent) or a flat fee. In some cases, a strategic partner will not be willing to pay a referral fee (for example, if they are already booked up with work at their full fee).

If you have a referral fee arrangement with your strategic partners, it's wise to have a written agreement to protect yourself. Another situation where an agreement is needed is if you offer inclusive services or package deals for your clients with one price tag. In this situation, the client will pay you and you pay the providers. (Image consultants who use this system don't usually cover the cost of clothing and accessories.)

When you take on the role of coordinating the service and collecting payment, you might charge a higher referral fee, such as 25 percent of the cost of the services. Note that this comes off what the strategic partner is paid, not added to the client's charge.

If you do have a written agreement with a provider, make it as specific as possible. Outline exactly what services you are expecting and what the exact cost will be. Don't leave room for a service provider to add to their bottom line at your client's expense. This scenario shouldn't happen very often, though, because it will mean the end of your relationship with that provider who may be penny-wise but pound-foolish.

On the next page, you will see an example of an agreement used by Image Group International. Make sure you consult with an attorney when preparing your own agreement to ensure it covers everything you need.

IMAGE CONSULTANT'S / COACHES AGREEMENT WITH SERVICE PROVIDER

I.   Parties and Purpose:

_____ (hereinafter called "Image Consultant/Coaches") hereby engages _____ (hereinafter called "Service Provider") to render _____ services and provide goods for the benefit of Image Consultant's / Coaches client, (hereinafter called "Client".)

II. Description of Supplier's Performance:

Service Provider shall provide Client the following goods and services as directed by Image Consultant / Coach.

_____

III. Time For Performance:

Work pursuant to this agreement shall begin on _____ and be completed by _____.

IV. Payment to Supplier:

Service Provider shall bill Client and look exclusively to Client for payment. A copy of the bill shall be provided to Image Consultant/Coach.

V.   Referral Fee to Image Consultant / Coach:

Upon completion of payment Service Provider shall pay to Image Consultant/Coach ___% of the sale pre-tax payment by Client to Service Provider.

VI. Receipt:

I acknowledge receipt of a fully completed copy of this contract.

_____   _____
Service Provider   Date

_____   _____
Address   Tel No:

_____
Email:

_____   _____
Image Consultant/Coaches Name and Signature   Date

_____   _____
Address   Tel No:

_____
Email:

©2003 - Image Group International
Asia – Pacific Head Office: 47 Darling Street, Victoria, Australia
Tel: +613 9820 4449 Fax: +613 9820 4441
Email: info@imagegroup.com.au
Website: www.imagegroup.com.au

4. Developing Your Skills

4.1 Your Own Image

As an image consultant, people will look to you for an example of how they should ideally carry themselves. After all, you're the expert! Taking care of your own image is as important as creating the right looks for your clients.

Image consultants have to lead by example. You are selling "image," so it's important to represent to the world what you're trying to encourage in your clients. You can't tell your clients to dress smartly and then show up to meetings in sweat pants and a t-shirt.

Image consultants have to look good at all times, whether they are going to the grocery store, a business meeting, or the gym. You always have to be well-dressed and well-groomed — you never know when you will run into a client or potential client.

Apply everything you've learned in chapter 2 on image to yourself. You can be your own image consultant in the beginning and identify the colors and clothing styles that best suit you. A sharp wardrobe is important in this business, and by wearing the correct clothing you can add an exclamation point to what you're telling clients.

You need to practice speaking and writing well to ensure potential clients see you as competent, knowledgeable, and confident in your abilities. All of these things – from the clothes you wear to the words you say – impact others' impression of you. Image consultants may even be held to a higher standard and judged more critically. If clients are expected to trust your word, you have to show them you know what you're talking about.

Consultants do not all need to be size fours with perfect physiques. They do need to project a positive image and dress well for their body type. A consultant who is heavier can perhaps better serve a different market than one who is a size two. Consultants of different ethnic backgrounds can offer different perspectives as well. Each consultant has an insider's perspective on the issues facing a person of a certain background, body type, or ethnicity, and clients sharing these challenges may feel more comfortable hiring them.

Spending time on pampering yourself – by taking a dance class to improve movement and grace or getting a regular manicure – are positive steps to becoming an image consultant as well.

4.2 Skills You Need to Succeed

Knowing the services provided by an image consultant is only half the battle. Identifying the skills required to provide these services is the other half. It takes organization, knowledge, flexibility, and great people skills to find success in this field. This section outlines some of the skills required to become a great image consultant and some resources to strengthen these skills.

4.2.1 Visual Sense

Good image consultants have the ability to really see their clients. These professionals have a strong sense of balance, line, and design. This talent allows consultants to assess their clients' wardrobes and eliminate pieces that do not work while infusing the closet with more appropriate, dynamic, and flattering articles of clothing.

Many people have the misconception that image consulting and color analysis are essentially the same thing. While understanding a person's color type and how to use it to make them look great is a large part of many consultants' jobs, there is much more to the career. You have to be able to establish the client's season, suggest shades and tones that would work for their season and features, and then help bring these colors into their closets and makeup kits. Consultants accompany clients on shopping excursions to show them the styles and colors they should buy to make every new wardrobe choice count.

Image consultants have to keep abreast of the latest fashion and style trends. Being up on the hot colors and styles of the year is part of their job. They also need to be aware of what styles are appropriate for different body types as well as different purposes. A work suit serves one purpose while a party dress serves another and blue jeans yet another. Consultants need to be well-versed in all levels of dressing and provide wardrobe options to meet all segments of a client's lifestyle.

Consultants must have a vision for their client based on an assessment of the person's body type and coloring. Experienced consultants learn to make this assessment in a matter of minutes while novice consultants may take more time to analyze a client. Just by looking at an individual, image consultants should be able to picture the proper hairstyle, colors they should be wearing, essential wardrobe pieces, and the best cosmetics to accent the features and coloring. These suggestions help the client look their best all the time.

To improve your visual skills, consider taking professional training programs (see section 4.4). Also use the resources in Chapter 8 of this guide.

4.2.2   Interpersonal Skills

An image consultant has to be a people person. That means you must have strong interpersonal skills in order to be successful in the field. Here are some important skills that help turn an image consultant into a great image consultant.

Relationship Building

Relationships are at the backbone of any image consultant's business. If clients do not feel connected and comfortable with you, they are going to find a consultant with whom they do. If a potential client is trying to decide on a consultant to work with, all things being equal, they will choose the person they like and trust most. Being likeable, friendly, and sincere are important ways to establish, build, and maintain relationships. Clients who like you will often transfer that positive feeling and impression to your work.

You will deal with some very personal issues — issues about which most people can become defensive or sensitive. At times, you may have to ask clients to abandon many of the things they are accustomed to and step out of their comfort zone. This can be scary and intimidating for anyone, and having a consultant who is trustworthy and non-threatening can make these transitions smoother and easier.

To build good relationships, an image consultant needs to have a positive attitude. Cheerful, sunny consultants will attract people and put clients at ease with the consultation process. In a career that addresses what is wrong with a person's style or behavior, it's important to also offer positive feedback. This prevents clients from feeling attacked or like they have been doing everything wrong.

It can be a difficult job to point out faults and help reverse them. The best strategy in dealing with this difficulty is for image consultants to be honest and considerate of their clients. This respect shows your client that you are working with them to bring about a desired end result. Your credibility and experience will be reason enough for your clients to trust you and accept your suggestions. A good relationship between you and your clients makes it easier for them to risk letting go of and replacing their previous habits and style.

If this is an area you want to improve, a great resource used by many professionals is the book *How to Win Friends and Influence People,* by Dale Carnegie.

Speaking Skills

When you are fine-tuning another person's image, you have to be prepared to practice what you preach. It's not enough to tell clients that they should be articulate, well-spoken, and great conversationalists. You have to show them how by embodying all those traits yourself. No one is born with all these talents — you have to learn about them and work on them, just like you'll advise your clients to do.

Voice coaches and even friends and family members can be great sources of feedback about what you need to work on in this area. They can point out speech issues you may not notice, including using slang terms, incorrect grammar, and voice quality and tone. And of course you can use the techniques described earlier, such as videotaping yourself, for helping your clients.

If you are going to be presenting training programs, public speaking experience can help with delivery as well as nerves in front of strangers. There are numerous courses offered to help people with these skills, and enrollment in one may help improve your presentation skills. Also consider joining Toastmasters, a national organization that helps people develop public speaking skills. To find a chapter near you, you can check your local phone book, call their world headquarters at (949) 858-8255, or visit **www.toastmasters.org**.

Listening Skills

Good listeners pay close attention to their conversation partner and show interest in what is being said. This is a crucial talent for image consultants to possess. You have to listen to your clients to determine what they need and expect from your professional relationship.

For the most part, good listening skills are rooted in common sense, but these skills are often forgotten in the heat of conversation. Here are a few tips to help improve your listening skills:

- Don't interrupt. Allow the other person to finish their thought before jumping in with your ideas and opinions.

- Don't assume you know what the other person is going to say. You might miss their point if you are wrong. Listen carefully to what they are saying.

- Keep an eye on your conversation partner's non-verbal cues for signs of emotion, including irritation, excitement, anger, or confusion.

- Ask questions to make sure you understand what the other person has said.

- Don't be distracted by what is going on around you. Such factors as loud noises, the other person's misuse or mispronunciation of a word, or an uncomfortable room temperature can all affect your listening.

- Let the other person know you are listening by using non-verbal cues as well as phrases such as "I see."

- Paraphrase what the other person has said. This allows you to confirm that you understood what they said correctly to avoid misunderstandings later.

Reading People

Listening goes far beyond hearing the words your clients say. Clients will tell you what they want or need, but they may not use clear and exact wording. Image consultants have to be able to read between the lines. You will have to learn to interpret what is being said as well as how it is said to determine the best way to counsel each individual client. This requires a knack for reading people.

A client's non-verbal communication may give you a truer sense of their opinions about what you've said or suggested. It can also give you an opportunity to ask follow-up questions. These queries can elicit a response that your client may not have offered otherwise. See section 2.2.1 for more information about non-verbal communication.

4.2.3 Organizational Skills

It's important to keep your business well-organized. The following are skills that can help you keep track of everything you need to be an image consultant.

Detail-Oriented

Image consulting is all in the details. When consulting, you look at the big picture as well as the individual details that make it up. From the inflection in a client's voice to the type of shoe they wear, the details are what you are being paid to notice.

If you are not equipped to help a client in a given area (such as diction) you should have a list of other professionals (such as voice coaches) accessible. Be sure your referral is deserved — never refer a client to anyone you haven't personally checked out or worked with.

It's a good idea to keep a binder or file folder that contains research materials in the areas an image consultant addresses. This could include newspaper and magazine articles about such topics as the latest fashions and the changing world of business and dining etiquette. This will help you make sure you are providing your clients with the most up-to-date information available.

Image consultants also need to stay on top of their appointments and meetings. Office supply and electronics stores sell various software programs that can help you schedule your week and prevent you from missing important appointments. There are also hand-held organizers that you can use on the go to avoid forgetting about an appointment made while out of the office.

Image consulting is a creative career. Creativity and organization do not always go hand in hand. A systematically organized person may not possess the creative skill set that makes for a good image consultant. That does not give you permission to operate in chaos.

Gloria Starr of Global Success Strategies works in an office with a computer, and has a separate office for consulting with clients and conducting meetings. She also has formal dining and living rooms to accommodate etiquette and meet-and-greet lessons. The offices seen by clients are kept neat and organized. The work office may be another story, but no one else sees it. Starr establishes a high level of organization in public while operating within a system that works well for her in her personal office.

Many consultants are hired to conduct seminars and corporate sessions. Starr determines her level of organization by the profession and personality types of her clients. If the attendees are engineers or accountants, she knows to provide and closely follow a workbook. If the seminar is for sales representatives or marketing executives, she knows that they will expect her to address their immediate and varied concerns rather than following point by point in a workbook.

Time Management

The life of an image consultant is busy. There are many clients to counsel and only a limited number of hours in the day. As a consultant becomes more experienced, they could begin to work for clients in other countries as well. This can be a challenging test of their time management skills. You can take steps to better manage your time.

One way to do so is by keeping a logbook that records everything you do and how long you spend at each activity. This will give you an accurate account of your priorities and some areas that are taking up more time than is necessary. You can get rid of some activities that are wasting time and allot additional time to more important tasks.

Prioritizing your responsibilities can help manage your time. Assign each task one of the four following categories:

- Urgent and important

- Non-urgent and important

- Urgent and non-important

- Non-important and non-urgent

By doing what is both urgent and important first, you can make sure to address high-priority responsibilities. Many people spend time on non-important tasks because they are either urgent or easy to do. Finishing these tasks can give a sense of accomplishment. However, important but non-urgent tasks that are postponed because they are difficult have a way of re-emerging as urgent and important ones.

Create a to-do list and stick to it. Prioritize your errands on this list. Those tasks in the "A" column have to be done that day. The "B" column list are those tasks that can be done after the "A" list but that need to be done within a day or two. The "C" list is everything else that is left over. This prioritizing will help you keep on track for each project.

There are many resources available on time management, including *Creative Time Management for the New Millenium*, by Dr. Jan Yager.

4.2.4   Other Skills

Flexibility

A good image consultant needs to be able to go with the flow. Every day is different. Each client introduces new challenges and demands a slightly different approach to meeting these challenges. It is not a 9-to-5 job, and you need to be able to accommodate the schedules of your clients. Consulting is also not an office job. You will sometimes work out of an office, but at other times you will be at the shopping mall or in the client's office or home. This requires a level of flexibility.

Image consultants also need to search their creative banks to properly and effectively serve their clients. They have to find solutions for a number of problems or challenges — solutions that are tailored to each individual client. Clients are often going through major changes and consultants have to be sensitive to and aware of this transformation.

A person seeking an image overhaul because they are up for a prestigious promotion may have different needs than a client who is going through a divorce. As a consultant, you will wear many hats — stylist, therapist, linguistic coach, and cheerleader. You need to adjust to these varied roles easily and interpret from your client which hat to don.

Self-Marketing Skills

Having knowledge about image is incredibly important, but unless you get hired, these talents will go to waste. Successful image consultants are those who can market themselves. Just like with any product, it is key to have brand recognition. Your name is no different. Consultants have to work hard to get their names into circulation in order to attract clients. It takes time and high visibility to develop a successful business. An impressive website, effective advertising, and, in the end, word of mouth are important ways of building a solid client base.

Self-marketing can be tough for many people, but it is a necessary part of running a business. You need to network often and effectively. You need to be comfortable introducing yourself and explaining what you do at every turn. Hand out business cards, collect other people's cards, and follow up with those who expressed interest in the services you offer. It's amazing how many people will be interested in your profession and want to know more about what you can do for them or perhaps for their friends, colleagues, and family members.

Another self-promotional method is presentations. Offer to meet with a group of executives to outline what you could do for them, the company, and their employees. To present your case for being hired, show them what they will gain and why it is important to be image-conscious.

Another option is to pursue speaking engagements at conventions or conferences, or within associations and organizations. This gets your name and services out to a large number of people at once. Once you are an established consultant, these organizations may seek you out to speak. Until then, pound the pavement, promote yourself and your product, and watch the results.

See chapter 6 of this guide for detailed advice on marketing yourself and your business.

4.3   Ways to Learn Image Consulting Skills

The good news about this exciting profession is that opportunities to learn your trade and hone your skills are literally everywhere. Although there are college programs, certification programs, and professional courses you may take to learn image consulting (more about those later in this chapter), they are just a start. Certainly these programs can shave years off your learning curve, but once you become certified, you will want to spend some time developing your presentation and fine-tuning your program. Here are a few ideas to get you started.

4.3.1   Information Interviews

A fun way to learn about your profession is to get out there and talk to people in the field. Not only can you ask questions, but the interviews are also an opportunity to practice your people skills and an incentive to improve your own image as you aim to impress your peers.

Image Consultants

One of the best places to learn about image consulting is from other image consultants. People in the profession – which is, at its core, a helping profession – are warm, helpful, and eager to share their stories with others who may want to nudge their way into the field.

Although you may not want to contact image consultants in your immediate area (you would be their competition, after all), the Internet makes it exceptionally easy to find the phone numbers and e-mail addresses of image consultants from around North America.

Try finding consultants who live and work in communities similar to yours. For example, if you live in a small town in Illinois, you may find an interview with someone in the suburbs of Cleveland more helpful than one with an image consultant in Los Angeles, a much larger market with a diverse clientele and generally higher fees for services. Professionals in the field will often answer with honesty and candor such questions as:

- How did you learn the skills needed for image consulting, and how would you suggest I learn them?

- How did you get started? Where did you find your first clients?

- Did you find it helpful to earn certification before you started taking clients?

- What types of questions do you ask clients before you begin their color analysis and image makeover?

- What are your fees?

- How long did it take before you could make a living at full-time consulting?

- What is the number one piece of useful advice you could give a new image consultant?

When you contact a consultant, be wary of using the phrase "information interview." So often, people who ask for such interviews are either seeking a job or are trying to sell goods or services. Though you'll be doing those very things later on, what you want now is some casual and candid conversation to help you get started in your new career.

You need not be too formal when asking — simply state that you are considering entering the field of image consulting and that you have a few questions, then ask if you may schedule a brief phone interview to ask these questions. If a phone interview isn't convenient, ask if you could list some questions and correspond via e-mail. You'll be delighted to find that more often than not, your request will be granted. However, we found that some image consultants expect to be paid for their time to provide information about getting started in this career, so make sure you clarify in advance whether there will be a charge.

After the interview, be sure to send a warm thank you note to the consultant. Not only are you grateful for their graciousness and helpfulness, but you also never know when professional contacts will be useful in the future — either for networking, support, or perhaps even a job. Be sure to stay in touch with those professionals you meet in the early stages of beginning your career.

Strategic Partners

Vendors and strategic partners are excellent sources of information. Interview several different kinds to get a feel for which are the most knowledgeable and which will be the most willing to work with you.

Meet with a variety of clothing vendors, hair stylists and cosmetics suppliers to find the right suppliers for you and your clients. They are easy to find — take a trip to your shopping mall or a nearby fashionable shopping district, and look in the Yellow Pages in your phone book. Don't be afraid to ask friends and families to recommend their favorite dress shops, suit shops, and hair stylists. Once you find a few vendors you would like to meet with, you can glean a plethora of helpful information from them.

Makeup Artists

Although you will be an expert on your clients' coloring and lifestyles, a cosmetics supplier can introduce you to their products and let you try them before you offer them to clients. They can give you tips on application and can let you familiarize yourself with every product. You will likely need a variety of cosmetics suppliers, as not every vendor will have every type and shade of makeup to meet every client's needs.

Ask the cosmetics supplier to recommend makeup products and tips for you to see how well they understand their business, and to determine if they will respect your wishes when you say you want a different color or application.

The relationship with cosmetics suppliers can be tricky, because in some markets they have erroneously been given the title of image consultant. If you can't work out an agreement with a cosmetics supplier who will work with you, don't fret! You simply need to meet with a few in order to better know their product lines. Make it clear that if you establish a good working relationship, you would like to purchase from them regularly. Ask about the lines they carry, and their prices (and of course any discounts for being a regular customer), but don't expect them to provide cosmetics makeovers. You need to establish a relationship where you are clearly in charge and you are both working toward the same goal — pampering and helping your clients.

Clothing Vendors

Striking a balance can be tricky, but remember, you are the suppliers' client and your needs are the most important, because you are the expert in your own clients' lifestyles, body types and color needs.

For example, you want to deal with a clothing vendor who knows all the comfortable, fashionable and trendy colors and fabrics. But those fabrics and colors may not be what's best for your client. So get a feel for which stores and salespeople are comfortable with you taking charge while at the same time offering information on products that may interest you and your clients.

Be sure to meet with specialty clothing vendors, such as those who specialize in larger sizes, casual wear, and formal wear. Meeting with vendors before you bring clients to them is an excellent opportunity to find out what they have to offer, in terms of styles, colors and fabrics.

But you should also form an understanding with the salespeople you work with that what you need is someone to bring clothing to you, in a variety of sizes. You want them to pamper your client the way you do, and to pay full attention to you and your clients while you are there.

It often helps to make it clear during the first meeting that you expect no commission, but appreciate any discounts the store has to offer. Very often, establishing your expectations and letting the salesperson know you don't expect a "cut" of their commission can help establish a trust and rapport.

Hair Stylists

Perhaps the easiest, but most sensitive, relationship to establish will be the one you forge with hair stylists. Finding stylists to interview is as simple as asking your colleagues, friends and family members which stylists they have visited and liked, and why they liked them.

Make an appointment with the stylist, and ask if you can observe them at work. When you explain that you are starting a career in image consulting and have heard wonderful things about them, and that you would like to bring clients, chances are very good you will get a warm welcome and enthusiasm.

Plan on spending a few hours to half a day with the stylist. Watch how they treat their own customers. Do they touch them? Are they warm and professional? Do they listen to them before making suggestions? How well do they pay attention to their customers? How do their finished styles look? Are they what the customer asked for? Were their suggestions helpful in creating the perfect style for the customer?

If you are uneasy about the answers to any of the questions, don't be afraid to simply offer the stylist a genuine thank you (after all, they were kind enough to let you observe), but then leave at the scheduled time. However, if you are confident in their skills and personal traits, ask if they would have time to do your own hair. If not that day, perhaps they could make an appointment for you to return. If you like the finished product, then you are on your way to a great working relationship.

During the interview, you will also want to find out how to best work with each supplier or service provider. Ask such questions as:

- What days do you typically work, and what hours are you available? Are you available at other times, as well?

- How much time does it usually take to get an appointment?

- What are your prices and/or fees (depending on the product or service)? Do you offer a discount to image professionals?

- Where appropriate, ask if there are catalogs available, or a website you can check to stay abreast of new products (particularly with cosmetics suppliers).

After meeting with every vendor or service provider, be sure to send a thank you note immediately, and stay in touch with each until you are ready to start bringing clients.

4.3.2   Volunteer Work

Volunteering your time is an excellent way to learn your trade and sharpen your skills before you start taking paying clients. Getting exposure, recognition, and networking is crucial to your business, and there is no better time invested than in working with a variety of people and groups. Volunteering your time in the beginning will not only help you learn your profession, but it is also a great habit to establish early.

The image consulting profession is, at its core, a service profession, and most consultants continue to do pro bono work at least once a month throughout their careers. It's a great way to show you care about your community, have heart, get some name recognition and, in some cases, attract media attention (worth its weight in gold, in terms of newspaper and television exposure).

Friends and Family

You may not realize it, but you have a host of volunteers right under your nose already. Your family and friends are terrific choices as your first "clients." Most image consultants will tell you to start with individual consultations before moving on to groups, and there are no better individuals than people who already know you and care about you.

Until you learn the skills needed to work with people you may not know as well, your close friends and family will give you the chance to make your presentations, do color analysis, hone your skills and make plenty of mistakes (and they will forgive your imperfections and let you start over without thinking any less of your skills).

Be sure to treat your family and friends the same way you would treat a client who may be a stranger to you. You want to make an earnest effort to learn skills and to gain confidence before you start working with other audiences. Perfect your color analysis skills as well as your tact and diplomacy skills (after all, it may be even harder to tell your mother she's been wearing the wrong colors for the last two decades than it would be to tell a stranger, but your mother will forgive you if you're too blunt).

Before you meet with each client (volunteer or otherwise) you should have a consultation to help determine what information to present, and on what areas of the client's image to focus. The more information you have ahead of time, the more effective your presentation will be.

Don't skip important steps, like that "first meeting" used to figure out what the client's needs and goals are. Everything you learned in chapter two should be utilized when working with family and friends.

Don't forget to work with the men in your life, too. Your father, neighbor, brother, husband or boyfriend all can help you learn skills to work with men, who may have similar goals as female clients but express their wishes completely differently.

When you complete a session with a family member or friend, ask them to fill out the same feedback form you would of any other customer. Ask the same questions listed in section 3.5, under "Follow Up." Use the information provided to tweak your presentation and gain confidence and skills.

Once you feel you're ready to work with a less familiar audience, ask your friends and family members to give you names of their friends who might be interested in your services.

Charitable Organizations

You'll be able to find charitable organizations who would welcome your pro bono services. When you meet with the decision makers for such organizations, explain that you are training to become an image consultant and would like to offer your services, free of charge, to help you learn your profession.

Describe the services you can provide, and how you intend to do so. Before the meeting, be sure to prepare an agenda and have appropriate materials to make the presentation. You can also offer to give a sample presentation, tailored to the group's potential needs.

With groups, you will more likely work on one specific aspect of image, since you won't have the time or resources to do such things as total makeovers and wardrobe evaluations for even small groups.

Although the opportunities to volunteer with groups are as endless as your imagination, here are a few ideas to get you going:

Church Groups

Consider contacting a women's church group and performing color analysis and cosmetic makeovers.

Business and Professional Clubs

You can find these organizations through your chamber of commerce or your city's community resource office. You could suggest a presentation in which you discuss the most flattering clothing styles for different body types and lifestyles. With a smaller group, you can also perform individual color analysis and body type analysis.

College Students

The possibilities for students are endless. Contact the local university's placement or student activities office. Propose presentations on job-seeking etiquette, business dinner etiquette, dressing for job interviews and the first job after college.

Women's Shelters/Women's Help Organizations

These organizations can be found in the Yellow Pages, or through other social service agencies. Consider making a presentation on interviewing for a job, using sample outfits from the local thrift store or a local charity (such as a clothing donation project like My Sister's Closet). Another terrific idea would be to ask students at a local beauty college to help with the presentation and create new hair styles for the clients.

This is an excellent opportunity for you to contact the local news media and ask them to do a feature story on the event. But don't try contacting the news until after you have made at least one presentation like this. You want to be sure your skills are what they should be before you invite the media.

When meeting with women in shelters, it is very important to avoid making any assumptions about their career history, educational level, or social skills. Often, women in shelters are college-educated, employed, professional women who have experienced one catastrophic event which led to their current situation.

Cancer Patients

Contact the local hospital's public relations department, which can direct you to the right person to present your proposal. Propose a presentation on maintaining image and balancing career, family and chemotherapy.

In this case, a series of presentations may be best. For example, one session could be about looking your best when you're not feeling your best. Another could be about finding flattering clothing when nothing fits quite right due to weight loss, or when pain makes it difficult to dress. Another session could address hair loss and the decision to cover with hats, scarves, or wigs.

Prior to your presentation, it is very important to meet not only with administrators but also with nurses or caregivers who best understand what image issues are faced by people receiving cancer treatments.

One outstanding volunteer opportunity can be found at The Associates Image Enhancement and Support Center, located at the Chao Family Comprehensive Cancer Center at UCI Medical Center in Orange, California. Its website is **www.healthcare.uci.edu/cc2.asp**.

According to the site, "The center provides advice and help to men and women with appearance-related problems. Patients include individuals affected by cancer, burns, traumatic injuries, lupus, scleroderma and serious skin conditions. Volunteers will provide hair consultation for complete or partial hair loss; assist with selecting and fitting wigs, hats, turbans and scarves; and offer corrective makeup application and skin care tips."

The program's coordinator, Barbara Quayle, says, "At a time when women are at a crisis and have a tremendous amount of stress in their lives, the image enhancement program eases their anxiety by providing a nurturing environment where we offer them [image services] in a very private and beautiful environment... where everybody understands."

There are a handful of similar programs at other medical facilities. For a list of cancer centers across the country, see the site for the National Cancer Institute at **http://cancercenters.cancer.gov/cancer_centers/cancer-centers-list.html**.

Presentations to Organizations

Virtually any charitable organization, or every cause you are interested in, will provide opportunities to volunteer your services. It's just a matter of defining how your services can help a variety of audiences. For example, you could approach your local Parent-Teacher Association to propose a fun presentation on care-free hairstyles for every face and every lifestyle (perfect for busy parents).

Just as with individual clients, the more information you have before making a presentation to a group, the more effective you will be, and the happier the clients will be. In addition to asking questions similar to those you would ask individuals, ask questions such as:

- What types of goals should I focus on?

- How many people should I expect, and when will you have a final count on attendees?

- How will you plan on promoting the event? You may offer suggestions such as using their calendars and newsletters, bulletin boards, personal invitations and posters on-site.

- Where would the presentation take place? What types of resources will be made available for me to use (i.e. a chalkboard, a microphone for presentations to larger groups, a nice flat empty wall on which to hang visual aids, electrical outlets and screens if you're making a PowerPoint presentation)?

- Are there any special needs I should consider?

Be sure to ask attendees to fill out evaluation forms, and look for opportunities to maintain contact with clients who may eventually be paying customers. Most of all, take your time, perfect your presentation, make lots of contact with people, and have fun.

4.4 Educational Programs

Although you do not need a degree or certificate to become an image consultant, you may learn more efficiently and effectively by taking a training program. Formal educational training can also help enhance your credibility. Educational opportunities are available through several types of programs. They include:

- College or university degrees or courses

- Professional certification programs

- Continuing education courses

In addition to offering on-site programs (where students are required to appear in person for classes), various organizations also offer distance learning opportunities.

What to Look For

It's important to select the program that best suits your needs. If you enjoy the interactive aspect of attending classes, then a traditional classroom setting will probably work best for you. If working according to your own schedule and pace is more important, then distance learning would be a better fit. If you would rather learn by experience from others in the field, you may want to enroll in a mentoring program. If cost and time commitment are key factors in your choice, you should carefully assess the available options. You can spend hours to days to years, and hundreds or thousands of dollars taking a program.

While all of these aspects are important to consider when you are evaluating educational opportunities, you can also ask a few questions to help you decide if a program is worth your time and investment. In the following section, you'll find a list of various programs. In the meantime, here are questions to ask when gathering information from interviews with instructors or former graduates of the program.

Is the Program Accredited?

A number of educational programs are accredited by official organizations that are recognized for their educational standardization. Accreditation means that the program has met certain educational standards. (Even if a program is not accredited, you may still find it useful for your career training, depending on your goals).

Is the Program Recognized in the Profession?

You can answer this question best by asking professionals in the field about the program's credibility and reputation. If you conduct informational interviews with image consultants, as discussed in section 4.3.1, ask them their opinion of the program you are evaluating.

What Areas Does the Program Cover?

To ensure you are satisfied with your educational investment, make sure you know the type of material you'll be learning from a program. As there are several different niches in image consulting where you can specialize, you may not yet know the area of the business where you'd like to concentrate. Or you may have a very clear idea of what area of expertise you'd like to learn. Both approaches can help you narrow down the best options for you.

If you haven't yet determined what type of image consulting you'd like to do, you may want to find a program with both comprehensive image consulting and business courses. These programs can provide baseline knowledge of all aspects of the business and may help you determine where you'd like to specialize. It also can help you decide if there are areas where you would like to continue your education.

These programs would include, for example, courses in presentation skills, core business classes like marketing and small business management, wardrobe and closet organization, communication, business and social etiquette, design, speech fundamentals and merchandising.

If you know what your area of expertise will be, you can also select programs with a more focused approach in the various disciplines. This would include programs that concentrate on areas like color analysis, corporate dress, non-verbal communication, media training or makeup, to name a few.

Who is Offering the Program?

Find out who will be teaching you. How are they qualified to teach, and what are their credentials? Check out how long they've been in education and/or the field of image consulting, as well as the teaching style they use and whether you're comfortable with it. If you are taking a program from a company, find out how long it has been in operation. You can also contact the Better Business Bureau to find out if there have been any complaints lodged against it.

4.4.1 College Programs

Having a degree or college coursework in either image consulting or a related field can help make a good impression for both present and future clients, colleagues, the media, and the public-at-large.

While numerous organizations offer degrees and/or coursework related to image consulting, only a very limited number of degree programs currently offer specific concentrations in image consulting.

If a school's location precludes you from attending the programs, you may be able to find local programs that might not be image consulting-specific, but do offer degrees or courses that can be useful and applicable for starting your career in image consultation.

Below are three colleges that offer image consulting programs. Also consider checking your local junior college, college or university for course offerings in business, communication, psychology, marketing, and fashion merchandising.

An additional area of study to consider is education. According to veteran image consultant Sherry Maysonave, founder and president of Empowerment Enterprises, you can't go wrong with a degree in education because the field of image consulting lends itself so well to the educational process. Even when working one-on-one with individuals, you're educating them.

You can visit the Peterson's Education Portal site on the Internet at **www.petersons.com** to help you in your search for degree programs and coursework in general disciplines that would relate to image consulting. To search for schools, visit the site and look under the following majors for school location information: Marketing Operations (which includes the sub-discipline of Fashion Merchandising), Communication (you can search in sub-disciplines Public Relations and Organizational Communication), Education and Psychology.

Skyline College

One college that offers an image consulting degree program is Skyline College in San Bruno, California. Within the school's Business Division, in its Fashion Merchandising program, you can major in image consulting while obtaining an Associate's degree in science. The degree program – a two-year program if attending full time – covers general core fashion, business and psychology courses, along with image consulting-specific courses.

The college also offers an image consulting certificate program, which is a one-year certification program that concentrates on the fundamentals of image consulting, from fashion courses to speech courses, as well as business basics. The cost of Skyline's certificate program starts at about $780 U.S. for California residents and varies for out-of-state and international students.

E-mail: **meadows@smccd.net**

Website: **www.skylinecollege.edu/programsofstudy/ business/fashionMerchandising.html#icert**

George Brown College

George Brown College in Toronto, Ontario, offers a certificate program in image consulting. As part of the continuing education department, this fashion program teaches image consulting with instruction covering wardrobe, style, color, makeup, and personal development. It also covers etiquette, human relations, starting your own business, reading and using nonverbal communication, and your personal presentation. Each of the six courses in the certificate program takes fifteen hours to complete and costs around $187 Canadian.

E-mail: **cefashion@gbrownc.on.ca**

Website: **http://coned.georgebrown.ca/owa_prod/ cewskcrss.P_Certificate?area_code= PA0007&cert_code=CE0093**

Fashion Institute of Technology

A certificate in image consulting is offered through FIT's School of Continuing and Professional Studies in New York. To earn this non-credit certificate, students must complete 141 hours within 24 months. Program courses cover both the knowledge needed to become an image consultant – including a study of great designers, makeup and hair, wardrobe, color, personal shopping, and fashion – as well as the business side of the job, such as business essentials and creative business planning.

E-mail: **conted@fitnyc.edu**

Website: **www.fitnyc.edu**

4.4.2   AICI Certification Programs

The largest international organization of professionals offering image consulting services is AICI, or the Association of Image Consultants International. AICI offers three levels of certification in image consulting in addition to educational opportunities at its yearly educational conference during April or May, where consultants of all levels can train with industry veterans. AICI chapters also offer members educational days for additional training opportunities.

The different levels of AICI certification are listed below. For more information about any of these programs contact AICI:

E-mail: **info@aici.org**

Website: **www.aici.org**

FLC — First Level of Certification

According to AICI, this program was created for individuals who have not had access to professional credentials in image consulting and are looking for ways to advance their business, level of knowledge, experience and expertise.

The FLC requires passing a written examination covering the fundamental issues that every image consultant needs to know, according to AICI's website. The exam is very similar in format to those offered by many professional associations and there are no pre-existing requirements for work and formal educational/training experience. However, you are required to be a member of AICI to take the exam.

Currently, the FLC exam is administered only once each year, in conjunction with AICI's Annual Conference in May. When details about the year's annual conference are posted, you can complete the online (or hard copy) registration form to register for either the FLC exam alone or the FLC exam and conference.

From year to year, the exam changes in content, but not in focus, to a certain degree, according to AICI. AICI strongly recommends that those interested in starting or enhancing their business should regularly study books and combine them with accredited training. AICI has a recommended reading list on their website, which will help you prepare for the current year's exam.

After attaining AICI's FLC level, the organization offers more advanced levels of certification. Each year at AICI's annual conference, the organization offers a free session that provides a walk-through of requirements for these certifications. The certifications include:

CIP — Certified Image Professional

This type of certification requires experience and preparation of a comprehensive portfolio after being involved with image consulting services for a sufficient number of years. The certificate is earned based on a points system, with points assigned to various categories that applicants complete, including: education, performance, industry recognition, organizational activities, contributions and promotion.

CIM — Certified Image Master

This is the highest certification level that AICI offers and it requires more extensive education and experience in many of the same categories as the CIP.

4.4.3   Other Training and Certification Programs

Numerous organizations and individuals offer training and certificates in image consulting. Several programs also offer follow-up mentoring and coaching services after completion, which can help further enhance your learning. On the pages that follow, you will find a list of programs, in alphabetical order, that you may want to look into. For tips on choosing a program, review "What to Look For" at the beginning of section 4.4 for pertinent questions to ask yourself when evaluating a certificate program.

> **NOTE:** We cannot say whether any of the programs listed in this guide will be right for you. You are the only one who can make that decision. Program costs and other details can change, so make sure you confirm information about any program before registering.

ColorStyle Institute

Using hands-on techniques, demonstrations, and instruction, trainees will learn about color and style. This company offers many levels of courses for mastering issues of coloring, body and skin types, wardrobe, and style. Prices vary depending on the course.

E-mail: **info@bodybeautiful.net**

Website: **www.bodybeautiful.net/training_schedule.php**

Conselle Institute of Image Management

Conselle offers image management educational training and certification. Their 14-day on-site training program consists of two seven-day segments on comprehensive image management topics and running a business, plus 15 months of mentorship and coaching following the course. The company offers a flexible attendance plan, and a flexible payment plan is also available.

E-mail: **judith@conselle.com**

Website: **www.conselle.com**

Donna Fujii Institute

This training program prepares students to practice color analysis and image consulting. Trainers present a multiethnic analysis method that helps consultants complement all skin tones. The institute offers two- and six-day courses. The two-day course involves sixteen hours of instruction in color theory and allows students to practice on people with different skin types and coloring. Tuition for the two-day course is $495, which includes course materials. The six-day course is an extensive program in which students learn and practice color mixing, analysis, style, and wardrobe. Tuition is $3,490 including materials.

E-mail: **donna@donnafujii.com**

Website: **www.donnafujii.com/df_html/training/index.html**

Empowerment Enterprises

Empowerment Enterprises offers a Certificate in Communication and Image Consulting. Their comprehensive program covers major areas like color analysis, body types, wardrobe analysis, wardrobe and closet organization, how to pack for travel, speaking skills, business/marketing skills, and other aspects of running a business. They have on-site training programs in New York and San Francisco that run for nine months, though the classes can be staggered throughout this period. Edward Latson is the contact.

E-mail: **edward@casualpower.com**

Website: **www.casualpower.com**

Global Success Strategies, Inc.

Global Success Strategies, Inc. offers a Certificate in Impression Management, Image and Style and a Certificate in Etiquette and the Business and Social Graces. Training programs take place in Charlotte, North Carolina. Each program lasts for five days and covers techniques for working with clients, diplomacy strategies, sales and marketing skills, business tools and skills, and communication topics. It also includes mentoring services for several months after completion of the program. Each program costs $8,500, or $16,000 for both.

E-mail: **expert@gloriastarr.com**

Website: **www.gloriastarr.com/training.htm**

Image Group International

Established in 1989, Image Group International is an Australia-based, award winning organization with representation in New Zealand, southeast Asia, the U.K., and the U.S.A. They train individuals and Fortune 500 corporations on image, managerial and non-verbal communication skills, media skills, color analysis, protocol and etiquette, inner image, grooming principles and wardrobe strategies. They offer a Train to Be a Corporate Image Advisor certification program for professionals considering becoming qualified and accredited corporate image advisors or lifestyle, business and executive coaches.

E-mail: info@imagegroup.com.au

Website: www.imagegroup.com.au

The ImageMaker, Inc.

The ImageMaker offers a home study image certification and a Seminar Leader certification. The correspondence course can be completed in as little as a few weeks, although most students spend an average of two to three months. The course can be taken on-site when requested — call or e-mail them for more information.

Classes offered include Business Strategic Planning, Marketing Your Business, Color Analysis, Fashion and Style, Figure Analysis, Etiquette, Posture and Poise, Makeup and Skin Care, Non-Verbal Communication, and Business Casual. Courses also include unlimited mentoring services. The Home Study Mentoring Program is $4,050. The cost of the Certified Seminar Leader program is $4,050. If both are taken at the same time in a package called the International Image Certification Program, the cost is $5,050.

E-mail: imagemaker@bellsouth.net

Website: www.imagemaker1.com

International Image Institute

This program, located in Richmond Hill and Toronto, Ontario, Canada, offers clients training in such areas as etiquette and human relations, color analysis, image management for men and women, presentation, and developing a consulting business. Training classes are offered three times through the year — spring, autumn, and winter. Trainees can design their own programs to accommodate their interests and needs. Courses range from one-day programs to six-day courses. Prices range from about $300 to $1,950 Canadian. They also offer distance certification training.

E-mail: karenbrunger@imageinstitute.com

Website: www.imageinstitute.com

Lindquist Associates

Trainees can study at home, one-on-one with trainer Debra Lindquist, or in a small group to become a consultant. Lindquist offers four modules that cover extensive color analysis, clothing, psychology, and your own image as a consultant. Trainees are certified after completing each of these modules.

E-mail: **debra@lindquistassociates.com**

Website: **www.lindquistassociates.com**

London Image Institute

This school offers two programs, a Fast-Track Certificate Program for beginners in the industry and an Executive Course, which is an advanced program that includes teaching and training techniques for giving seminars and workshops. The Fast Track course takes place on-site in New York. The eight-day classes cover a basic foundation in image consulting, including color, body, style and line analysis; men's wear, wardrobing, personal shopping, individual consultations, business development, and media training. The Executive Course, which takes place in Atlanta, is seven days long, with four months of follow-up coaching. Contact the institute for information about tuition costs and payment plans.

E-mail: **info@londonimageinstitute.com**

Website: **www.londonimageinstitute.com**

S.T.A.R. Power Image Consulting Certification Program

Trainees complete a five-day training and apprenticeship program that teaches the skills of the trade including personal style, shopping, etiquette, and marketing your business. After the week is up, the student can take advantage of six months of free e-mail or telephone coaching by founder Ashley Rothschild when needed.

E-mail: **ashley@rothschildimage.com**

Website: **www.rothschildimage.com**

Continuing Education Courses

There are a variety of resources that offer continuing education opportunities. These classes and programs can enrich your training and prepare you for an image consulting career. Continuing education is an ongoing process, according to many industry veterans who say they regularly take courses to broaden their knowledge and expertise. It's important to stay current not only on the ever-changing fashion and technology aspects of image consulting, but also the components of education and transformation.

The most industry-specific continuing education opportunities include single courses in topics such as style, how to be a consultant, image and personal development, presentation skills, etiquette, color, and wardrobe basics. These will often come from individual image consultants who offer programs, as well as programs from professional associations, such as AICI.

To find image consultants offering programs at the local level, check in your Yellow Pages under "image consultants" and contact them to see if they offer any continuing education courses.

Also, see if other consultants offer mentoring assistance. With this type of continuing education, an experienced image consultant will provide one-on-one assistance and guidance for those new to the field.

AICI and its regional chapters also offer education days, where they provide classes in various areas of image consulting. However, course availability will depend on the size of the chapter and how active it is. To find a chapter close to your area, you can go to AICI's website (**www. aici.org**), where they provide links to various chapters' websites all over the world. The links will provide further contact information so you can determine if there are opportunities near you.

AICI also offers a variety of courses and seminars at its annual conference. For instance, courses at a recent conference ranged from the basic "The ABCs to Run a Successful Image Consulting Business" to topics like "Body Talking," "Can You Strike It Rich Working With Celebrities?" and "European Makeup and Style." All courses are included in the general conference registration fee. Many of these sessions and courses are taught by experienced image consultants who charge significantly higher fees for their training on an individual basis. The conference can provide you with their instruction at a significantly reduced cost.

Another place where you can explore opportunities at the local level is to contact the continuing education department of your local college or university. While they may not offer image consulting-specific courses, they probably will offer some coursework in areas applicable to image consulting, including psychology, education, fashion merchandising, basic business courses, nutrition, communication, and speech.

You may also find courses applicable to image consulting from other local institutions. They include:

- Business courses from local women's organizations
- Business courses from your Chamber of Commerce
- Beauty and skin care courses from local beauty schools, cosmetology schools or modeling agencies

4.5 Related Work Experience

You have given all your friends makeovers. You have just helped your mother get a new job. Three women from her bowling team are begging for your help, and your father wants you to work with him on his presentation style. It's time to start getting paid for this!

There are several paying jobs that will prepare you, and even train you, to become an independent image consultant. You'll learn all about these jobs and how to get hired in this section. It covers the types of employers you will encounter, how to find job openings, the materials you'll need for your job hunt, and how to prepare for the all-important interview, including salary expectations and following up. You'll also learn about a job you can get working along with an image consultant group as a specialist or assistant.

4.5.1 Types of Employers

Plenty of employers have jobs to fill that are related to image consulting, and there are employers who do hire in-house image consultants, although they may call them something else. Whether you are interested in a "stepping stone" job to give you some experience (and valuable contacts) in the field before you launch your own consulting business, or you want to build a stepping stone into a satisfying career, there are many choices for you.

According to the Association of Image Consultants International, by far the most jobs for image professionals are offered by major retailers and by companies that provide products for the major retailers.

There are, however, other possibilities...

Fashion Retailers

The Bureau of Labor Statistics predicts that there will be nearly 600,000 new retail jobs by 2014, which translates to average growth for retail sales workers over the next few years. Retail has many excellent entry-level opportunities that do not require a college education.

Retailers in this category include, among others, Bloomingdale's, Nordstrom, Neiman-Marcus, Saks Fifth Avenue, Macy's, and Barney's New York. All the major department stores have websites with a link to their career pages where you can view job openings at their stores all over the country. You can apply for a job directly online or submit your resume for future consideration.

- *Barneys New York*
  www.barneys.com/Jobs/JOBS,default,pg.html

- *Bloomingdale's*
  www.bloomingdalesjobs.com

- *Macy's*
  www.macysjobs.com

- *Neiman-Marcus*
  www.neimanmarcuscareers.com

- *Nordstrom*
  www.recruitingsite.com/csbsites/nordstrom/index.asp

- *Saks Fifth Avenue*
  www.careersatsaks.com

Large retailers hire beauty advisers, cosmetics associates, sales associates, and personal shoppers (sometimes called lifestyle consultants, or, simply, consultants) — all good jobs to pursue while training to become an image consultant.

Beauty advisers and cosmetics sales associates work at the makeup counters on the main floor of the store. They help customers choose makeup products and demonstrate how to put them on during individual sessions. They keep records of their clients' purchases and notify them of new products.

Both sales associates and personal shoppers assist customers in purchasing fashions and accessories. The most experienced associates work in the "executive" sales departments of their stores (the Fifth Avenue Club at Saks, for example) and have extensive knowledge of designers, fitting, and color. Personal shoppers must develop and maintain a "book" of clients whom they shop for and notify of upcoming sales or special finds. The larger their book, the higher their value to their employer.

Meet Kevin. Kevin is an exclusive consultant at Macy's flagship store, formerly Marshall Fields, in Chicago. He had been at Fields for seventeen years, having started in the gourmet foods department. Over the next twelve years he worked his way through the store as a sales associate, eventually working in every department but menswear. Kevin became well-known for his excellent customer skills and good taste. At one point about five years ago, he was asked by upper management to become a consultant (an exclusive personal shopper), which, he says, is "the top tier outside the design studio."

Beauty Salons and Spas

Beauty salons and spas hire hair dressers, makeup professionals, estheticians, nail technicians, and massage therapists. Like the retail jobs listed above, these jobs can be careers in themselves, or stepping stones to a career in image consulting. They all involve helping clients look their best, and any one of them could be expanded upon to encompass the full palate of image consulting.

According to Larry Oskin, president of Marketing Solutions, a marketing, advertising, and public relations firm specializing in the beauty industry, the current trend in cosmetology is toward all-encompassing beauty training. Hair designers and cosmetic artists, for example, are receiving training not only in makeup and hair care, but also in color analysis, wardrobing, and body typing. Thus, many hair designers are also likely doing image consulting work as well.

Salons and spas that offer image consulting will likely advertise it as "total image makeovers," and the people who do it will usually be called "total image consultants." As Oskin says, the problem is mostly one of semantics. When looking for salons and spas that hire image professionals, he advises to look for the biggest facilities that offer a wide variety of services beyond hair cuts and manicures, then call and ask if they do "total image makeovers."

According to the Bureau of Labor Statistics, in 2006 there were 825,000 people employed in the personal care industry. Your local telephone book is the best way to find a facility near you, or you can try the National Accrediting Commission of Cosmetology Arts and Sciences (NACCAS) website (**www.naccas.org/Pages/JobandResumeBank.aspx**).

Beauty Product Sales

Many image consultants break into the field by starting as an independent beauty consultant selling a line of popular cosmetics and skin care products. These companies offer training materials, support, and a variety of incentives (such as new cars, trips, and expensive jewelry) to help their consultants succeed.

As an independent beauty consultant, you set your own hours and run your own business. Some companies such as Avon go all-out in an effort to help their sales associates take their careers to the highest level. Avon also offers insurance and retirement plans, and has a college internship program.

Major companies in this industry include Avon, BeautiControl, Color 1 Associates, Color Me Beautiful, and Mary Kay. Check out the career sections of the websites of the following beauty product companies for more information about how to get started, costs, training, incentives, and benefits.

- *Avon*
  www.avoncompany.com/about/career.html

- *BeautiControl*
  www.beauticontrol.com/contactus.htm

- *Color Me Beautiful*
  www.careersinbeauty.com

- *Mary Kay*
  www.marykay.com/sellmarykay/default

Weight Loss Centers

Weight loss centers are another area where image professionals can find employment. Weight loss counselors help clients set weight loss goals, track their progress, and celebrate their successes. The weight loss industry is, well, huge, and many opportunities abound in this rapidly growing field.

LA Weight Loss Centers, Jenny Craig, Beverly Hills Weight Loss & Wellness, and Weight Watchers are national weight loss chains. Careers in weight loss are easily explored via the following company websites:

- *Beverly Hills Weight Loss & Wellness*
  www.beverlyhillsweightloss.com/franchising.php

- *Jenny Craig*
  www.jennycraig.com/programs/faq-oos.asp#1

- *LA Weight Loss Centers*
  www.laweightloss.com

- *Weight Watchers*
  www.weightwatchers.com/about/ldr/index.aspx

Advertising Agencies

Advertising agencies are a good choice for the image consultant who is more interested in developing the image of a business, as opposed to an individual. You may find work as an assistant account executive, where you will get a chance to work with clients, study the market and follow up on client services. There are more than 22,000 advertising agencies in the United States, with most of the large firms located in New York, Chicago, and Los Angeles. Most agencies, however, employ fewer than ten people and are located all over the country.

To learn more about advertising jobs and the companies that have them, try the following websites. American Advertising Agencies has an annotated list of top agencies in more than 20 U.S. cities at **www.american adagencies.com**. The American Advertising Federation (**www.aaf.org**), American Association of Advertising Agencies (**www.aaaa.org**), and the American Marketing Association (**www.marketingpower.com**) are the professional associations for this field.

The sites below list careers in advertising, communication, creative services and management:

- *AdAge.com Career Center*
  http://jobs.adagetalentworks.com/jobseekerx/ SearchJobsForm.asp?ft=bas

- *Talent Zoo*
  www.talentzoo.com/advertising-jobs/index.php

Public Relations Agencies

Public relations agencies are an excellent choice for image professionals who have a background in journalism or broadcasting as well as business. Media trainers are image pros who assist their clients in dealing effectively with the media.

Public relations agencies also hire account assistants and executives. Account executives handle one or more accounts, working closely with the client on writing, media contact, and placement. Communication consultants work for public relations agencies or for corporations, usually in the human resources, communication, marketing, or public relations department.

As in advertising, most of the big public relations firms are located in New York, Los Angeles, Chicago and Washington, D.C., with smaller firms all over the country. The field of public relations specialists is predicted by the Bureau of Labor Statistics to have much faster than average growth over the next six years, although stiff competition is predicted for entry-level jobs.

The Public Relations Society of America (**www.prsa.org**) and the International Association of Business Communicators (**www.iabc.com**) are the professional associations in this field. Both include job listings on their websites.

Large Corporations

Some image consultants have combined savvy business knowledge with exceptional image skills to become corporate image consultants, either helping to enhance the professional image of executives, develop or remake the image of the company, or both. Most corporate image consultants work for themselves, however, and contract their services to companies. Lauren Solomon, one of the first image consultants ever to be hired as an in-house image professional, says that opportunities for in-house image pros are "almost non-existent."

Corporations recognize the importance of image, but generally "bring it in from the outside," Solomon says. Whether they classify it under "learning and development," "scope of diversity," or "interpersonal skills," Solomon says it is still more common for corporations to turn to an American Marketing Association program or a Dale Carnegie course than to hire an in-house image consultant, and she calls the handful of companies that have tried it "purely visionary."

Solomon's job (at Chase Manhattan Bank) was actually created especially for her by a senior executive after he found out she'd been doing informal image sessions with some of her company colleagues (she was in the marketing department at the time). He was so impressed with her work (her colleagues were walking advertisements) that he asked her to put together a plan.

Four years later, however, a company merger left her "in between." If she wanted to stay at the company, she would have to go back to marketing. She chose image consulting and today runs her own firm, LS

Image, Inc., located online at **www.lsimage.com**. She also teaches "The Brand Called Me," a mandatory mini-course at New York University's Stern School of Business, and has written a book, *Image Matters! First Steps on the Journey to Your Best Self.*

Medical Offices

Plastic surgery is hot right now, with an increasing number of younger people seeking to make changes in their appearance. Some well-known plastic surgeons, such as Manhattan plastic surgeon Dr. Stephen Greenberg, have added image consultants to their staffs in an effort to make their business more of a "one stop shop."

Lisa Kaufman, marketing director for Dr. Greenberg's practice, put it this way: "Once you have a cosmetic procedure (and many women have more than one) you want to know what to do with it." Some changes (like liposuction) can be extreme, giving the patient a whole new body type. Dr. Greenberg's office contracts with professionals to help patients with fashion, makeup, and hair. Visit **www.greenbergcosmeticsurgery. com** to check out the practice for yourself.

Another cosmetic surgery company, Personal Image Centers (PIC), employs patient care coordinators, preferably with an image consulting background. At PIC, the patient care coordinator walks the patient through the entire process, from selecting the surgery to recovery.

According to the general manager at PIC's Connecticut branch, doctors are recognizing that they need someone to help answer patient questions, coordinate and schedule services and procedures, and generally hold the patient's hand and help them get everything they need. PIC prefers working with image consultants in this capacity because they already have "good customer service skills and a knowledge of cosmetic surgery and procedures." Dermatologists and cosmetic dentists may offer similar services.

Image Consultant Groups

Most traditional image consultant businesses are one-person operations. If they need a service that they can't provide, they seek out "strategic alliances" with other professionals. For example, an image consultant in business for herself might do her clients' makeup, but make an arrangement with someone else who does hair.

There are also a large number of "specialty" corporate image consultant businesses founded by people with expertise in a particular area such as speech, media relations, advertising, training, and branding. These agencies hire people with experience in the related specialty.

To find Certified Image Professionals and Certified Image Masters in the United States and 11 other countries, see the website of the Association of Image Consultants International at **www.aici.org**.

Other Possibilities

Transgender Services

Transformation Shops, located in the United Kingdom, has on-staff image consultants to assist its transsexual and transgender clientele. To find out more, visit **www.transformation.co.uk** (site contains nudity). Similar shops exist in the U.S. and can be found by searching online for "transgender" or "transvestite" and "image consulting."

Political Consultants

Political campaign resource firms, such as The Meridian Group in Austin, Texas, specialize in winning elections. Many include image consultants on their staffs. For a national list of political consultants, including media trainers, see the website at **www.politicsmagazine.com/win-loss 2010**. (Also see the resources listed in section 6.1.2.)

Hair Replacement Centers

Hair replacement centers, such as Hair Club for Men (**www.hairclub. com**), a national company with facilities in 36 states as well as Toronto, Nova Scotia, and Puerto Rico, hire image consultants (whom they call stylists) to assist their clients as they select hair options. Hair Club's stylists are expert hair designers recruited from top salons and trade shows who work with clients to achieve their optimum look.

Eyewear

The Eye Boutique (**www.eyeboutique.com**), an eye clinic in Schaumburg, Illinois, has on-staff image consultants to help customers select the perfect eyeglass frames.

"Most women these days look at eyeglasses like a piece of jewelry," says Diana Reynolds, president of The Eye Boutique. And they feel more comfortable with another woman helping them to select frames that are suitable for the shape of their face and their skin tone.

Some frame manufacturers have literature to help educate eyewear employees on how to help customers select frames that are right for them, but Reynolds says she has had no trouble finding people with optical experience who also have some image training. "This is just something that has evolved," Reynolds says.

Community Colleges

Community colleges and trade schools hire experienced image consultants to teach classes on topics such as wardrobe, makeup, hair, designers, color, fashion forecasting, menswear, and business essentials. (See section 6.3.3 for tips on teaching image consulting.)

For a directory of community colleges near you, visit **www.community-college.org**.

Job Listing Sites

Although there are no online job boards specializing in image consulting, general job listing sites abound on the Internet, and most allow you to post your resume, set up a job search profile, and receive an e-mail when a job matching your criteria is listed. In addition, listings for jobs such as beauty advisor, cosmetics associate, and sales associate are plentiful, and, these are all good jobs to get your foot in the door.

You can check the classifieds in more than 4,000 U.S. newspapers at Newslink (**http://newslink.org/news.html**). Employment 911 (**www.employment911.com**) searches over 100 online employment sites, such as Monster, HotJobs, CareerBuilder, and America's Job Bank.

4.5.2 How to Create a Job

This route may have more to do with putting yourself in front of the luck ball than anything else. As Thomas Jefferson said, "I'm a great believer in luck, and I find the harder I work the more I have of it."

You may be able to create a full-time job for yourself as an image consultant at the company you already work for. You must show your employer that there is a need for your skills in this capacity (or impress them with your informal colleague makeovers, à la Lauren Solomon).

One way to do this would be to develop a relationship with a company as a self-employed image consultant, and then at some point suggest that, because of their growing needs, you could better serve them by coming on staff full time. Such a move would take a great deal of understanding about the company, its needs, and its top management, and would most likely be impossible before several months, if not years, of working together. Ideally you would have such a close relationship with the major decision makers that they would offer the job to you.

Another way to create a job for yourself would be to take a stepping stone job (as a sales associate or makeup person, for example), prove yourself an indispensable asset to your employer in that capacity, and then, when the time is right, suggest that you be allowed to expand your job by taking on additional responsibility. You must be able to explain how such a change would benefit your employer (what's in it for them?). The most desirable benefit would be bringing in new business or increasing the business of current customers.

A third way to create a job for yourself would be to develop an expertise in a particular area (familiarity with cosmetic surgery procedures and physicians, or an extensive knowledge of eyewear, for example) and, through networking and information interviewing, contact business owners in your target area to pitch your ideas. Again, you need to persuade the business owner that hiring you would be good for business.

Networking

By far, the majority of image consulting jobs go unadvertised. In fact, 80 to 95 percent of all jobs go unadvertised. Advertising a job costs money.

Going through a recruiter costs even more money. Even after hiring "the best" of the applicants, there is no guarantee that the new hire will perform as expected. All of these are reasons why most companies prefer to hire people either with whom they already have a relationship, or who have been recommended by a trusted colleague.

What this boils down to for the jobseeker is one word: Networking. If you are serious about getting a good job that will help you use your current skills and develop new ones – all while rewarding your efforts at an attractive rate – you need to view the job hunt as a job in itself and apply yourself to it with all the effort that a future employer would expect you to give their company.

To be effective at networking, you must be organized and diligent. Networking is work, make no mistake, but it doesn't have to be painful. After all, as someone attracted to image consulting, chances are that you are already a people person — that is, you enjoy meeting and talking with people. That's networking in a nutshell.

The trick is to always be looking for new contacts, following up on the contacts you make, and ensuring that those contacts stay current. This can be done easily by keeping a "tickler file" to remind you to call or e-mail certain people at certain times, by remembering birthdays or anniversaries, and by attending functions where you are likely to run into your current contacts or meet new ones.

Don't forget the possibilities on the Internet. Participating in forums and chat groups (such as YoungPRPros, a forum under Yahoo! Groups at **www.youngprpros.com**) is a great and easy way to network. For more details about how to network, check out Monster.com's Career Advice on Networking (**http://career-advice.monster.com/job-search/professional-networking/jobs.aspx**) or "The Art of Career and Job-Search Networking" from Quintessential Careers (**www.quintcareers.com/networking.html**).

Information Interviewing

Sometimes making contacts isn't that easy. Perhaps there is a particular company you would like to work for or a particular person whom you think could help you, but you just haven't had the chance to make contact with. That's when you need to bite the bullet and simply contact the person directly by writing a polite letter asking for an information interview. Explain your interest in the person or company and express your desire to learn more.

Even if the person you contact doesn't have the time to meet with you personally, you've at least gotten your foot in the door and established a contact that you can refer to in the future, perhaps when you do finally meet them at an event, or meet one of their colleagues. In addition, there is always the chance that the person may recommend someone else with whom you can meet. For more about information interviews, see section 4.3.1.

4.5.3   Job Hunting Materials

Your resume and cover letter are important tools in helping you get the job interview. In this section you will find advice for creating both of them. Keep in mind that the range of careers in image consulting is too broad for there to be one "right" way to do a resume and cover letter. The resume of a public relations specialist, for example, is going to look a lot different from that of a top hair designer. No matter what your background; however, the key is to focus on your skills and match them to what the employer is looking for.

How to Prepare a Resume

The type of resume that works best when focusing on skills over job history is the functional resume. In a functional resume, you list the skills you have acquired – formally or informally, through work, school, volunteering, or hobbies – that are applicable to the job. (Skills that are not relevant to the job, even if you're a pro, are unnecessary and will clutter up your resume.) Group your skills under appropriate headings, such as customer service, sales, wardrobe or color analysis.

Your work experience section, listing dates of employment, job title, and employer's names and addresses, comes after the skills section. The education section comes next and includes dates attended, names of schools, majors and degrees earned. If you have any professional credentials or affiliations (related to the job you are applying for), list these next. You do not need to conclude with "References available upon request." It is assumed that you will be able to provide references if they are asked for, and so it is gratuitous to say so.

Sample Resume

Jennifer Jobseeker
1212 Maple Lane
Gary, Indiana 46403
555-555-5555
jjobseeker@online.com

Skills Summary:

- Excellent communication skills

- Consistently meet or exceed sales quotas

- Extensive knowledge of a variety of designers, styles, and fashion periods

Courses In:

- Color and body analysis
- Psychology

- Wardrobing
- Clothing design and style

- Fashion personalities and styles
- Men's wear

Retail Sales Experience:

- **Sales Associate**
  2008 to present
  Great Big Department Store, Great City, NY
  Duties: Assisted sales and received merchandise in a variety of departments including Cosmetics, Linens, Housewares, Fashion Accessories, Luggage, and Better Dresses

- **Sales Assistant**
  2006 to 2008
  The Gap, Great City, NY
  Duties: Assisted sales, received merchandise

Education:

- Certificate in Image Consulting
  Fashion Institute of Technology

- Bachelor's Degree, Psychology
  Great City University, Great City, NY

Affiliations:

- Student Member
  Association of Image Consultants International

- Volunteer
  The Women's Alliance (a national organization providing professional attire, career skills training, and related services to low-income women seeking employment)

The resume should differ depending on the type of employer you are applying with. Someone applying to a major retailer, spa, salon, or an image consulting firm should emphasize knowledge of and experience in what AICI calls the "core curriculum" of the image consultant:

- Color and body analysis

- Fashion personalities and styles

- Clothing design and style (knowledge of construction and fit)

- Wardrobing (how to put a wardrobe together)

- Basic psychology

- Men's wear

- Basic business skills

Someone applying to a public relations firm for a position as a media trainer would emphasize writing and visual skills, while someone applying for a position as a corporate image consultant would play up their knowledge of corporate training or branding. If you want to teach image consulting at the community college level, your experience as an image consultant is actually what you would emphasize because you are being hired for your expertise in your field, not your teaching ability.

If you need additional help writing a resume, there are countless sites on-line. The CareerBabe Resume Tutorial (**www.careerbabe.com/resume. html**) and eResumes (**www.eresumes.com/eresumes.html**) offer good advice on electronic resumes. You can find helpful articles at **www.fabjob. com/advice.html#resume**.

How to Prepare a Cover Letter

The basic job of the cover letter is to get the employer interested enough in you to call you in for an interview. Your writing style, word choice, and message all reveal something about you that the employer judges, consciously or unconsciously.

Like your resume, your cover letter must be flawless in spelling, punctuation, and grammar. Always try to address the cover letter to a specific person (making sure to get their name and title exactly right). Never direct your letter to "To Whom It May Concern" or "Dear Sir or Madam." If the ad does not give a name, make a call to the company and attempt to find out. If you still can't come up with a name, try:

- Dear Director of Personnel

- Dear Human Resources Manager

- Dear Director of Marketing

- Dear Employer

If you are applying for an advertised position, the first paragraph of your cover letter should mention where you saw the ad (include date of publication) and what position you are applying for. If you are applying for a job you heard about from a colleague, the first paragraph should mention that person's name and your connection to them as well as the position you are interested in.

The second paragraph is where you tell the employer why you're qualified; that is, outline your academic and professional qualifications.

Sample Cover Letter

1212 Maple Lane
Gary, Indiana 46403
555-555-5555

September 25, 2011

Ms. Francine Hireme
Human Resources Director
The Best Department Store Anywhere
2424 South Main Street
Anycity, NY 23232

Dear Ms. Hireme:

My neighbor Steve Onager, a sales manager at The Best, suggested that I write to you about the executive consultant position you are seeking to fill.

As you will see from my enclosed resume, I have extensive experience in retail sales and am currently attending classes at the Fashion Institute of Technology in pursuit of a certificate in image consulting.

As a sales associate at Big Huge Department Store, I take great pride in helping my customers select just the right outfit for any occasion, including accessories and shoes. In a short time I have built up a regular following of customers who ask specifically for me, and oftentimes, other sales associates will ask for my fashion advice as well.

I would welcome the opportunity to meet with you to discuss the executive consultant position. I will contact you in ten days to arrange a convenient time. Please feel free to contact me before then at home or by e-mail (jjobseeker@online.com). I look forward to speaking with you soon.

Sincerely,

Jennifer Jobseeker

The third paragraph is your chance to explain why you are the right person for the job. The most important point in this paragraph is to explain what you can do for the *employer* — not what *you* want! Be sure you address all the points mentioned in the advertisement. Try to work in any relevant facts you can about the company or industry.

The fourth paragraph is where you close your letter and express your interest in meeting with the person for an interview. Tell the employer when you will follow up (ideally within ten days), and then follow up. Be sure to include information where you can be reached during the day, and don't forget to sign your letter!

Online cover letter resources include Quintessential Careers' Cover Letter Resources at **www.quintcareers.com/covres.html**.

Other Materials

Other materials that will be important in helping you get the job will vary greatly depending on what kind of position you are applying for. Everyone should have a prepared list of references. (Use the same paper as you did for your cover letter and resume, and don't offer the list unless the employer asks for it.)

Personal shoppers need to bring their book of clients with them to show their potential employer that they have a following. Hair or makeup professionals should bring a portfolio of their work and be prepared to demonstrate their skills on a live model.

Always bring a briefcase. Make it a simple one that is easy to reach into and retrieve what you need. Put in extra copies of your resume and copies of your list of references. Also bring an attractive pen and a small pad of paper for note-taking during the interview.

4.5.4   Interviews

The job interview is your chance to clinch the job. Your resume and cover letter may have gotten you in the door, but the interview is where your personality and skills come together to make a lasting impression. You have to make sure that the impression is a good one by doing your homework, dressing appropriately, responding effectively to questions, and following up.

What Employers Are Looking For

An image consultant's personal appearance, style, and presentation are their bread and butter. Employers want to see people who are clean and neat, speak clearly, have good posture and manners, and present a professional image.

Of course, right before a job interview isn't the time to give yourself a makeover. You need to be comfortable with yourself and what you are wearing, and if you are trying to adjust to, say, a new hairdo, you may come across differently from what you intended.

Consider seeing another image consultant at some point early in your job search. It isn't as easy to see or evaluate your own shortcomings, or positive points, for that matter, as it is someone else's. You may get some good tips, but you will also get to see how another image consultant does their thing, which is always valuable.

Image isn't the whole package, however. Lynne Marks, president of London Image Institute and co-author of the book *The Perfect Fit: How to Start an Image Consulting Business,* watches her potential hires closely to see how they interact with people.

"How well they can explain concepts simply and clearly (which is sometimes very hard to do) is very important," she says. Above all, she looks for self-confidence and the ability to work with and read people.

"There's always a little bit of selling" in helping people make decisions about such things as clothing and makeup, Marks says. This involves "a bit of give and take" between the consultant and the client, with the consultant being able to intuit when to push and when to let up.

Kevin, the consultant with Macy's in Chicago, agrees. "You have to be comfortable talking to people," he says. "You have to be able to extract [personal] information casually, through normal chit chat" because the more you know about your clients, the better you can serve them. Kevin does this by sharing information about himself. This helps open people up, and they start sharing information in return.

Following are some specific skills and experience sought by major employers in recent advertisements seeking beauty advisors, sales associates, and sales counselors. Remember that these jobs can be stepping stones to image consulting.

LA Weight Loss Centers

- Persuasive

- Energetic and enthusiastic

- Outgoing and confident

- Team player

- Motivating

- Customer service oriented

Burdine's

- Enthusiastic

- Strong communication skills

- Work well in a team environment

Bloomingdale's

- Outgoing personality

- Strong phone skills

- An understanding of cosmetics is helpful

- Prior selling experience is helpful, but not essential to success

Researching the Company

Preparing for an interview involves many things. First, you need to do as much research about the company as possible. Chances are, most of what you learn will not become a topic of conversation during the interview, but as the interviewer is telling you something about the company – perhaps as they are walking you back to their office to interview you – you may have the chance to say, "Yes, I read about that on your website," or, "Yes, I read that in your annual report."

This is always impressive because it shows the employer you took the time to learn about the company on your own. Beware of spouting off too much about what you learned, however. After all, you are not there to prove you know more about the company than the interviewer.

Your first stop for company information should be the company's website. How they present themselves on the website will also tell you something about them. If possible, try to find some information about the person who will be interviewing you.

If you are hungry for more, check out websites for company overviews and histories, key people, financial information, and industry news and trends. Some of these websites include Hoovers Online (**www.hoovers.com/free**) and Inc.com 500 (**www.inc.com/inc5000**).

What to Wear

Marks advises image consultants to dress in "updated classics" both for the job interview and on the job. You should wear something current, but not too trendy.

"You have to remember that, first and foremost, you are a business professional and you are an image consultant second," she says. "You should never wear anything so faddish that nobody could understand what you're trying to say."

Women should wear a skirted suit. The skirt length should be a little below the knee (never above!). Blouses should be a light (white, off-white) color. Shoes should be polished (no scuffs or rundown heels!) and low heeled. Keep makeup to a minimum, with colors in the neutral range. Do not bring a purse. Keep essentials in a small clutch that will fit easily into your briefcase.

Men should wear a dark navy or grey two-piece business suit. Wear a white button-down dress shirt with a conservative silk tie that matches the colors of your suit. Your shoes should be polished and should match your belt. Your socks should match your suit and be long enough not to show bare legs when you sit. Do not wear any jewelry, and make sure your beard, mustache, and nose hairs are trimmed.

Whatever you wear, the fabric should be the best you can afford – wool or silk or a high quality blend – and it should fit perfectly (pants not too long, skirt not too short, blouse not too tight, jacket sleeves not too long). See a tailor if you have to, but get it right. Your clothes should look like yours, not like you borrowed them from your roommate.

Accessorize carefully. Again, you want your overall look to be polished and professional. Don't wear anything that draws undue attention to itself or gets in the way (no noisy bracelets, happy face ties, or giant hoop earrings). Do not draw attention to any body piercings beyond simple ear piercings for women. Keep your cologne or perfume to a minimum. And remember, as Dr. Joyce Knudsen, AICI-CIM, image consultant and president/CEO of The ImageMaker, Inc., says, "Your best accessory is your smile."

Get a manicure (men, too). Keep it simple (no extra long nails, sequins, pictures, etc). Just clean, neat hands. Make sure you use deodorant and antiperspirant. Stash some breath mints in your briefcase.

The night before your interview, lay out everything you will be wearing. If you are wearing stockings, make sure you have an extra pair for your briefcase, in case you put your thumb through your first pair. Set your alarm for the appropriate time, and get enough sleep.

Interview Questions

There are two basic styles of interviewing today. The traditional interview uses broad-based questions, such as "Tell me about yourself," or "Why do you want to work for our company?" How you respond to these open-ended questions tells the interviewer how well you communicate. (Does your answer sound pat and rehearsed? Do you go on and on? Can you be succinct yet interesting?)

The behavioral interview asks about specific past behaviors in an attempt to gauge how well you would perform on the job. "Tell me about a time when you were confronted with an unexpected problem," is a good example of a behavioral question. When confronted with these types of questions, always be sure to describe the situation, tell what you did, relate the outcome, and finish with what you learned from it.

Take time to think through the answers to some common interview questions. Don't memorize anything (except for your "commercial") — your answers should sound natural. But have an idea of what you want to say. Below are typical questions with tips on how to answer.

Tell me about yourself.

Avoid giving personal information. Write a one-minute "commercial" (see section 6.3.2 for an example) focusing on education and experience. Practice it until it sounds natural.

Why are you looking for a new job?

Keep answer positive, in terms of where you want to go, not what you want to get away from.

What are your short-term and long-term goals?

Short-term goal is getting the right position; long-term is where you want to go in your profession.

What are your strengths?

Discuss three or four strengths as they relate to the position you are interviewing for and give examples.

What are your weaknesses?

Again, avoid personal information. Pick a "weakness" that the employer might actually see as a positive, or admit a real weakness, but explain how you're taking steps to correct it.

Why have you had so many jobs?

Give acceptable reasons, but focus on the fact that you're ready for a permanent position.

What kind of salary do you expect?

Say that you'd prefer to delay a discussion of salary until you've been offered the position. If pressed, indicate that you would expect to be paid a rate comparable to your experience.

Describe your ideal supervisor.

The real question is, "Can you work with me?" Avoid launching into a diatribe against a former supervisor. Focus on the positive qualities that you appreciate in a boss.

Why should I hire you?

This is your chance to reiterate your skills and relate them to the position you are applying for. If you are confident about your skills, it will show.

You can find more information at FabJob.com to help you make a good impression during an interview. Visit **www.fabjob.com/advice.html# interviews** for advice on what to say and do during an interview.

Don't forget that you should ask questions as well. After all, you have a legitimate reason: Do you really want to work here?

Asking questions demonstrates your interest in the company and the job and makes you a proactive – not a passive – job seeker. It gives the interviewer a sense that you are not just a doormat to hire and use, but an intelligent individual with desirable skills. Following are some good questions:

- What is a typical day for someone in this position?

- How will my performance be measured? By whom? How often?

- How would you describe the company's management style?

- Does the company support ongoing training and education for employees to stay current in their fields?

- What challenges will the company face in the near future?

- How does this department fit in with the organization? How is it perceived by the rest of the company?

Creating a Prep Sheet

Another way of preparing for an interview is to create a prep sheet. Divide a piece of paper into three columns. In the first column, list each job requirement mentioned in the advertisement (or your perceptions of the job requirements for an unadvertised position). In the second column, list corresponding qualifications and experience (be specific). In the third column, briefly tell the "story" behind the experience.

This is a good way to prepare for a behavior-based interview, and it will provide you with something to talk about when the interviewer says, "Tell me about yourself."

Interview Do's and Don'ts

Do

- Know exactly where you are going and how long it will take to get there

- Arrive about ten minutes early

- Speak up

- Turn off your cell phone or pager during the interview

- Ask questions, but never about salary or benefits until you've actually been offered the job

- Be courteous to the receptionist

- Be aware of your body language (and the interviewer's)

Don't

- Chew gum or smoke

- Badmouth your current or former employers

- Sit down until you're offered a chair

- Lie or swear

- Act desperate for a job, but do show interest

- Be afraid to talk about yourself

Discussing Salary

Never bring up money in a job interview. From the employer's point of view, you already have some idea of what the salary range is and find it appropriate or you wouldn't be applying for the job. (If you don't know what the salary range is, asking during the interview makes it painfully obvious that you haven't done your homework, something that tells the employer a great deal about how much you care about getting the job.)

Some salaries are fixed. Sales associates, for example, generally earn a fixed commission that is not negotiable. If you are an entry-level applicant, there is not much you can do but take it or leave it. Realize that your true benefits will not be in monetary remuneration, but in experience, which is often much more valuable. Once you have a certain level of experience, you will be in a better position to negotiate salary.

For salary information, try looking on the Internet. JobStar (**http://jobstar. org/tools/salary/index.php**) has links to over 300 salary surveys plus tips on how to negotiate your salary.

Following Up

Always mail a typewritten thank you note within 24 hours after your interview. (Very neat handwriting on simple stationery is also acceptable.) If you interviewed with three people at the same company, send all three a polite note thanking them for their time.

Remind the interviewer of the position you interviewed for and the date of the interview. Reiterate (briefly) your qualifications for the position and state your interest in it. If possible, mention something the two of you discussed during the interview. This will help the interviewer to remember you and make you stand out from the crowd. Close by thanking the interviewer for their time.

Following is a sample thank you note written by someone applying for an image consultant position at an image firm.

Sample Thank You Note

1212 Maple Lane
Gary, Indiana 46403
555-555-5555

October 13th, 2011

Ms. Veronica Employer
Human Resources Director
Your Best Image, Inc.
35 Broadway, Suite 111
Chicago, Illinois 60606

Dear Ms. Employer,

Thank you for taking the time on Monday to discuss the image consultant position at Your Best Image, Inc. with me. After meeting with you and discussing the company's operations, I am further convinced that my background and skills coincide well with your needs.

I appreciate the time you took to go over all the aspects of working at Your Best Image, Inc. It is obvious that you care about the fulfillment of your employees just as much as the fulfillment of your clients. I know I would learn a great deal from you and would enjoy working with you.

As we discussed, I agree that image consulting takes a certain passion that goes beyond mere appearance. As a consultant for your firm I would strive to bring out the inner best in my clients, guiding, not pushing, them to self-actualization.

I look forward, Ms. Employer, to hearing from you concerning your hiring decision. Thank you for your time and consideration.

Sincerely,

Ms. Jobseeker

Gloria Starr

5. Starting an Image Consulting Business

If you have decided to start your own business as an image consultant, congratulations! You've already taken the first and most important step toward success. This chapter will walk you through the basics of starting a business and address specific issues relating to image consulting. This information will help you to proceed smoothly and with confidence as you get started in your own business.

5.1 Getting Started

Starting and running your own business is not for the timid — any entrepreneur will tell you that. It takes guts, determination, persistence and confidence. It also requires a dream that you just can't let go of. You must want to build a successful business in order to make it happen.

If you've decided that you meet those criteria, you can join the ranks of entrepreneurs who have poured their hearts and souls into creating successful businesses.

Nobody who has started their own business will tell you that it's easy. It's not. For people with dreams and vision, however, it's the only way to go. Having your own business gives you the opportunity to do the work you love — not for somebody else, but for yourself.

You'll be making a lot of important decisions in connection with starting a business, and there are many legal and practical matters you'll need to address. Don't be afraid to ask for help along the way.

A good source of help available in many communities is the Service Corps of Retired Executives (SCORE). Partnered with the U.S. government-affiliated Small Business Administration (SBA), SCORE is a 13,000-member organization of retired businesspeople who volunteer to work with people who are planning, or have started, small businesses. Check with their website at **www.score.org** to find a SCORE location in your area, or call your local chamber of commerce, which often works hand-in-hand with SCORE groups.

The following websites are also good resources for starting a business:

- The Small Business Administration (**www.sbaonline.sba.gov**) is an excellent resource with advice on business licenses and taxes as well as general information on starting a business.

- The Canadian government (**http://canadabusiness.gc.ca**) offers information about taxes, financing, incorporation and other topics.

- Nolo.com is another useful resource. Nolo publishes legal information presented in plain English. Their website also offers free advice on other small business matters. Visit **www.nolo.com** to find out more.

5.1.1 Creating a Business Plan

One of the most important tools you'll need when starting and building your business is a good business plan.

A business plan serves two purposes. It's a guide for you – and anyone who may work with you – of how you want your company to progress and grow. It also serves as a sales tool, should you decide to seek funding for your business.

If you're fabulously wealthy and have all the money you could want to begin and grow a business, you don't have to consider the possibility of using your business plan to attract funding. However, you'll still need a plan to serve as your roadmap.

Your original business plan will guide you as you start out, and will keep you on course as your business progresses. But it is not written in stone. As your business changes and grows, your business plan will probably need some tweaking. Perhaps, for instance, the description of your business will change as you branch out into different areas of image consulting. Or your management plan will change when you discover you need to add a personal shopper to your staff.

A business plan doesn't have to be overly complicated, and there are some good models available to use as guides. Many entrepreneurs use the United States Small Business Administration's (SBA's) business plan outline (**www.sba.gov/content/templates-writing-business-plan**) as a model. The Canada Business website also provides a sample business plan at **www.canadabusiness.ca/eng/86/4878**.

Basically, the main body of your business plan will be divided into the four sections listed below:

- a description of your business
- your marketing plan
- your financial management plan
- your management plan

In addition to those parts, your plan should include the following extra material and information:

- an executive summary
- supporting documents
- financial projections

- a cover sheet

- a statement of purpose

- a table of contents

If the prospect of writing a business plan sounds daunting or confusing, hang in there. We'll take a closer look at each of these parts.

Description of Your Business

A description of your business is just that — a description of the business you plan to start and run. The trick is to include the unique and special things about your business so that everyone who reads your business plan will know you're on to something really fabulous.

You'll need to state in this section that, as an image consultant, you'll be operating a service business. Get specific about the services you'll provide. If you will specialize in executive coaching and business etiquette, for instance, state that in your description. If you will focus on personal dress and grooming, include information about what those areas involve, and point out why your services are important. The idea is to paint a picture of the business you plan to start.

You should also explain what the legal structure of your business will be. Will you have a sole proprietorship, for instance, or perhaps a partnership? You'll learn more about legal structures a little later in this section of the chapter.

Also in this section, you'll need to explain why your business will be profitable, and how your image consulting business will be different and better than any others in the area. What do you plan to offer that will have clients beating down your doors, begging you to be their personal image consultant?

TIP: When writing your business plan, pay close attention to spelling and grammar, and try to write clearly and concisely. You don't want to make reading the plan a chore.

Describe your business hours. As an image consultant, you'll most likely need to have flexible hours to accommodate the schedules of your clients. But if you plan only to work from 10:00 a.m. until 2:00 p.m.

three days a week, you should make that clear. Also, you should identify the planned location of your business, the type of space you'll have, and why it's conducive to your business.

Conclude the description of your business by clearly identifying your goals and objectives and supporting them with information and knowledge you've acquired about being an image consultant. This is important, because it's here that you're explaining exactly why you're starting this business and what you hope to accomplish with it.

Your Marketing Plan

How well you market your business has a lot to do with the degree of success you'll experience. The most important elements of a good marketing plan are defining your market and knowing your customers.

You don't want to limit yourself to a very narrow market, because that can affect your chances of getting funding, as well as limit the scope of your business once it's underway. So if you're going to specialize in executive coaching and business etiquette, your market should be the entire corporate community, not just one area of it. Your marketing plan should paint a picture of a wide and ready market, just waiting for your image consulting services.

Knowing your customers is important because it allows you to identify their likes and dislikes and tailor your services to accommodate them.

Your marketing plan also must address the areas listed below:

Competition

Businesses – yours included – compete for customers, market share, publicity and so forth. It's smart to know who your competitors are and exactly what they're doing. In order to provide services that are different and better, you need to look carefully at your competitors' products and services, how they're promoting them, and who's buying them.

Pricing

You'll learn more about setting fees later in this chapter, but know that you should address it, at least briefly, in your business plan. This section should consider factors such as competitive pricing, costs of labor and materials, overhead and so forth.

Advertising and Public Relations

Many people think that marketing is all about advertising and public relations. While they are important components of marketing, they are only pieces of the puzzle. You need to think about how you'll advertise your business, making sure that whatever means of advertising you choose accurately portrays the image you want to convey. You are an image consultant— you need to properly convey your own image!

Your Financial Management Plan

Financial management is crucial to running a successful business. Your business plan should describe both your startup costs and your operating costs. The startup budget includes all the costs necessary to get your business up and running. Operating costs are ongoing expenses, such as advertising, utilities, rent and so forth.

Remember to include the following items in your budgets. Notice that some expenses overlap on the startup and operating budgets.

- *Startup budget:* Legal and professional fees, licenses and permits, equipment, insurance, supplies, advertising and promotions, accounting expenses, utilities, payroll expenses.

- *Operating budget:* Make a budget for your first three to six months of operation, including expenses such as: personnel (even if it's only your own salary), insurance, rent, loan payments, advertising and promotions, legal and accounting fees, supplies, utilities, dues and subscriptions, fees, taxes and maintenance.

Your financial management plan also should address the accounting system you plan to use. Many small business owners conduct their own accounting, using software such as Quicken or QuickBooks (**www. quickbooks.com**), while others hire someone to set up a system.

Your Management Plan

Managing a business, no matter how big or small it is, requires organization and discipline.

Your management plan should be carefully thought out, well-written, and address issues such as:

- Your background and business experience, and how they'll be beneficial to your image consulting business.

- The members of your management team (even if you'll be the only member).

- Assistance you expect to receive (this can be financial help, consulting and advice or whatever).

- The duties for which you and any employee or employees will be responsible.

- Plans for hiring employees, either now or in the future.

- A general overview of how your business will be run.

The Extras

In addition to these major areas, your business plan should include the extras mentioned earlier:

- *A cover sheet:* This identifies your business and explains the purpose of the business plan. Be sure to include your name, the name of the business and the name of any partners, if applicable; your address, phone number, e-mail address and other pertinent information.

- *Table of contents:* This goes just under your cover sheet and tells what's included in your business plan. Use major headings and subheadings to identify the contents.

- *Statement of purpose:* This is important because it summarizes your goals and objectives. A statement of purpose should sum up your hopes and dreams.

- *Executive summary:* Basically, this is a thumbnail sketch of your business plan. It should summarize everything you've included in the main body of the plan.

- *Financial projections:* This is just an idea of how much money you'll need to start your business, and how much you expect to earn. Remember to support your projections with explanations.

- *Supporting documents:* Include your personal (and business, if applicable) tax returns for the past three years, a personal financial statement (get a form from your bank) and a copy of a lease or purchase agreement if you will buy or rent office space.

A good business plan will require some time and work on your part, but it's really essential to getting your business off on the right track. If you make the effort to draw up a good plan now, you can be confident that it will pay off in the future.

5.1.2   Choosing a Business Name

Some entrepreneurs love the prospect of naming their business, while others agonize over the task. Either way, the name you choose is an important part of what your business will be, so you'll want to put some thought into the process.

Experts disagree about whether a business name should be vague, allowing an image to be built upon it, or concrete and informative, allowing potential customers to know right away what you're offering them. Most experts do agree, however, that customers like names that are meaningful and easy to understand.

Something like "Dream Makers Image Consulting," for instance, is preferable over ADLJR Image Consulting. Customers can understand and remember Dream Makers, but trying to remember ADLJR is like trying to pull a phone number or address out of your head.

If you have the financial resources, you could hire a naming professional to help you choose the right name for your company. Known as name consultants or naming firms, these organizations are experts at creating names, and can help you with trademark laws.

> **TIP:** Business names don't have to be trademarked, but having them trademarked prevents anyone else from using the same name. Trademark laws are complicated, so if you think you want your company name trademarked, it's a good idea to consult a lawyer with expertise in that area.

Most people starting a small business don't have the money necessary to hire professional namers. The cost of these services can range from a few thousand dollars to upwards of $35,000. Some people get a group of friends together and brainstorm names. If somebody comes up with a really good one, you'll probably know it right away.

Let's look at the names of some real-life image consulting firms:

- Total Image Consultants

- Prime Impressions

- About Face Image Consulting

- Here's Looking at You Image Consulting

- Image Impact

- Image Makers on the Move

- London Image Institute

- Optimum Image

- Première Impression

When it comes right down to it, you know best the services you plan to offer and the image you want to convey. Think it over and choose your name carefully, because it will send a message of your intent and business tenor to prospective clients.

In most jurisdictions, if you operate under anything other than your own name, you are required to file for a fictitious name. It's usually just a short form to fill out and a small filing fee that you pay to your state or provincial government. You can find links to the appropriate government departments for filing your name through the Business.gov website at **www.business.gov/register/business-name/dba.html**.

Before registering a fictitious name, make sure it does not belong to anyone else. You certainly wouldn't want to spend your initial investment money, only to find out you couldn't legally operate under a name you had chosen because someone else owns the trademark.

So do some research on the names you like. You can do an online search of the U.S. federal trademark database (**http://tess2.uspto.gov**) to find whether a name has already been registered. You can also visit the

Nolo.com Small Business Legal Encyclopedia mentioned at the beginning of this chapter for good advice on trademarks and other matters to consider before choosing a business name.

5.1.3   Legal Matters

Details, details, details. You may feel like you're ready to get your business up and running, and are getting frustrated by all the decisions and paperwork you need to deal with. While they can be a source of irritation, legal matters concerning your business are extremely important and must be taken seriously.

Types of Legal Structures

The first legal issue to consider when starting a business is the form of ownership it will have. The resources at the start of this chapter have further information on business structures. Excellent advice is also offered at **www.sba.gov/content/incorporating-your-business**.

Basically, there are four forms of ownership: sole proprietorships, partnerships, limited liability companies and corporations. Let's have a look at what these terms mean.

Sole Proprietorship

If you decide your business will be a sole proprietorship, the buck stops with you. It doesn't mean that you don't have to deal with other people or that you can ignore rules and laws. It just means that, ultimately, the responsibility for the business lies on your shoulders.

The good news about a sole proprietorship is that you get nearly total control of the business and all the profits. The bad news is that you also get full liability for all business debts and actions.

More good news about a sole proprietorship is that it's the easiest business structure to set up. All you need to do is apply for an occupational business license in the municipality where your business will be located. The SBA has information on how to do just that. Visit **www.sba. gov/content/obtaining-business-licenses-permits** to learn how.

Usually the license doesn't take long to be processed, and you can begin operations fairly quickly. If you're in business by yourself, your Social Security number can serve as your taxpayer identification number. If you have employees, you'll need to request a taxpayer identification number from the Internal Revenue Service. Don't worry — someone will be happy to send you one!

On the bad news side of a sole proprietorship, you run the risk of becoming isolated. If you choose a sole proprietorship, consider joining an association for image consultants, your local chamber of commerce, or some other professional organization.

Sole proprietorships are extremely common and popular among small business owners. Obviously, much about them is appealing. The nature of image consulting certainly lends itself to the sole proprietorship form of ownership. Unless you really want a partner or have another reason for setting up a different form of ownership, you should take a close look at a sole proprietorship.

Partnership

When two or more people decide to start a business together, they enter into something called a partnership agreement. There are two types of partnerships: general partnerships and limited partnerships.

A general partnership is when two or more people get together and start a business. They agree on how to conduct the business and how the profits, risks, liabilities and losses will be distributed between them.

> **TIP:** Partnerships don't have to be divided equally between all the partners. All partners, however, must agree on how the profit, risk, liability and loss will be divided.

A limited partnership is when one or more partners invest in the business, but are not involved in the day-to-day operations. Limited partners are investors, which makes them partners, but they have limited say in the hands-on operations.

An advantage of a partnership is that they have more financial clout than sole proprietorships, because more assets are available than with just one person. Another advantage is that in an ideal situation, you and your partner will balance out each other's strengths and weaknesses. And working with a partner who you like can be a lot of fun. On the flip side, many businesses have turned sour because partnerships have gone bad.

TIP: If you decide to form a partnership, think very carefully about the person you choose as your partner. Make sure you each understand the other's expectations and goals.

If you're thinking of forming a partnership, be sure to consult a lawyer and get a partnership agreement that covers all contingencies. The less that's left to chance, the stronger and more stable your partnership will be.

Corporation

When you incorporate a business, you form a corporation that's legally separate from yourself. Instead of the business being in your name, it's registered in the name of the corporation, and the corporation is responsible for all its business activities. Even if you start the business, once it's incorporated, you're considered an employee and a stockholder instead of a personal owner.

The good thing about having your business incorporated is that it limits the liability of each stockholder to the amount of their investment in the business. If the business fails or is found liable in a lawsuit, the corporation is responsible — not the members of the corporation.

Let's say that you and a partner each put up $100,000 to start an image consulting firm. Now, imagine the unimaginable. Something so terrible happens that you find yourselves liable for a half million dollar lawsuit. If your company is a partnership, sorry Charlie, you're responsible for coming up with a half million dollars. If your company is incorporated, you and your partner can't be held liable for more than the $100,000 you have invested in the business.

While that's clearly an advantage of incorporation, there's a downside to incorporating your business, as well. A good amount of paperwork and legal work are involved, and more people are involved than with other forms of ownership.

Many new owners of small companies do not incorporate their businesses and everything works out fine, while others feel that a corporation is the only viable option for their businesses. See the Small Business Administration website listed at the beginning of section 5.1 for more information about incorporating a small business.

Limited Liability Company

A limited liability company is like a corporation, except it's not incorporated. It is legally separate from the person or persons who own it, and offers some protections that a partnership does not. Partners in a limited liability company get the same personal financial protection as those in a corporation. However, a limited liability company can't sell stock or have shareholders or a board of directors. Regulations regarding limited liability companies vary from state to state, so do your homework if you're interested in this sort of ownership.

Registering Your Business

Regardless of what form of legal structure you choose for your business, you'll need to have it registered, at least at a local level. This is not a difficult task. All it normally entails is filling out some forms and paying an annual license fee. Contact your municipal or county office for more information about registering your business. Or, check out the information on business licenses at the Small Business Administration's website mentioned earlier in this section.

Retail businesses that collect sales tax must be registered with their state's Department of Revenue and get a state identification number. All businesses that have employees need a federal identification number with which to report employee tax withholding information. If you are self-employed, you'll pay a self-employment tax to contribute to your Social Security fund. Contact the Internal Revenue Service office in your area for more information.

5.1.4   Insurance

As you know, insurance is necessary in life — including business. And, as you also know, insurance can be a complicated business. Anyone starting a business should sit down with a trusted insurance agent and determine together what kinds of insurance you need — and don't need. You also should check out the National Association for the Self-Employed (**www.nase.org**), which offers reasonably priced insurance plans for self-employed people. State Farm has a program available specifically for home-based businesses. Visit State Farm's website at **www.statefarm.com/insurance/business/homebus.asp**.

If your business will be located in your home, you're most likely already covered with homeowner's insurance. However, it's a good idea to update your plan to provide coverage for office equipment and other items that aren't included in a standard plan.

> **TIP:** Make sure you have the insurance that you need, but don't let a salesperson talk you into buying all kinds of extra riders and policies that you don't need. Develop a good understanding of what you need, and stand firm when a salesperson tries to talk you into buying more than that.

Also be sure to ask an agent about your auto insurance if you'll be using your personal vehicle on company business. If you're liable for damages in an accident that occurs while you're conducting business, your business could be at risk. Ask about special coverage that protects your business in those types of circumstances. Other insurances to ask about include:

Liability Insurance

Laws regarding liability change all the time, so get the latest information regarding them. Nearly all businesses require liability insurance.

Property Insurance

If you're working from home, you probably already have this insurance, although you should check to make sure it covers all your valuables. If your business will be located in a building other than your home, you may need an additional policy. If you rent space, you'll need property insurance only on the equipment you have in your office — the owner of the building normally would pay for insurance on the property.

Disability Insurance

If you become sick or otherwise disabled for an extended period, your business could be in jeopardy. Disability insurance would provide at least a portion of your income while you're not able to be working.

Business Interruption Insurance

In the event that your property or equipment is damaged or destroyed, this type of insurance covers ongoing expenses such as rent or taxes until your business gets up and running again.

5.2   Setting Up Your Office

Compared to tasks like buying insurance and applying for business licenses, setting up your office may seem like a stroll in the park. It's important, though, to put some thought and effort into your office, for you're likely to be spending a lot of time there.

If you're going to meet with clients in your office instead of going out to them, it's particularly important that your office be properly located and impressive. After all, image consultants have to pay close attention to the image that they convey.

5.2.1   Location

Your personal circumstances and finances will largely dictate the location of your business. If you know that your business will be based in your home, then the location issue becomes a moot point.

If you plan to meet your clients in their homes or offices as opposed to having them come to you, your home very well may be the ideal location for your office. Just be sure to check with your municipality about any regulations that might impact a home office. If your office is in your home and you plan to meet with clients there, be sure that the office is separate, or can be isolated from the rest of the house. It won't do for you to try to conduct business while the house phone is ringing and the family dog is barking.

If you're going to rent space and meet with clients in that space, however, think about what location makes sense. If most of your clients will be located in a particular area, it makes sense to rent office space in that area. You want to be as accessible as possible for your clients.

If customers will have to travel to get to you, consider the parking situation around your building. Is the area in which you're located safe? Is there adequate lighting? How about handicapped access? Does the neighborhood project the image that you hope to convey?

Remember to consider your plans for the future of your business when renting or buying office space. If you plan to begin offering seminars in a year, for instance, does it make sense to rent a tiny office now? Of course, you could always rent meeting space for a seminar, but it's worthwhile to consider such contingencies now.

Some realtors specialize in matching businesses with target opportunity areas. Check with some of the larger realty firms in your area to see if this type of service is available.

And remember, no matter how anxious you are to get your office furnished and your business up and running, take your time and do your homework before renting space. Many people have encountered problems and headaches because they neglected to thoroughly check out a property and rental terms before leasing. For good advice on what to consider before renting space, visit the Nolo.com link at the beginning of this chapter.

5.2.2 Telephones

In our increasingly technological world, telephones are still necessary and vital tools for businesses. If you're going to have an image consulting business, you'll need to have a phone line designated for the business, and only for the business. It simply won't do to have your 12-year-old son answering when a client calls and shouting to you that you're wanted on the phone.

A fax line also is desirable, although e-mail can accomplish much of the same business as a fax machine. If you have a fax machine, you probably could have it installed on the same phone line as your Internet service instead of dedicating a separate phone line to it.

Nearly everyone has a cell phone these days, so if you don't have one, think about getting one. A lot of business gets taken care of via cell phones between client visits or while you're stuck waiting in a traffic jam. A cell phone is good for notifying your client that you are stuck in a traffic jam and running late for your appointment.

TIP: If you don't want to be interrupted, turn your cell phone off or turn it to vibrate. And use it safely. If you talk while you're driving, you should have a hands-free system in your car.

Using Your Phone System Effectively

Once you get the phone system that you need, it's up to you to make it work for you. One way you can do this is to make sure you've got a great message on your voice mail or answering machine. Instead of saying something ho-hum like, "Hi. Thanks for calling Dream Makers Image Consultants. We can't come to the phone right now, so please leave your name and phone number, and we'll get back to you as soon as we can," go for something more memorable and imaginative.

How about this:

> "Hi there. Thanks for calling Dream Makers. We're out right now changing someone's life for the better by teaching them how to make a great first impression. Your call is really important to us, though, so please leave your name and number, and we'll get back to you before the end of the day."

Some small businesses change their message every day to let clients and potential clients know when they'll be available. That probably isn't necessary, but if you're going to be unavailable during a vacation or something similar, be sure to record an appropriate message letting everyone know that you're away and when you'll be back. Of course, your clients should have already been informed that you'll be away.

If you're away from your office but will be available on your cell phone, leave your cell phone number on your office answering machine and encourage clients to reach you at the mobile number. Do not, however, interrupt a meeting with a client to take a call on your cell phone.

How you handle yourself on the phone is just as important as the message on your answering machine or voice mail. Some telephone tips are listed below.

- Always identify your business and yourself when answering a call or placing a call.

- Speak with confidence. Avoid overuse of words such as "like" (as in, "Like, can you tell me when he'll be back?"), "stuff" (as in, "I just wanted to pass along some stuff I heard.") and so forth. Remember, you're a professional who runs your own business. It's important to act accordingly, especially considering the nature of your work.

- Try to not keep a client or potential client waiting on the line while you check information or take another call. Remember that everyone's time is valuable. Instead, say something like, "I'll need just a few minutes to get my hands on that information, Gene. Can I find it and get right back to you?"

- When leaving a message for someone else, be concise and clear about why you're calling. Nobody appreciates having to listen to a long, rambling message.

- As an image consultant, you're well aware that first impressions count, and you only get one chance. When making an important call, think ahead about what you'll say and the impression you hope to convey.

A final word about telephones is to avoid the temptation to get more bells and whistles than you need. It's important to have a good, adequate system, but extras can add up quickly in cost, and you probably just don't need them.

5.2.3   Furnishings, Equipment and Supplies

As with any new venture, it will take you a little while to determine exactly what you need and how to make your business run as efficiently and effectively as possible.

Furnishings

If you don't plan on meeting with clients in your office, you don't have to be quite as fussy about how you look. In your business, however, an office that promotes the image you want to convey is a necessity. So, whether you're working from home or renting office space, you'll need to furnish it to impress.

If you're working within a limited budget (as most start-up entrepreneurs are), be creative with your furnishings. Sure, you could run out to Ikea – known for its reasonably priced, stylish-looking furniture – and get yourself set up. However, if you can identify your own style, and are willing to look around for pieces that express that style, you may come up with a far more interesting office.

Why not check out some auction houses or secondhand furniture shops? Who knows what great antique desk might be waiting for you, sometimes for about the same price as one from Ikea? Other ideas to consider for your office include:

- Be creative with fabric for curtains. Make coordinating pillow covers, or have someone make them for you.

- Create a mood with lighting. Soft light from table and floor lamps is much more appealing than fluorescent lights.

- Look for one-of-a-kind items (like a great vase) to create interest and give your office a focal point.

- Choose a couple of nice pieces of art for your walls.

- You'll need to have a filing system, but that doesn't mean you need metal or heavy oak filing cabinets. Check out secondhand furniture shops for filing alternatives. Use your imagination.

- Add some personal items, such as a family photo or two or the candy dish that's been handed down to you from your grandfather. These items give personality to your office. Remember that you're starting an image consulting business — not an accounting firm. Have some fun with your office and make it warm and inviting.

Equipment

Because it's vital that your clients are able to contact you at their convenience, you'll need equipment that will allow you to stay connected. You've already read about the importance of a good phone system with either voice mail or a reliable answering machine. And we've considered the value of a fax machine, as well.

Because e-mail is the means of communication of choice for many people these days, and because you'll need an Internet connection, you'll definitely need to have an adequate computer. And you may want to consider a high-speed connection to the Internet, especially if you foresee that you'll be accessing the web frequently.

You probably also will need a copier. While you're just getting your business up and running, however, you might want to consider a system that combines a computer printer with a fax machine, copier and scanner. You'll also want to be sure that you have something like a flash drive to allow you to back up files.

As an image consultant, a digital camera will be an important tool. A digital camera will allow you to send high-quality electronic photos to clients online. You can do this with a regular camera and a scanner, but you might not get the picture quality that you would with a digital camera. Prices on digital cameras have decreased and will continue to, so you should do a little shopping around before you buy one.

Office supplies are easy to find and can be purchased at a variety of locations. Staples and Office Depot are competitively priced, and may deliver if you buy in quantity. And don't overlook online shopping, which is becoming increasingly popular.

The stationery and business cards you select will help to convey the image of your company, so look around and give some thought to what you want. This is an area in which you probably don't want to cut corners, for your stationery will say a lot about who you are and what you can do. You can order personalized stationery from Staples or a similar store, or you can work with a printer in your area.

Remember that the price goes down on stationery and related items when you order bigger quantities. If you're not sure how long you'll be in your current location or anticipate other possible changes in the not-so-distant future, however, resist the temptation to order 5,000 cover sheets and the same number of envelopes. It's better to pay a little bit more for items you'll use than to end up with useless stationery because the information is wrong.

Image Consulting Supplies

As discussed in chapter three, you will also need supplies for your image consultations, such as drapes, body measurement tools, color swatches, etc. See section 3.2.1 for information about image consulting supplies and links to suppliers.

5.3 Employees and Contractors

If you're starting your business as a sole proprietorship, then you won't need to immediately address the issue of employees or contractors. Down the road, however, chances are that you'll need some help. Let's take a look at exactly what is an employee, and what is a contractor.

5.3.1 Employees

Basically, an employee is a person you hire to perform specific tasks for a specific amount of time during each pay period. You pay your employee a mutually agreeable amount of money at regular intervals in exchange for their services.

You may also extend benefits to an employee, such as vacation leave, health insurance, life insurance, disability insurance and retirement benefits. You'll need to pay payroll taxes on behalf of an employee, such as local, state and federal withholding taxes, Social Security taxes and federal and state unemployment taxes.

Employees might be expensive, but when you need them and find good ones, they become your company's most valuable assets. Regulations concerning payroll taxes, unemployment and worker's comp pay vary within the United States and Canadian provinces. Before you hire someone as an employee, it's a good idea to get some additional information concerning regulations, taxes and so forth. Check out the sites listed below for more information:

- *Canada Business*
  (Click on "English," then "Hiring and Managing Staff")
  www.canadabusiness.ca

- *U.S. Internal Revenue Service*
  (Search for "employees and contractors")
  www.irs.gov

- *U.S. Department of Labor*
  www.dol.gov/opa/aboutdol/lawsprog.htm

Finding Good Employees

So, how do you find an employee when you need one? There are several routes you can take, including running an ad in the classified section of your area newspaper, working with an employment service, or seeking help on an online site such as Monster.com.

If you need help for just a limited time, you might consider contacting a temporary employee service. These services provide employees on a temporary basis. You pay the service, and the service pays the employee. It also provides benefits to the employee and takes care of payroll, taxes and so forth.

You'll probably need to pay more to the service than you'd pay to a permanent employee, but if you only need help for a limited amount of time, it's probably worth it.

5.3.2 Contractors

Some business owners prefer to work with independent contractors rather than permanent employees. An independent contractor is a person who agrees to perform a particular job for a fee. It's understood that the contractor is not a permanent employee, and will stop getting paid when the agreed-upon work is completed or your agreement with the contractor otherwise ends.

Advantages to small business owners are that they don't have to offer benefits to independent contractors, or pay Social Security or unemployment taxes or workers' compensation for independent contractors. This can save an employer almost one-third of the cost of a permanent employee who gets benefits.

If you're serious about hiring one or more independent contractors and you really want to cover all the applicable bases, pick up a copy of *Hiring Independent Contractors: The Employer's Legal Guide,* by Stephen Fishman, an attorney. It includes all sorts of legal information and sample contractor agreements.

Again, there are certain tax-related matters that apply to contractors, so be sure to check the sites listed above for specific information.

Getting the Most from an Independent Contractor

The single most important piece of advice to remember when hiring a contractor is to make sure you and the person you hire have the same understanding about the work to be done, when the work must be finished and how much you'll pay for the work. In other words, make sure that you and the contractor are on the same page.

Be sure that the person you're hiring is reputable by asking for the names of others for whom the contractor has worked. Contact those people and ask for their input.

Never hire a contractor until they have signed a written agreement detailing services to be performed, delivery dates, amount of pay and so forth. There are websites, such as **www.findlegalforms.com**, from which you can download and print off independent contractor agreements for a fee.

5.4 Financial Matters

There's no getting around it — financial matters are at the heart of every business. With all the uncertainties associated with starting a business, you can be sure of one thing: You will need money to get your business up and running, and to keep it operating smoothly.

5.4.1 Start-Up Funding

Fortunately, an image consulting business doesn't require a lot of inventory that must be purchased in advance, or large warehouses or manufacturing facilities. It doesn't require too much equipment, and you probably even can get away with working from your home.

Still, there will be expenses involved. Your job is to figure out how much money you'll need and where you're going to get it. To figure out how much money you'll need to start up, go back to your business plan. Remember that it's your roadmap. Take a look at the financial management plan section. Much of the information you need to figure out start-up expenses should be included.

In addition to money needed to actually get your business started, you should try to have about six months of operating cash in reserve, if possible. So, if you figure that you need $5,000 to get your business up and running, and $1,000 a month to keep it operating smoothly, you should try to have between $10,000 and $12,000 available in advance.

If you're wondering where in the world you're going to come up with that much money, consider these possible sources:

- *Your personal savings:* This includes bank accounts, 401(k) funds or other retirement savings, mutual funds, money market accounts and stock accounts. Just be sure that you don't spend so much of your personal money that you can't meet your personal expenses.

- *Credit cards and lines of credit:* These are great vehicles for stop-gap money — that is, money you need right away to pay for something that you know money is coming in for. But try not to use credit on a long-term basis. You'll end up paying costly interest that can really drag down your business.

- *Collateral:* A lender often will agree to loan you money if they are assured they'll get something of value in the event that you default on the loan. A business just starting up can't count as collateral, so you'll probably need to put up personal assets like your house or your car. It's a guarantee to the lender that they'll get their money – and the interest on it – back.

- *Private venture capitalists:* These are companies that invest money into private business ventures. However, they'll charge you interest, and often want a say in how you run your business.

- *Private placement firms:* Sometimes called "money finders," these firms will try to get money from business investors on your behalf. Of course, they don't perform this service for nothing. They usually take a percentage of the money they find for you, or you have to agree to pay them a percentage of your profits.

- *Family and friends:* Borrowing from family and friends can be tricky, but if you know someone who has money and is willing to loan it to you, it might be worth considering. Just make sure you have a legal agreement that outlines repayment terms and so forth. And make it clear that the loan doesn't give the family member a right to tell you how to run your business.

- *Lending institutions:* These include traditional banks, credit unions, savings and loans and commercial finance companies. Be sure to compare interest rates and terms of lending to see which institution offers the best deals. Be prepared to write a proposal outlining why the bank should lend you money, how you plan to repay it, and why your image consulting business is going to be the best.

Regardless of where you go for money, be well-prepared. Have an extra copy of your business plan available for the potential lender's inspection, and be able to speak clearly and concisely about your plans and goals.

Keep these tips in mind when asking someone for funding:

- Get an introduction or referral. If you can get someone who is respected in the community to introduce you to a potential lender, it gives you credibility and a big advantage.

- Be prepared. Be able to discuss all aspects of your business plan, your long-range goals and your prospective market.

- Be professional. Shake hands, speak with confidence and look the person you're talking to in the eye.

- Dress to impress. You're going to be an image consultant. Be sure you look the part.

- Be receptive. Even if you don't end up getting any money from a prospective lender, you may be able to get ideas and suggestions. Perhaps they will have some pointers regarding your business plan, or some suggestions about steering your business in a particular direction. Don't be afraid to ask questions, either.

Remember that if someone agrees to loan or give money to your business, they're doing so because they believe in you and what you can do. When you ask someone for money, you need to sell yourself and your ideas. Make sure you have a great sales pitch.

Some good advice about financing can be found at the SBA and Nolo sites listed at the beginning of section 5.1. Also look into the SBA business assistance programs. The SBA has a Loan Guarantee Program that provides loans to small businesses.

5.4.2 Keeping Track of Your Finances

Once you've rounded up enough money to start your image consulting business, you'll need to figure out how you'll track your finances. Tracking finances carefully is very important for a couple of reasons. One is that being sloppy about business finances can get you into big trouble with clients, not to mention with the government when tax season rolls around. It's also big-time important to be particular about your finances because it's the best way to know how your business is doing.

Keeping close watch over your company's profit and loss statement, balance sheet and cash flow statement will keep you constantly on top of financial triumphs and stumbles. Imagine, for instance, that a client owes you $2,000 for work you've completed, another owes you $600 and yet another owes you $3,200. All of the payments are overdue. You owe your computer fix-it guy $750, the office supply store $250 and your $2,000 monthly rent is due at the end of the week.

If you're not carefully watching your finances, you might not realize that it's possible your bills are going to come due before you're paid for the work you've completed. Knowing exactly how much money you need and how much is due allows you to react to the situation before it becomes a problem. You can get on the phone and request payment immediately so that you can meet your obligations.

Keeping up with the finances of a small business shouldn't be much more difficult than keeping up with your personal finances. But it's a good idea to have some help. Many small businesses rely on Quicken's Premier Home and Business software program to manage finances. You can find out more about this software at **http://quicken.intuit.com**.

Getting a business credit card shouldn't be difficult if your personal credit history is good. If you've had credit problems, though, you might run into trouble establishing business credit. To check your credit report (everyone who's ever had a credit card has one), go to one of the big credit agency companies like Equifax (**www.equifax.com**) or Experian (**www.experian.com**).

An important bit of advice concerning your business finances is to make sure you keep them separate from your personal finances. You'll need to get a business credit card and separate bank accounts. Do not be tempted to mingle your business and personal accounts. And be sure to keep copies of receipts, invoices, payments due, payments received and so forth. The better your record keeping is, the less chance there is that you'll encounter financial problems.

5.4.3 Taxes

Most experts, and probably most entrepreneurs, will encourage you to consult a good accountant, certified public accountant or tax lawyer to walk you through the complicated path of business taxes.

You'll be taxed differently depending on the structure of your business. If you're a sole proprietor in the United States, you'll be taxed as an individual. You'll simply file a Schedule C with your personal tax return. You might be eligible for investment tax credits and other tax advantages, so you definitely want to talk to someone who can tell you exactly what you're entitled to.

Partnerships are taxed the same way as sole proprietorships. Income or loss from the business is passed on to the partners, who include it on their personal tax returns. Corporations pay taxes on earned profits.

If you're a sole proprietor with no employees or pension plans, you don't need to have an employer identification number, which is used for tax purposes. Partnerships and corporations do need such numbers, which are assigned by the IRS. If you need an employer identification number, you'll need to fill out IRS form SS-4.

You'll also need to file a form to figure out how much Social Security tax you'll pay. Canadians need to work out how much they pay to the Canada Pension Plan. If you're used to working for someone else, you may be in for a bit of a surprise concerning the Social Security tax. When you're employed, your employer pays half of the tax and you pay the other half. When you're self-employed, however, you need to pay both halves of the tax, and it can be daunting. You'll need to figure in the extra tax when you set your prices.

If you have employees, you'll have to pay half of their Social Security contribution, plus withholding taxes and perhaps federal and state unemployment taxes. Some websites to check out to learn more about taxes include:

- *Canada Revenue Agency*
  www.cra-arc.gc.ca/menu-e.html

- *Internal Revenue Service: Small Business/Self-Employed*
  www.irs.gov/businesses/small/index.html

- *Canada Business*
  www.canadabusiness.ca

Remember, taxes are complicated business and you're probably better off letting a professional help you negotiate the territory.

5.4.4   Setting Fees

A stumbling block for many entrepreneurs is what to charge for the products or services they provide. It can be particularly challenging to set a price on a service. You need to consider the nature of your market and how much the market is willing to pay for your services. And you'll also need to think about the kinds of profits you want to make.

TIP: When setting fees, be sure to figure in all of your expenses and overhead. You won't be able to figure out how much profit you want to make without knowing all your expenses.

Karen Brunger, owner of International Image Institute, has a logical method of figuring out what to charge clients. She considered three criteria: required income, value perception, and social and competitive environment.

Required Income

You want to set your fees so that you'll be able to make a living. According to Brunger, a typical consultant works two and one half billable days per week. That works out to be 125 billable days per year, or 750-1,000 hours per year. After you calculate your required new income, you should add 30 to 40 percent to cover expenses and then another 30 percent for taxes.

For example, let's say you're aiming in your first year to bring in $30,000, and you expect to work the typical two and one half billable days per week your first year. Assuming a six-hour day, that comes out to be 750 hours per year. So $30,000 divided by 750 hours is approximately $40 per hour, or $240 per day. But this is before we accounted for expenses and taxes.

Expenses: $30,000 + ($30,000 x .35) = $39,600

Taxes: $39,600 + ($39,600 x .30) = $51,480

This gives you the total gross income the business needs to generate. You then divide this number by 125 to get the per day rate, or by 750 to get a per hour rate.

Per day rate: $51,480 ÷ 125 days = $412 per day

Per hour rate: $51,480 ÷ 750 hours = $69 per hour

So if you want to make $30,000 income your first year, you'll need to charge at least $69 per hour, or $412 per day.

Of course, you will charge certain clients like corporations more. But these calculations will help you figure out how many hours you'll need to work per week and how much to charge on average for your time to reach your income goals.

> **TIP:** Nothing says you can't raise your prices as your first year progresses. In fact, you should, especially if the economy improves, when you gain experience, or if you receive further specialized training in your field.

Value Perception

Don't be afraid to charge what your services are worth, even when you're just starting out. "You must honor your expertise and charge appropriately for it in order to attract money and clients," advises Evana Maggiore, of Fashion Feng Shui. "I increased my prices according to my increase in confidence level. I soon discovered that people were willing to pay whatever I believed I was worth."

You may want to ask your first clients what they felt your services were worth. "I used that as a guideline of how high I could go," says Brunger. "The response was $1,500 for a wardrobe audit, plan, and personal shopping, which took one day."

You can include this question on a feedback form for all your clients. You may also use this information to help you decide how and when to increase your prices as you become more experienced.

Social and Competitive Environment

The area in which you're located will affect what customers will pay for your services. You're a lot more likely to draw high-paying customers in a city than you are in a rural farm town. Of course, your required income level will also be more or less depending on where you live, so this will work out for you and your clients fairly.

You also need to consider what your competition is charging for similar services. It's best to stay in the same range as your competitors, unless something about your services sets you apart from other image consultants. If the going rate for image consulting in your area ranges from between $100 and $125 an hour, you'd better have something really special going for you if you decide to charge $150 an hour.

So, what are beginning image consultants charging these days? Anywhere from $50 to $100 per hour, depending on education, location (rural or city), and local competition. We'll talk more about what experienced image consultants are charging later in this section.

Typical Fee Arrangements

Now you have an idea of how much to charge per hour or per day in order to meet your income needs. But how does this translate into a fee schedule? The most common ways for image consultants to charge for their services are one or more of the following:

- A fee based on the service being offered

- An hourly fee

- A daily or half-day fee

- A percentage

Service Being Offered

You may decide to charge your clients per service. If you've already figured out how much you need to charge per hour to meet your required income, you'll want to base your fees on how much time you usually spend with a client.

Here are some sample services and sample prices for each service.

Service	Fee
Color analysis	$75–150
Makeup and wardrobe consultation for a photo shoot	$175–200
Two hour spa treatment	$175
Image, style and color analysis	$350

Fees based on a service make the most sense if you'll be offering just one service for a client, or services that don't take much time. If you'll be working more in-depth, hourly or daily fees may make more sense.

Hourly Fees

An hourly fee is a common way for image consultants to charge for their services. Usually the image consultant tells the client the per hour rate, and the estimated amount of time the service will take.

For example, let's say you're offering an at-home wardrobe analysis. You may tell your client your fee is $90 per hour, and an at-home wardrobe analysis will take somewhere between two to four hours. You would have them sign a contract up front that would spell out all of this.

Here are typical time frames for different services you may offer:

Service	Time Frame
Image, Style, and Color Analysis	A 2- to 3-hour consultation, plus 3 to 4 hours for a written report
At-Home Wardrobe Analysis	Average 3 hours
Updating Your Look Within a Budget	Average 3 hours
Personal Shopping	Average 3 hours
Full Day Consultation	Average 6 hours
Business Casual Seminar	Two-hour session
Dressing for Networking and Interview	Two-hour session

Typical hourly rates for individuals range from $50 per hour (for a beginning image consultant) up to $250 per hour. Corporation fees range from $100 per hour for dress code consultations or working with individual employees, or up to $500 per hour for a seminar or class.

If you charge by the hour, you could also charge for your travel time and time that you spend writing reports. However, some professionals do not charge for local travel, or charge a lower fee for travel time. Consultants who interviewed for this guide charged on average $40-50 per hour for travel, plus expenses.

Daily Rates

Some individuals and corporate clients will hire you for more than just one service. They may be looking for a full makeover, or you may be offering a seminar or other corporate training program. For them, you may want to consider a daily fee (also known as a per diem). You may charge the same as you would with a per hour client but invoice it as one day's work, or you may charge less per hour to encourage clients to hire you for longer periods of time.

Here are some average payment rates:

Length of Consultation	Fee
Full day (up to six hours)	$1,500 for individual $2,000 for corporation
Half day (up to three hours)	$700 for individual $1,000 for corporation

Fees for training programs are typically charged by the day. Fees vary, but it is not unusual to charge several thousand dollars a day for a training program. As you will read below, consultants may charge anywhere from $1,000 to $12,000 or more per day.

However, if an organization has a specific amount budgeted, and it's a topic you specialize in (meaning you won't have to do a lot of extra research), you might decide to be flexible on the fee.

Your own fees might be based on such factors as: how much in demand your services are, how much you want to earn, what your expenses are, and what your competitors charge. Generally, a lower fee will result in more work, and it will be time to raise your fees when you have more work than you can handle, or if you want to work less. In some cases, raising fees may help you get work by signaling to employers that you are an experienced professional. (An employer may associate low fees with little experience.)

Percentage

There are two situations when an image consultant will charge a percentage-based fee: personal shopping and referrals.

For personal shopping, this method involves charging clients a percentage of the price of the merchandise you buy for them (before taxes), if you offer your client personal shopping services. You will most likely use this in combination with your consultant fees.

Generally, the fee will vary depending on the total amount spent. While the percentage amount usually ranges from ten to 25 percent of the retail price, you may charge as little as five percent for a large purchase and as much as 30 percent for a small purchase.

Some image consultants charge a referral fee. Whenever they refer someone to another expert, the expert pays the image consultant a percentage of their price. For example, if you refer someone to Hair Styles Rock salon, assuming you have worked out a deal with them to receive a ten percent referral fee for any clients you send them, you would receive ten percent of whatever they charge your client.

Referral fees usually range from five to 15 percent. It is based on what you've worked out with other professionals. You benefit both monetarily and professionally, since your clients get expert instruction and care when needed, and the referred business receives new clients. Your referral fee is like a marketing expense for them.

Experienced Image Consultant Fees

Listed below is a sampling of what real image consultants charge for a variety of services. Anne Sowden, managing director of Toronto-based Here's Looking at You Image Consulting, offers a variety of services for individuals and corporations. Some of the individual services include:

- Image, style and color analysis
- Dressing for networking and interviews
- At-home wardrobe analysis
- Updating your look within a budget
- Personal shopping
- Successful business casual dressing

Sowden generally offers potential clients a no-charge preliminary consultation, at which time she performs a needs assessment. She then sets her fees based on the needs assessment. If a client requests a color analysis as part of an overall consultation, for instance, the charge for the analysis is $75. If the color analysis is the only service requested, the charge would be $150.

Sowden's hourly fee for an overall consultation including a range of services is between $125 and $175, depending on her travel time. In addition to individual services, she offers various corporate seminars, which range in price from $1,500 to $2,000 a day.

Joyce Knudsen of The ImageMaker also offers a variety of services for individuals and businesses. Those services range from executive image services to etiquette to modeling. Knudsen requires potential clients to come in for an initial consultation at a specified fee, at which time they decide from which services the client would benefit. From there they develop an action plan. Knudsen charges an hourly fee of $175, and says that her total fee for services could be anywhere from $1,000 to $2,000.

Gloria Starr, of Global Success Strategies, says she prefers to charge by the project, rather than the hour. Starr, whose client list includes names such as Destiny's Child, Princess Cruise Lines and Levi Strauss, is well known and respected in the image consultant business. Her prices reflect that respect.

Personal consultations are billed by the type of service required. Services include personalized color analysis, wardrobe consultation, figure analysis, extreme makeovers, and so forth. According to Starr, the cost of the services ranges between $200 and $3,500.

Corporate services, which include keynote speeches, two-hour seminars and half-day and full-day programs, range in price from $5,000 to $12,000. She also offers extensive training for corporate clients, including focus groups, assessment profiling tools, executive interviews and coaching and so forth. These types of training are billed on a project basis, ranging from $20,000 to $150,000.

The upper ranges, Starr explains, would be for a large health care or technological organization which has requested training on image and etiquette for its sales team, group sessions for administrative assistants, assessment profiling and coaching for executive teams. Starr advises image consultants just starting out to be patient concerning fees. Over time, she says, you'll get a better feel for the average price of various services, and for what you're comfortable charging for each service.

Finally, remember that just because you set certain fees for your services doesn't mean they can't ever change. If you find out people aren't hiring you and you think it's because your fee is too high, try lowering it. Consider larger economic factors, as well. In a shaky economy, image consulting may be an area in which people decide they can cut back on the services they've been getting and save some money.

Raising your prices may also bring in more clients. In the corporate world, the impression is that the more you charge, the better your services are. The same can go for individual clients. As Karen Brunger of the International Image Institute explains, "I had as much work as I could handle, so I raised my fees to cut down on clients. Rather than losing clients, however, I got even more, and I also got 'easier' clients who were more willing to pay my fee. I find it ironic that whenever I raised my fees, people complained less and were more willing to pay me and trust me."

5.4.5   Arranging Payment

Regardless of at what rate you set your fees, you want to be sure that you'll get paid in a timely manner. Unfortunately, many small business owners find that collecting what they're owed can be challenging, and sometimes downright unpleasant.

The most important thing is to arrange for payment before you perform any service. A sample client contract is found in the next section of this chapter. You can use it as a model or find another contract, but be sure that you and your client agree to its terms before you perform any service.

Methods of Payment

You need to decide in advance the methods of payment you'll be able to accept. If you want to be able to accept credit cards, you'll need to set up a merchant account. To accept Visa or MasterCard, you may have to work with a bank to get an account set up. Or you can get set up online at a site like Yahoo.com (**http://smallbusiness.yahoo.com/merchant**).

You also can be set up to accept debit cards, which deduct your payment directly from your client's account at the bank and deposit it into your business account. Discover and American Express set up merchant accounts nationally and internationally without the requirement to work with a local institution.

You should know that being able to accept credit cards comes with a price. You'll pay either a percentage of every credit card payment, or a monthly fee, depending on what arrangements you make. Still, many clients will expect to pay with credit cards, and it could jeopardize your business if you're not able to accept them.

Accepting online payment is an option and is accomplished by setting up an account with a service such as PayPal (**www.paypal.com**). However, since you'll be working closely and personally with clients, it probably isn't necessary to establish online payments. Personal or business checks are another method of payment, and generally a safe way for you to get what's owed to you.

Writing an Invoice

To get paid, however, you first have to bill a client. To do this, you need an invoice on which you'll list the services that have been provided, the agreed-upon fee for those services, and other pertinent information.

Sample Invoice
(on your letterhead)

Date: Date on which invoice is sent

To: Name of client
Street address and apartment number
City, state and zip code
Client's phone number
Client's e-mail address

Services:	Fee:
Coaching on communication skills	
4 hours at $75 per hour	$300
Total Due:	$300

Also include special payment instructions, such as that payment is expected within 30 days. If a client doesn't pay within the time requested on the invoice, then send another invoice, noting that payment is expected with a shorter time, perhaps five or ten days. This gives your client a reminder to quickly make the overdue payment.

If a bill is not paid within 60 days, you'll need to contact the client again. You can do this in writing, either in an e-mail or snail mail. If you send a letter, you should make arrangements with the post office to get confirmation that your client actually received it. E-mails are a little harder to track, and easier for someone to deny getting. You can call the client, but be aware that they are likely to avoid your phone calls.

If the matter remains unresolved for 90 days, you may have to contact a collection agency about getting your money for you. Or you can consider taking the matter to a small claims court. You may or may not need a lawyer to do this.

Corporate Clients

Corporate clients are often invoiced at the end of a training program, or they can be invoiced monthly if services are ongoing. A challenge with invoicing on a monthly basis is that corporations normally expect at least 30 days to pay, and some wait 60 or 90 days before putting a check in the mail. Some image consultants interviewed for this guide said they invoice their corporate clients a month in advance, with payment due on the day of service. This gives the company time to process your invoice, and you get paid in a timely manner.

Your invoice should be on your letterhead and include the following:

- The client name and contact information
- The date of the invoice
- A purchase order number (if the client gave you one)
- Services you provided
- Any expenses and taxes payable
- The total amount due
- Terms of payment (e.g. "Payable upon receipt")

Sample Corporate Invoice

(on your letterhead)

Date: July 25, 2011

To: Jane Jones
Human Resources Department
City of Sunnyday
123 Main Street
Sunnyday, CA 90211

Re: Professional ImageTraining Program

Design of Seminar	$ 1,500.00
July 22, 2011 Workshop Delivery	2,000.00
July 23, 2011 Workshop Delivery	2,000.00
Subtotal	5,500.00
7% tax *(include your own tax rate here)*	385.00

Total: Please pay this amount   **$5,885.00**

Terms: Payable within 30 days
Thank you for your business.

TIP: To ensure you are paid by corporate clients make sure you have a contract in place.

5.5 Client Contracts

A client contract is very important to your business. It ensures that you and your client have the same expectations and can help protect you. Your contract or agreement should spell out what services you will provide for the client, when you will provide them (the dates between which or by which your services are to be completed), as well as when and how you are to be paid. The contract should also include your company name and address, as well as the contact name, company name (if applicable) and address of your client.

On the pages that follow you will find two sample contracts. Before using a contract, make sure you have it reviewed by your attorney.

Sample Services Agreement

THIS AGREEMENT is made this *[date]* day of *[month]*, 20__.

BETWEEN
[insert name of your client] (the "Client"); and *[insert your name or your company's name]* (the "Image Consultant"), collectively referred to as the "Parties."

1.1 Services

The Image Consultant shall provide the following services ("Services") to the Client in accordance with the terms and conditions of this Agreement: *[Insert a description of the services here]*

1.2 Delivery of the Services

- *Start date:* The Image Consultant shall commence the provision of the Services on *[insert date here]*.

- *Completion date:* The Image Consultant shall *[complete/cease to provide]* the Services *[by/on]* *[insert date here]* ("Completion Date").

- *Key dates:* The Image Consultant agrees to provide the following parts of the Services at the specific dates set out below: *[insert dates here, such as the date for the wardrobe consultation, the fittings, replacement of items that do not fit, and so on]*.

1.3 Site

The Image Consultant shall provide the Services at the following site(s): *[insert details here if applicable, such as client's home, your office, etc.]*

1.4 Fees

As consideration for the provision of the Services by the Image Consultant, the fees for the provision of the Services is *[insert fees here]* ("Fees"). The Client *[shall/shall not]* pay for the Image Consultant's out-of-pocket expenses comprising *[insert here, if agreed]*.

1.5 Payment

The Client agrees to pay the Fees to the Image Consultant on the following dates: *[also specify whether the price will be paid in one payment, in installments or upon completion of specific milestones].*

The Image Consultant shall invoice the Client for the Services that it has provided to the Client *[monthly/weekly/after the Completion Date]*. The Client shall pay such invoices *[upon receipt /within 30 days of receipt]* from the Image Consultant.

Any charges payable under this Agreement are exclusive of any applicable taxes, duties, or other fees charged by a government body and such shall be payable by the Client to the Image Consultant in addition to all other charges payable hereunder.

1.6 Warranty

The Image Consultant represents and warrants that it will perform the Services with reasonable skill and care.

1.7 Limitation of Liability

Subject to the Client's obligation to pay the Fees to the Image Consultant, either party's liability arising directly out of its obligations under this Agreement and every applicable part of it shall be limited in aggregate to the Fees. The Image Consultant assumes no liability due to the quality of items or services purchased for the Client.

1.8 Term and Termination

This Agreement shall be effective on the date hereof and shall continue until the completion date stated in section 1.2 unless terminated sooner. If the Client terminates this agreement for any reason before the scheduled completion date, the Client will reimburse the Image Consultant for all outstanding fees and out-of-pocket expenses.

1.9 Relationship of the Parties

The Parties acknowledge and agree that the Services performed by the Image Consultant, its employees, sub-contractors, or agents shall be as an independent contractor and that nothing in this Agreement shall be deemed to constitute a partnership, joint venture, or otherwise between the parties.

1.10 Confidentiality

Neither Party will disclose any information of the other which comes into its possession under or in relation to this Agreement and which is of a confidential nature.

1.11 Miscellaneous

The failure of either party to enforce its rights under this Agreement at any time for any period shall not be construed as a waiver of such rights.

If any part, term or provision of this Agreement is held to be illegal or unenforceable neither the validity or enforceability of the remainder of this Agreement shall be affected.

This Agreement constitutes the entire understanding between the Parties and supersedes all prior representations, negotiations or understandings.

Neither Party shall be liable for failure to perform any obligation under this Agreement if the failure is caused by any circumstances beyond its reasonable control, including but not limited to acts of god, war, or industrial dispute.

This Agreement shall be governed by the laws of the jurisdiction in which the Client is located.

Agreed by the Parties hereto:

Signed by: _____

On behalf of: _____

[the Client]

Signed by: _____

On behalf of: _____

[the Image Consultant]

Sample Training Contract
(on your letterhead)

Client

Jane Jones
Human Resources Department
XYZ Corporation
123 Main Street
Sunnyday, CA 90123

Purpose

To deliver a Training program for XYZ Corporation.

Details

The training sessions will be presented at the XYZ Center in Sunnyday. The training will consist of seven half day (three hour) sessions scheduled to take place from 4:30 p.m. to 7:30 p.m. The session topics and dates are as follows:

Fundamentals of Effective Communication	April 27
Advanced Interpersonal Communication Skills	May 4
Dressing Professionally	May 11
Dining Etiquette	May 18
Business Etiquette	May 25

The trainer will be Irma Image. In the event the chosen trainer is unavailable for a particular session, Irma Image Services will send a suitable and equally qualified trainer.

Client Responsibilities

- facility arrangements

- A/V equipment

Trainer Responsibilities

- printed materials for each participant

- delivery of training

Fees

Per session fee (based on 12 participants): $1,200.00 plus tax, payable within ten days after each session.

Actual billing may vary should the number of attendees exceed those quoted above. The minimum amount of program fees above, based on client's statement of numbers is binding, even when fewer participants actually attend.

If prior to the commencement of the program, dates are postponed or sessions cancelled, Irma Image Services shall be paid the appropriate postponement/cancellation charge as noted below. (This does not apply to rescheduling of the order of topics or session start/end times, which may be changed on request.)

Days Prior to Scheduled Program	Postponement/ Date Change	Cancellation of Program
30-90	10%	25%
11-29	25%	50%
10 or fewer	50%	100%

Signature and Date

_____

Jane Jones
Human Resources Dept.
City of Sunnyday

_____

Irma Image
President
Irma Image Services Ltd.

_____

Date

_____

Date

6. Getting Clients

When Toy Russell decided to start an image consulting practice, she was in a good position to attract high-end corporate business. For 15 years she'd worked as a makeup artist in television and motion pictures and was well-acquainted with many people in the film industry.

She'd parlayed her work as a model and her cosmetology license into a makeup production-trainee job at ABC TV and had worked her way up through "the industry" so effectively that when she requested testimonials and photographs from stars she'd worked with over the years – Paul Newman, Joanne Woodward, Halle Berry, Dick Cavett, and Eddie Murphy, to name a few – they were happy to oblige.

Armed with a professionally designed brochure and A-list entertainment-industry credits, Russell brought her expertise to bear on consulting contracts with TV stations all over the country, where she counseled local on-camera personnel on everything from posture to makeup to color to wardrobe. The roster of satisfied clients led to the referrals and repeat business that kept her profitably busy between film gigs.

Not every image consultant will get the Hollywood jump-start that Toy Russell got for her practice. Even so, there are many different kinds of marketing strategies, and if you go about it systematically, you can establish a credible image for yourself as an image expert that will enable you to attract clients, build a reputation as a pro, and get that referral engine roaring.

Being effective at attracting clients starts with identifying the most likely prospects and focusing your marketing efforts in a way calculated to lead to signed contracts. You'll find that, in this business, marketing is not a one-size-fits-all proposition; the needs of various market segments may be highly specialized and vastly different. For example, what on-camera TV anchors need may be radically different from the needs of a back-office computer programmer who's moving into the executive suite but whose current wardrobe makes him look more like a shipping clerk than a vice president.

The point is that you may have to adjust the way you approach client prospects based not so much on what you're selling as on what they're buying. Keeping that in mind may help you choose target markets wisely and shape your marketing techniques appropriately.

6.1 Choose Your Target Markets

Before you start trying to sell your services to client prospects, you should decide which types of clients you want for your consulting practice. These are your "target" markets.

Novice image consultants are often tempted to say they want any client who is willing to pay. Avoid the temptation. The image needs of clients are as diverse and idiosyncratic as human nature itself. That makes it costly and time-consuming to market your services to "everyone." Indeed, client prospects – especially at the lucrative corporate level – are more likely to respond positively to you if you position yourself as a specialist who connects with their needs.

When you're just starting out, of course, you may not be in a position to sell a specialty, since profitable specialists trade on track record, and you have to start somewhere. You might have individual or corporate clients or individual clients who want to upgrade their position in a corporate setting. Nevertheless, as soon as you can, focus your business-building efforts on the target markets that are most suited to your interests and expertise. As you get more business you will be able to be more selective about the projects you undertake.

Getting to that point requires you to be aware of the characteristics of various target markets and of the implications of those characteristics for your marketing strategy. This section covers a variety of markets with tips on marketing to them. Later in this chapter, we will explore marketing techniques in detail.

6.1.1   Business Markets

Job Seekers and Promotion Seekers

John T. Molloy's classic book *Dress for Success*, which lent momentum to the image-consulting industry (he claims his book made the whole industry possible), brought into popular discourse the linkage between career success and personal presentation and projection in the corporate workplace.

Unapologetically conservative, classic, and class-conscious in his wardrobe recommendations for upwardly mobile corporate employees, Molloy argued that careful attention and adherence to what amounted to a corporate uniform would help them get better jobs, make more sales, bring in more business, etc. He deplored faddish, trendy accessories and classic-wardrobe substitutions and took image consultants, fashion designers, and even retail clerks to task for enabling or encouraging clients to make wardrobe choices that deviated from his research and ideas.

On the other hand, Molloy acknowledged that dress-for-success norms vary across industries. By itself, a corporate uniform offers no career guarantees but is a key element of a totality of image. For example, a man who springs for a Brooks Brothers suit but whose hair is unstyled and who could use a manicure is unlikely to get the promotion he wants. The weight of evidence sides with the view that a person can more successfully advance their career if their personal image is consistent with the image favored by the people who do the hiring.

The job-seeking target market is distinguished by a specific goal, and to achieve that goal this market needs to present itself to its own market – people who hire – by demonstrating an image consistent with what they expect to see in the workplace. Surprises won't go over well with the market niche that the ambitious job seekers are targeting. So between the idea of a job and the completed goal stands the image consultant whose judgment, guidance, encouragement, and hand-holding may make all the difference.

Be aware that some people in this category may have definite career goals and definite but misguided ideas about their image. You need to be prepared to educate clients about an effective image in a given industry and overcome resistance to changing mind-set, hairdo, and wardrobe to reflect the expectations of employment decision makers.

A benefit of dealing with individual job seekers as clients is that you may be able to market to them more or less informally. That can be a real plus, especially for consultants who are just starting to build a practice.

For example, you could start giving your advice to family and friends, then move toward friends of friends, then break into a meaningful network of referrals. Every job candidate who follows your advice and lands a good job will be able to trace their success in part to you. That makes for both testimonials and referrals which you can incorporate into your promotional materials.

Corporations

Whether it's a corporation or nonprofit organization, the first contact most people have with any organization is the person who answers the phone. At big organizations it may be a receptionist or switchboard operator. Some customers may have to deal with the customer service staff, which is often a key point of public contact for a corporation.

People in the media, meanwhile, may deal with other corporate personnel whose manner and appearance could use an image boost. Press liaisons and ombudsmen are one version of the public face of an institution. CEOs and other corporate officers may also be called on to appear on television or at a big meeting to give a speech or provide commentary.

The role of the image consultant in these kinds of relationships is to help the organization put its best face forward. You bring to bear much the same expertise that works for job seekers, executives, and the like, but your principal emphasis is on how the individual's image will benefit that of the organization. In other words, you image-consult the individual or group, but your objective is to enhance the image of the organization that employs the individual on its behalf.

The form that this kind of consulting takes may vary, depending on the needs of the project and depending on the thrust of your consultancy. Some image consultants might focus on grooming, color, and fashion, while others might coach personnel on optimizing their "TV-Q" via body language. For customer service personnel the image consultant's job may entail voice coaching and telephone or e-mail etiquette. The structure of consultation may vary as well. The higher the executive, the more likely you will be doing one-on-one consultation.

Image consulting is suited to various forms of corporate in-service training. For example, if there's a corporate customer service department to consult, you may be working with a group of employees and running your training session something like an acting class. Sales departments might benefit from an image-related refresher course. Corporations also run executive retreats, where seminars and workshops are offered on a wide variety of subjects.

The marketing question becomes how you get the consulting contract. In the corporate environment, and particularly among the Fortune 500 and other elite institutions, you'll find that there's really no substitute for in-person marketing efforts at the executive-suite level. You will want to use supporting materials as sales aids. Perhaps you advertise in trade publications. You may have brochures, press kits, PowerPoint presentations, and similar materials to support your marketing efforts. But that's just what these materials are: support. In-person chemistry is what will put you over when a corporate consulting contract is your objective.

Indeed, it may take more than one or two contacts before you can close a sale. There's the initial approach, perhaps followed by telephone tag, a direct-mail package, a proposal, and/or an in-person appointment. You may have to give a presentation a couple of times – perhaps to one person, perhaps to a committee – to convince the prospects that you can deliver what they need. The more you can control the structure of your presentation, the better.

Corporate business has a history of getting the most marketing mileage out of relationships of trust and confidence, and you have a better chance of developing those by being in the room and at the table with corporate decision makers. That's where membership in local civic organizations such as Rotary, the Chamber of Commerce, Kiwanis, Elks, etc., becomes so important.

Membership, by the way, means active participation in the objectives of the group, not just showing up for the luncheons. Serving on a charitable fund-raising committee with professional businesspeople is a relationship strategy that you can later translate into either direct business or referrals.

An important aspect of building relationships and being heard at the table is doing your homework. If you're targeting a particular industry, such as a high-tech firm with a story to tell, you'll want to be aware of which organizations the people in that business belong to and where and when they have their conventions and/or trade shows.

The Internet is loaded with information on publicly traded companies, but don't ignore the websites of privately held corporations, which may give you clues about corporate priorities and public outreach and help you identify whom to contact in order to make your sales pitch.

It may be worth the investment of traveling to some trade shows and conventions to establish yourself as a professional industry presence and to exploit opportunities to make all-important personal contacts. Section 6.3.2 describes cost-effective ways of doing this.

New Executives

Sometimes executive positions are thrust upon workers who may not have had to spiff up their image before landing a big promotion. But what's really more likely to set this target market apart from the previous one is that the subject of the image consultation and the actual client may not be one and the same person.

A CEO Gets an Image Makeover

In the early 1990s National Medical Enterprises, which later went public as Tenet Healthcare Corporation, was caught up in a highly publicized corporate scandal. Crisis-management PR firm Sitrick & Company authorized Steve Jaffe to help prep NME's newly-installed CEO to make a presentation at the annual stock-holders' meeting and field questions from the media.

The new CEO had been an executive at MGM Studios, and his transition to the executive suite of a health-care organization was a major risk not only for him but also for the corporation because of the differences in corporate culture between the entertainment and health-care industries. Image consulting was considered essential for making the transition a personal and corporate success.

"I told him what tie to wear, what suit to wear, what to say and how to say it," Jaffe recalls. "We practiced his speech, videotaping it and talking about the inflection of every word: where he should sound angry, where he should sound compassionate, how he should address the little old ladies and other kinds of investors who were bound to have questions."

Far from resenting the consultants' interference in the transition process, the new CEO cooperated enthusiastically. "As with all really good CEOs who seek consultation," Jaffe explains, "he wanted to know every detail. He wanted to know about his speech down to the word and how to orchestrate his entry into the meeting room. He even wanted to know what would be on the projection screen before he came in."

Jaffe's contribution to the CEO's image didn't stop with grooming and wardrobe. He was responsible for picking, from thousands of slides, the various images that would go on the video screen while stockholders came in and got seated at the annual meeting.

He also chose the music — classical and soothing, which "was intended to lull them into a comfortable state, almost the equivalent of a slow-working anesthesia. Then the guy was to come in and soothe their aching pocketbooks. So we did that, and he came in and was brilliant."

Did the transition work? The CEO remained in place for more than ten years. Steve Jaffe now heads his own successful crisis-management PR firm, Jaffe & Company Strategic Media Relations, located online at **www.stevejaffepr.com**.

A technically skilled employee who gets moved into management may not have the social skills or background necessary for presenting the proper image. Some corporations also have formal or informal dress codes. Accordingly, for a variety of image-related reasons, a corporation may hire a consultant to do the personalized, image-related equivalent of a full-scale public relations intervention in a corporate crisis.

The image consultant's role is to bring the new executive's image in line with executive-suite custom and practice so that they project an image that does the corporation credit. What form the work would take could vary tremendously from subject to subject.

Some subjects may need tips on shopping for the right wardrobe, while others may need to be coached on the protocols of ordering wine in a fancy restaurant or even on table manners. But although you'd work on a very personal level with the individual subject, the corporation – not the individual – would be your actual client.

Your marketing effort involves identifying the person or department at the company most likely to oversee an image makeover for new executives. The point of contact may vary from place to place. Marketing, public relations, and human resources departments are the likely candidates in most corporations, but sometimes it may make more sense to start with the CEO, who can always delegate downward.

In some cases, you might target the corporation indirectly through such third parties as outsource PR firms, ad agencies, or media consultants. What is critical, ultimately, is to identify, impress, and cultivate whoever has authority to make deals.

Spouses of Executives

For this target market, the client could be the corporation or the individual. Let's say a new executive has gone through a successful image makeover and is rubbing elbows with top-level peers both professionally in the executive suite and socially at assorted country clubs.

High-end socializing puts enormous pressure on the spouses of executives to talk the talk, walk the walk, and look the look of the executive-level social class. It can sometimes be a rude awakening for the spouse of an executive when they are being scrutinized and gossiped about by colleagues and friends as a socially worthy companion.

Enter the image consultant to do the work that will enable the appearance of both Mr. and Mrs. Executive to reflect well on themselves and the corporation. It is a great mistake for a career-minded individual to underestimate the power of their spouse's appearance to affect the corporate culture's impression of the employee.

Some corporations may fund spouse consulting in whole or in part, which would make the corporation, not the spouse, your client. Alternatively, new executives who recognize the need to retool the appearance of their spouses may be willing to pay for consultation. In either case, this customer segment is likely to expect to pay top dollar for your services. It is important for you to shape your marketing efforts for this target market in a way that makes your offer clear and the scope of expertise that you claim credible.

One key aspect of your offer to this market segment may be confidentiality. The same corporation that is willing to fund an image consultation for the up-and-coming executive may expect the executive's spouse to be completely turned out in grooming, wardrobe, and social graces. So it may fall to the individual client to foot the bill.

Confidentiality enters the picture because the executive and spouse don't want everyone to start gossiping that the new kids in town aren't sophisticated enough for the big league. That's why word of mouth for an image specialist is so important. Client referrals are one version of that.

Another key is positioning yourself with other high-end service providers as a consultant who guarantees to offer image expertise confidentially. Stylists at the best salon in town, gym owners, interior decorators, architects, lawyers, stockbrokers, accountants, owners of fine clothing stores — these are businesspeople with whom executive fast-trackers and their families may have regular contact. The business-to-business link, which you would cultivate at Chamber of Commerce breakfasts and similar venues, becomes your bridge to the clientele.

Finding Clients Who Will Pay $5,000 a Week

Michael Thurmond, Body Makeover Specialist for ABC TV's *Extreme Makeover*, charges his spa clients $5,000 a week to supervise a six-week regimen of diet, exercise, and weight training that is meant to "sculpt" the body.

"This is targeted for people that can afford $5,000 a week and are pampered," says Thurmond, who is based in Los Angeles.

"Their menu is designed and redesigned as necessary. They don't have to think about it. The image is coming in as a caterpillar and coming out a butterfly."

For their money these clients get personal training, cooking classes, and follow-up support after they leave. Thurmond describes the program as "very much a high service offer."

Thurmond's spa market is made up mainly of higher-income women between 25 and 55, but he works with lots of men as well. Despite the pricey nature of the consulting and coaching services Thurmond provides, he encounters little price resistance.

"These people are baby boomers that are wanting to stay young and beautiful and have some leisure time, some money, and the belief that this is going to work for them," he says.

The production people at *Extreme Makeover* contacted Thurmond because of strong word of mouth from celebrities and others who had been through his spa program.

But Thurmond didn't start out at the top of the heap. A former competitive bodybuilder and longtime entrepreneur, Thurmond owns Provida Life Sciences Inc., through which he has reached the mass market for over 15 years. He calls his method Blueprinting, and he sells diet plans, exercise equipment, supplements, and services through Provida.

When Thurmond started to market his six-week body makeover, he took a fairly conventional approach to advertising and promotion. "I had a very strong product," he says, "something everyone in the world wanted, which was how to change how they looked quickly."

Using that as his hook, Thurmond bought print ads in *Los Angeles Magazine*, a four-color glossy monthly like many metro areas have. When that market proved to be limited, he switched to the *Los Angeles Times* and to *LA Weekly*, a community throwaway newspaper.

That's when things really took off. As he explains: "When I first started advertising in the *Times*, I had five to ten people on the phones, and they were ringing off the hook."

Lucrative as that market was, the high volume didn't last forever. So he invested in television. "You exhaust your market," Thurmond explains. "You have to change your venues."

Thurmond plowed profits into an infomercial that explained his system, and he got his products accepted by the Home Shopping Network. He credits before-and-after photographs and testimonials with enthusiastic viewer response. "The call-ins are so strong," he says, "that I did an hour [on Home Shopping] because the testimonials rolled in."

Thurmond also set up a 24-hour support line, which he says helped reinforce customer loyalty. "You make the benefit of the consumer your primary product," he says.

You can find out more about Michael Thurmond's Six-Week Body Makeover at **www.mybodymakeover.com**.

For additional information and tips on developing a wealthy client list, check out the latest edition of the book *Marketing to the Affluent*, by Thomas J. Stanley.

Sales Representatives

If a sales rep works exclusively by telephone or via e-mail, careful attention to personal image may not be their most pressing need. But in many industries, the time-honored tradition is for sales representatives to make personal calls on prospective and current clients. For those who make in-person calls on clients and prospects, the personal presentation is often as important as the wares being sold.

The whole matter has been complicated by new do-not-call regulations, which have cut into telemarketers' options and which may have the effect of putting more in-person reps on the road. This is complicated for the reps, but a marketing opportunity for image consultants.

Much about marketing to sales representatives overlaps and converges with marketing to corporate and individual clients. The consulting project might unfold in group venues – say, in-service training for the sales force of Acme, Inc. – or with individual salespeople who want to get ahead. Group consulting opportunities would be targeted in much the same way as you'd target any corporate prospect.

Individual sales reps might become clients via personal networking and referrals, or from ads that you place in trade publications. What really makes this a distinctive image-consulting customer segment is that you're marketing to marketers. So your offer and client service need to be effective and on point.

You also need to be a tireless networker. Many sales reps are people oriented, seeing virtually all new contacts as a stepping stone to new sales opportunities. So part of your marketing strategy must be to network in the same places they do — association conventions, regional sales meetings, civic organizations, etc. Sales reps also have insider networking meetings designed to help them improve their bottom lines.

An image-consulting workshop might be just the ticket to obtaining individual clients and/or a corporate assignment. Have a look at *Agency Sales Magazine*, published by the Manufacturers' Agents National Association (MANA), to get an idea of the territory. The magazine is online at **www.manaonline.org/html/agency_sales_magazine.html**. To find out more about MANA, visit **www.manaonline.org**.

Sales reps are completely familiar with prospects who raise objections to selling presentations, and, like them, you need to be prepared to meet objections. You need to be able to explain your opinions with expert confidence and reinforce that with a reputation for expertise. See section 6.3 for tips for positioning yourself as an expert.

6.1.2   Other Professionals

Litigators

Seasoned lawyers will tell you that the first time they appeared before a judge was one of the most frightening experiences of their lives. As one lawyer put it, "You know that you don't know what you're doing."

What lawyers know very well is that judges aren't in the business of training lawyers how to be effective in court. Many judges have definite ideas about how attorneys who practice before them should dress, walk, talk, and otherwise conduct themselves. You don't have to be an expert in the rules of civil or criminal procedure to know that judges can enforce their preferences for litigator behavior with contempt-of-court citations. That's where the image consultant comes in.

Of course, if you do know procedural rules, you're ahead of the game. Despite what you see in the movies, what real-world judges and juries want from litigators is no-nonsense presentation of the legal issues in a way that will hold everyone's attention. The role of the image consultant may include teaching the lawyer how to dress and groom properly, but the meat of the effort will be in establishing and maintaining a decorous and commanding courtroom presence.

While you might make use of video equipment with any of your markets, with no other segment will this teaching tool be more valuable than it is here. So if you're specifically targeting litigators, make sure that in your promotional materials you include something about the fact that you use video as a training tool. You'd record a client's speech to the jury or perhaps set up a role-playing exercise, then play it back.

Video is the consultant's best friend when it comes to pointing out clients' poor speech habits, voice timbre, and body language. Nothing is more sobering – or motivating – than watching one's own movements and hearing one's voice on screen. Video can also show clients how much they've improved after the coaching process. They'll see real differences in everything from how loudly they need to speak to the way they should hold their arms while they talk to a witness.

Much of what works with corporate prospects can be applied to this market. The actual consulting projects may be done with individual clients, but marketing the service might involve giving image-oriented seminars or workshops to groups at conventions or talking up your operation at networking "mixers" and other events.

To be a seminar leader, contact the people in charge of the convention and write a proposal that makes your case for becoming part of the program. Just as with other adult-education projects, the attendees in a group presentation will become part of your prospective client pool, so provide a jar for business cards and mailing list contact information forms for those who forgot to bring cards.

Use the *Encyclopedia of Associations* (available at your local library) to track down trade publications and meetings of lawyer organizations — not only of the American Bar Association, which by the way has a number of regional and state chapters, but also of regional organizations such as your state's trial lawyers association. All of these groups will have some version of regular conventions and other meetings, and most of them have a publication or outreach of some kind. All of their outreach represents marketing, advertising, and networking avenues for you to explore.

TV Reporters and Anchors

A journalism degree may be a plus, but TV reporters and anchors who are successful know how important their image, or "TV-Q," is to career longevity. The scene in the film *Broadcast News* where William Hurt coaches Albert Brooks about anchoring a program hints at the image-related issues that on-camera journalists confront. The film *The China Syndrome* devotes an entire subplot to the onscreen look of its anchor Kimberly, played by Jane Fonda.

In many local markets, however, there are no coaches. "Because of budget constraints," explains Toy Russell, "on-camera talent are left to their own devices when it comes to wardrobe, makeup, hair, and body language. In those places they also have to buy their own clothing. It's not provided by the station."

TV stations in search of better ratings, as well as on-camera individuals in search of a better career, are the targets of image consultants. Station managers are motivated because they get mail from viewers who feel entitled to comment on what the anchors are wearing, how they talk, or what their posture, makeup, or hair is like. Because the pool of on-camera talent may be limited in local markets, the image consultant is called in to help overhaul the talent that is now on the job.

Consultants with a background in TV, film, or theatre are most likely to be perceived as having the necessary credentials and credibility to make makeover suggestions. An image consultant who has strong credentials may, like Toy Russell, bring a career's worth of contacts to the business-building process. Even so, management rosters change constantly, and success in the entertainment business is all about who you know. So cultivating contacts at broadcast industry meetings and trade shows, backed up by smart use of direct mail, sales aids, advertising, and an Internet presence, has to be part of the game.

Look into meetings, publications (including membership directories), film festivals, commercial competitions, and journalism organizations for opportunities to give seminars and/or schmooze with colleagues, competitors, and client prospects. Most states have an association of broadcasters, but there are other subdivisions as well.

Politicians

If you're aware of the motion pictures *Primary Colors* and *The Candidate*, the TV show *West Wing*, or the nightly news, you already know that political consultants are big-time players in politics. A good portion of what political consultants do comes down to image consulting, whatever they might say about issues and action plans.

This is a high-end, high-stakes, well-seasoned specialty arena for image consultants if the clients are presidential and congressional hopefuls. But people also run for city councils and school boards and state legislatures, and where the public face is concerned they need very much the same media and speech training or wardrobe and grooming advice as corporate executives and spouse hunters do.

So there's no reason not to think of these people as reasonable market opportunities. You might be able to do workshops for aspiring candidates, which are sponsored from time to time by political parties. Obviously to accomplish this you'll need to mix it up with the polls and the leadership at various meetings of party organizations, such as:

- *Democratic National Committee*
  www.democrats.org

- *Woman's National Democratic Club*
  www.democraticwoman.org

- *Republican National Committee*
  www.rnc.org

- *Young Republican National Federation*
  www.youngrepublicans.com

When you deal with individual politicians, you find that what distinguishes them as clients is that image consultants may not be the lead service practitioners for them; issues and political advocacy will predominate. In other words, the real target of your marketing efforts for individual clients would be the consultants who run the political show for the candidate. That puts you back in the networking environment.

Look into the outreach programs of organizations like the American Association of Political Consultants (**www.theaapc.org**). Also become familiar with *Campaigns & Elections Magazine*, which maintains a directory of political consultants, products and services at **www.politicsmagazine.com/win-loss2010**. You should also check out the *Politics1 Directory of Campaign Products and Services* at **www.politics1.com/services.htm**.

Beauty Pageant Contestants

Phyllis George, Miss America 1971, became one of the most successful winners ever, parlaying her crown into a career as a sports broadcaster, food entrepreneur, Alzheimer's disease spokesperson, and book author.

But a little-known fact is that George had entered the Miss Texas pageant the year before and had come in second, apparently failing to impress one of the judges that year.

A lot of people thought she should have won and could have won Miss America that year. They urged her to try again. "What for?" she said. After all, she'd already won talent, swimsuit, evening gown, even Miss Congeniality. Eventually, though, she was persuaded and decided to try again the following year. The rest is history.

An unwritten chapter in that history is that the year between Phyllis George's first and second Miss Texas competitions included what is now called image consulting, courtesy of a family friend with a background in professional theatre. It helped give her the edge she needed to take Miss Texas and then Miss America.

More than 30 years later, pageant consulting has emerged from the shadows to become an important subspecialty in the image-consulting trade. Kimberly Aiken Cockerham, Miss America 1994, is an image consultant specializing in pageant interview preparation.

Your best advertising, of course, will be in the form of your track record. Consultants whose clients win use photographs on their websites and in their other promotional materials. But you will need to use other media as well. Although they serve a sharply defined market base, pageant consultants nevertheless have a significant Internet presence. That should give you an idea of at least one of the advertising vehicles you'll need to have if you specialize in coaching pageant contestants. Suited to You Total Image Consultants (**www.suitedtoyou.com**) is one example of a pageant consultant.

There are also numerous pageant magazines that can serve as promotional outlets. Several websites are gateways to a range of publications and other resources. For instance, you can check out *Pageantry* Magazine at **www.pageantrymagazine.com**. You can also find a list of pageant news bureau periodicals at **www.pageant.net/magazines**.

To find pageant clients, you'll have to do more than set up a website or place an ad. You'll need to go to the source and rub elbows with contestants or, in the case of pageants for children, their parents. The Miss America Organization holds an annual convention; it also has 51 chapters around the country. In addition, both service and proprietary organizations sponsor beauty pageants. Visit the Pageant Club (**http://pageantclub.com**) and the Pageant Center (**http://pageantcenter.com**) for state-by-state information on upcoming contests.

6.1.3   Individuals Who Want a Change

Singles Seeking a Partner

Tune in to *Queer Eye for the Straight Guy* or just do an informal survey at the water cooler for insight into the characteristics of this target market. Men and women who want to be in a committed relationship but who can't seem to get a date have highly variable awareness of the interlocking influences of grooming, body image, wardrobe, and self-presentation on the prospect of connecting with a partner.

The role of the image consultant in this market segment is to bring the client to a realistic picture of behavior, body image, and wardrobe, and then to work with the client to make over, transform, and optimize their presentation.

This may sound so straightforward as to be commonplace, but don't underestimate the investment that individuals have in their presented persona and the possibility that they may resist doing what's required to make a successful transformation of their image. As Freud explained a century ago, the ego is the agent of the facade that is the physical. Meanwhile, everybody has to cope with culturally determined values, and appearance – especially body image – counts for a great deal when it comes to selecting a life companion.

You can get some insight into the characteristics of this part of the market from John T. Molloy's book *Why Men Marry Some Women and Not Others*. Subtitled "The Fascinating Research That Can Land You the Husband of Your Dreams," it is an adapted version of his dress-for-success theory.

As an image consultant you need to tailor your promotional efforts to convey the message that the single seeking a partner has made the best possible decision in retaining your services. The consultant can't criticize what's wrong with the image-impoverished single but instead has to emphasize what's right with the decision to go for a new look.

You can get an idea of how to manage that fine line from body-sculpture expert Michael Thurmond, who says that his "big thing" was that "I always told the truth. I didn't tell them you could transform yourself overnight by taking a pill."

On the other hand, Thurmond says that clients stuck with his program for reshaping their body image because he built follow-up customer service into selling it. "When people feel that you actually give a damn, they respond," he explains. "People suffer from self-esteem and desire. My deal was that you can have what you want to a degree. You have to work for it, but it's doable."

In practical terms, this means that a consultant to this market segment will need to be conversant with a variety of diet and exercise programs and with the motivational cues that result in client buy-in to the transformational program. You'll probably also critique clients' wardrobes and – like the guys on *Queer Eye* – go shopping with them to optimize fabric, color, and line choices. The value of the personal-service benefit is hard to overstate, and if Thurmond's experience is anything to go by, it should result in strong word of mouth.

Transgender Individuals

This is a narrowly defined, highly specific market segment consisting of cross-dressers, transvestites, and transsexuals. Such persons have become increasingly visible in the culture in recent years. At a time when sexual identities have been strongly politicized, image consultants who are intimately familiar and completely comfortable with transgender culture are most likely to build a flourishing practice with this pool of client prospects.

Even if you're a consultant who has a high comfort level, though, be aware that image-related issues in gender-variant culture push a lot of people's hot buttons. That's because of what's often called the "social construction" of experience and the relationships between men and women in the modern world.

The hosts of *Queer Eye for the Straight Guy* have shown the mass market that it's possible to cross gender cultures and thrive, but don't be fooled into thinking that this doesn't present special challenges. Individual cases may present more complex issues for even the most expert image consultant.

Consciousness within this market segment of culturally – rather than biologically – determined gender roles implies that consultants will need to operate at an exceptionally high level of trust with their clients. To achieve that much trust may take extra effort on the consultant's part, since gender roles are so tightly tied to fundamental psychological and psychosocial experience. At minimum, you'll want to stay up to date about issues of concern to transgender culture.

From an image-consulting standpoint, body language is an issue. Spoken language may be an issue as well. No less significant would be such issues as shopping for role-appropriate clothing, as well as role-appropriate behavior, which – like gender roles, in the opinion of some experts – transgender clients might feel the need to learn.

One advantage of targeting a narrowly defined market is that the media serving it is also highly specialized. That means if you do national advertising, you can maximize your advertising dollars by using a "rifle" rather than "shotgun" approach (which is unusual for most smaller firms).

For example, you could consider print advertising in such publications as the *Advocate*, which has national reach but which does not have a particularly large "straight" readership. You can visit the *Advocate*'s website at **www.advocate.com**.

By the same token, you could consider online advertising on special-interest Internet sites. For additional leads to possible advertising outlets, a one-stop Internet source for gay, lesbian, bisexual, transgender (GLBT) publications published in cities around the country is located at **www.worldlingo.com/ma/enwiki/en/List_of_LGBT_publications**.

Click your way through additional advocacy organizations serving this market segment:

- *Transgender Forum*
  www.tgforum.com

- *Transgender Forum Community Center*
  www.transgender.org

- *The Renaissance Transgender Association, Inc.*
  www.ren.org

Women Seeking a Change

The mass media relentlessly bombard consumers with images of physical perfection as the ideal of beauty. Yet a vast amount of scholarly research has been devoted to the fact that the majority of women are dissatisfied with their body image.

In the mid-1990s the results of one survey showed that 40 percent of girls of ages 9 and 10 have tried to lose weight. Another found that by age 13, 53 percent are unhappy about their bodies. The BBC reported in 2002 that 70 percent of women who lived in affluent neighborhoods were likely to be dissatisfied with their body image. Eighty-nine percent of overweight women living in affluent neighborhoods were likely to report dissatisfaction with their body image.

Statistics like these add up to a market segment that in some ways may be positively desperate for an image consultant's services. Women may be seeking a change because they're tired of being run down or overweight. They may be on the rebound from a failed relationship that they attribute to their less-than-perfect body image. They may want to meet new people or look for a new job but may be fearful of rejection — and attribute their fears to their body image.

The role of the image consultant here is like that of a "life coach," who offers motivational support and guidance. If you're not a personal trainer or dietician, you may find yourself referring women seeking a change to a health club and a nutrition counselor — or receiving referrals from personal trainers and dieticians. Your job is to retool wardrobe, grooming, and body language in a way that empowers the woman to change.

The marketing effort for women seeking a change is likely to include a good deal of client support. Thurmond's success with his spa program, which charges clients $5,000 a week and takes six weeks, shows that affluent women are willing to pay for a radical makeover and reeducation in image management. But personal attention and handholding, both during the six weeks and after the process is complete, appears to account for the word-of-mouth enthusiasm for Thurmond's program.

"I realize the service idea may seem nebulous to some," he explains. "Why spend money and time taking care of these people after they're done with the program? But it pays off. If a [wealthy] client tells me 'So-and-so [a former client] recommended me,' that's a very strong reason for continuing that type of support activity."

Front-end marketing to this segment involves informing customer prospects of your existence. It could take the form of presenting workshops at meetings of civic clubs and church societies. Being a member of a country club or being friendly with people who are can also help you get the word out.

Also use your contacts in related businesses. Cultivate high-end boutique owners, department store clerks, personal trainers, exercise-equipment retailers, hairdressers, facialists, manicurists, and salon owners — all of whom might be persuaded to keep your cards or brochures on hand. Advertising or writing a column in a community newspaper can also give you visibility with likely readers. The real returns, however, will come when satisfied customers start telling their friends.

Cancer Survivors

When serious illness strikes, the effect can be psychologically devastating as well as personally and professionally costly. As was explained in section 4.3.2 on volunteering, image consultants can help cancer survivors and others with serious diseases look better and feel better about themselves.

With this market segment you need to exercise a bit of caution and judgment about how you promote your services. Reading about image-related services on a website is one thing; getting an image consultant's brochure or, still worse, getting a cold call from a consultant eager to sell image tips won't sit well with individuals who have been hit with a cancer diagnosis.

That's where the business-to-business marketing bridge kicks in again. Oncologists, surgeons, oncological counselors, and retailers of prostheses may be members of the same service organizations you are. In an environment free of emotional stress, you can network with the professionals and explain the services you offer.

You can also provide them with brochures that they can make available to patients as part of a package of treatment resources. The idea is to get the client prospect to call you. Your job then becomes bringing to bear great empathy as well as the consulting expertise that will indeed help the client deal confidently with the disease.

6.2   Promotional Tools

Your most important promotional tools will be business cards, brochures, a press kit, a presentation portfolio, and a website. Supplement these with sharply designed letterhead stationery, which you will use for direct-mail communications.

Think of each of these elements as reinforcing the others; indeed, you may be able to use some of the same copy on your website and in your brochures and press kit. The promotional package, in turn, reinforces your in-person marketing efforts. And all of these elements should credit your image as a professional.

6.2.1   Business Cards and Brochures

Business Cards

As a professional image consultant, you will need to have business cards that convey a professional image. Simply listing your name, telephone number and "image consultant" is not enough. Your card should say enough about you to give people an idea of what you can do for them. Include your specializations, your website so they can get more information, and consider a special offer, such as "Call today for a free half-hour consultation."

Consider using heavy textured papers, raised printing, and a professional design. Check around for prices at print shops or office supply stores. There are also a number of online suppliers of business cards. Vistaprint.com offers color business cards on heavy paper stock, available with a number of different designs. You can get 250 cards for free, and you only pay for shipping.

Pass your business cards out whenever it is appropriate. Make sure that you carry at least three or four business cards in your wallet or purse at all times. Give them to friends, relatives, people you meet at social functions, your mechanic, your dentist, your mail carrier. Mention that you are an image consultant when handing out your card, so that people will look at it later and make the connection. When you mail bills or correspondence, stick a business card in the envelope.

Brochures

You will have many opportunities to give out your business card, but there are also times to give out brochures — for example, when you give a presentation at a networking meeting or when people seem particularly interested in your services. You should also provide some to the companies with whom you do a lot of business in case someone asks them if they know an image consultant they could recommend.

Your brochure should contain your company name and contact information, including your e-mail and web address. It can also include some of the information you have on your website, such as:

- Benefits of hiring an image consultant

- A list of the services you provide

- A photograph of you

- Some testimonials from satisfied customers

If you're just starting out, the initial testimonials may come from friends you've helped with an image upgrade. Consider including photographs of clients as well — both "before" and "after" pictures.

Spend time on the copy and layout of your brochure, working with a designer if necessary. Save money by asking for help from college or art school students who can use your marketing project as their school project.

If you are printing only a few copies of your brochure, you may be able to find nice paper at your local office supply store which you can run through your PC's printer. However, because you are selling image, the paper and printer must be of excellent quality.

If you aren't able to produce brochures on your home computer, or if you need hundreds of brochures (for example, if you are participating in a trade show), look into having your brochures professionally printed. Check the Yellow Pages under "Printers," or use the printing services of your local office supply store.

If you can't afford a four-color press run, choose two-color printing, which can do justice to black-and-white photographs. But single-color printing just won't do for you. Shop around and get competitive bids, but don't skimp on quality.

> **TIP:** Spell-check and grammar check everything. Also check your phone number, e-mail address, and other contact information carefully to make sure clients can reach you.

A serious business-building effort will also call for a respectable print run, which is another expense. But if you're starting from scratch you'll be surprised at how quickly you'll be able to burn through 1,000 brochures, what with all the potential outlets for distribution: civic clubs, conventions, trade shows, direct-mail packages, press kits to the media, counter displays at beauty salons and health clubs, etc.

6.2.2   Presentation Portfolio

Bring along a portfolio whenever you make a formal pitch to clients, especially in the corporate community. Traditionally, a portfolio would include these elements:

- a brochure

- before-and-after photographs

- copies of letters or e-mail messages from satisfied customers (also excerpted in brochure testimonials)

- copies of press coverage of your business

- photographs of you giving a speech or working with clients

- items from your press kit (see section 6.3.5 on publicity)

You could create a video or DVD presentation that shows you in action as a consultant — either one that you have generated for an actual project or one that portrays you "consulting" with actors. If you use the real thing, of course, you need written permission from the client. The only drawback to using video is lugging the tape or DVD all over town. Besides, not all offices are equipped with VCR and DVD players.

Indeed, lugging around a big portfolio can be cumbersome as well. Solution? A PowerPoint presentation on a laptop computer. You can scan all of the visual aids that would normally be included in a portfolio, including video clips, for easy viewing on the laptop screen or projection on the wall. You can even add bullet-point slides to the mix.

Instead of carrying around a scrapbook that will eventually suffer from torn pages and scuff marks, you can carry around a sleek laptop, which, in addition to being convenient for you, enhances your personal presentation. When you've completed your pitch, it's a simple matter to leave an easy-to-handle brochure with the prospective client.

If you can't afford the PowerPoint option right away, you can still create a graphically compelling portfolio. But keep the computer option in mind as an upgradeable feature of your marketing plan.

6.2.3   Your Website

There is no getting around the fact that businesses of all sizes and in all industries have an Internet presence. A website serves as an index of professionalism to the corporate marketplace and to many individual clients these days.

If you're computer savvy and know how to create a website on your own, that's good. But if you're not a web design expert, go with the pros. Design glitches that can be tolerated when you're trying to nail down a good-looking brochure can turn into major problems when it comes to Internet media — as anyone whose computer screen has frozen at an Internet site well knows.

Ask for leads to web designers from friends and business colleagues who are satisfied with work done on their site. Check out their sites to see if you like how they look and how they function.

Another way to find designers is to go online and search for other image consultants. Click your way through a dozen or so sites of your colleagues in the trade. You'll see the difference in quality of design and ease of use from site to site. Many, though not all, include web design credits on the bottom of the homepage. Typically there's a link to the credited company, which can save you a lot of research time.

You can also find vendors in your local Yellow Pages or an online web services directory. Whatever method you use to get your Internet ball rolling, make sure you account for the following things.

Reserve a unique site name. Be prepared: It may not be the first – or even the fifth – one you choose. So many have already been taken. Also be aware that there is something of a secondary market in site names, as web-aftermarket entrepreneurs long ago stepped in to reserve catchy, market-oriented words. Be cautious, too, of offers that invite you to "bid" on a name or to buy it outright for several hundred dollars. Before you overpay, keep trying to come up with a unique name that works for your business that's not taken.

Choose a web "host," a company which enables you to use its computer capacity to store your site's data online. This company is your site's customer service rep. Some website designers and developers also offer that service.

Work with the website designer to lay out your site's pages, art, and text. You'll provide the text and art – maybe even the design – and decide how to organize your information. This is the creative process of website creation and will take the most time to complete. Be aware that graphics add to the time it takes for new pages to load. If you add motion and music, the effect is amplified. So don't go overboard on special effects. Focus instead on the total presentation — just as you would with a personal client.

One of the best ways to determine what design decisions you should make is to compare what's good and bad about the sites of image consultants that are already online, adapting what you like and avoiding what you don't like about them. You will need to set up links to a certain number of pages, the titles of which typically run down a left-hand column of the screen. Two pages are pretty standard on all sites: "Home," and "Contact Us." Additional pages might be:

- Our Services

- What's New

- Testimonials

- Who We Are

- Success Gallery

Home page design is crucial and can be frustrating if it's not user-friendly. Make a point of putting your complete company contact information – name, address, and telephone number – on every page. You'd be surprised at how many companies whose designers should have known better make users click "Contact Us" to get that information.

If you use the Internet a lot, you've probably found that the "Contact Us" page often defaults not to a street address and phone number, but to an e-mail form for the user. The trouble is, people who send e-mail to a site asking for information very often leave out crucial contact details (e.g., a phone number), which makes follow-up difficult.

So a smart move would be to create a link to a page that looks like a mailing-list form, with spaces for client prospects' contact information. People who fill that form in are diamond-studded leads for you, not only because they're asking that you get back to them but also because the form can be translated into your contact database. Don't forget to ask your web designer to make that page work.

Keep yourself in the loop with your designer. Build into the contract opportunities to test the site before you roll out with it. Have the site uploaded to the host's computer so you and your friends can call it up from a variety of different computers to make sure that it looks good.

Comparison-shop web design and hosting services before you make a commitment of any kind. That's because sites have varying degrees of complexity and capacity and are charged for accordingly.

Now you're up and running, and here come the calls, right? Not yet. Once people find your site, it can be an effective sales tool. But they have to know how to get there first, and they can only become aware of your website via other media, such as business cards, brochures, print ads, letterhead, press coverage, personal contact, etc.

However, registering your website with major online search engines is a good start. There are premium services that advertise exposure to hundreds of search engines for a fee – which can cost a couple hundred dollars or more – but paying to be listed on every single obscure search engine is, quite frankly, a waste of time and money. Most people regularly use only a handful, such as Yahoo, Google, MSN, and AOL.

6.3 Marketing Techniques

Throughout this guide, we've emphasized the importance of in-person marketing efforts and the fact that your image needs to be consistent with what you're selling. You're a walking advertisement for your operation. In this section you'll learn a number of ways to connect with prospective clients.

6.3.1 Referrals from Other Businesses

An excellent way to get referrals is to make contact with businesses like dating services and health clubs, explain your business concept, and ask if you can leave a stack of business cards and/or brochures at their facilities. Do the same with the types of companies listed in the Strategic Partners section, such as manicure and beauty salons or with individual operators who work in the salons.

While visiting in person can generate the best results, you may also want to phone them. Telemarketers know the value of working with a script, and if you're just starting out you'll want one as well. As you develop your script, keep in mind that you're selling benefits and improvements. So you have to convey confidence and expertise. Don't write a script that tells the person on the other end of the line what you need and what you want. Write one that explains what you can do for the person you want to talk to.

If you can, "warm up" the call. Using a referral is one method:

> "Hello, (NAME). This is Diane Daley at FremontImageCo. Jackie Barnes at Boutique Splendide suggested that I call."

If your call is intriguing and the company has identified clients in need of an image upgrade, you may be asked to send an e-mail or brochure that explains your service. If you don't get a response, don't worry. Just be polite and move on. If you hear an objection, express empathy for it but rework it to suggest the benefits of cooperation.

THEM:	We're not interested in doing that.
YOU:	I appreciate that. Other salons felt the same way until I showed them the business-building benefits of this collaboration. I'd like to show you, too. Would Tuesday or Wednesday afternoon work better for you?

If you get the person to say yes – or at least not an outright no – to something, you're more likely to get the appointment. The secret is to talk not about what you want or need but about the benefits that the person you're calling will realize.

If the answer is no, write a note that includes three elements: that you enjoyed the conversation, that you understand the decision, and that you're available if any of the service's clients happen to ask about image-related services. Also include your business card and a brochure.

If the answer is yes, make a definite appointment to deliver the materials to a specific person, and show up on time — dressed for success, of course. Be prepared to go over the materials you're delivering with the business owner. That will enable you to meet whoever's in charge and negotiate where your materials will be displayed. "Talking shop" with hairdressers and manicurists will make you and your presentation a good experience and will encourage them to give you a good placement and talk about you favorably with their clients.

Bring along a holder for the brochures and/or business cards, though some businesses may not want the apparatus taking up counter space. You should check back from time to time to replenish the supply and also to schmooze and keep the business contact alive.

It may occur to you to offer beauty operators or personal trainers a referral fee as discussed in section 3.7.4 as an incentive to get them to push your service. But if you are working with a lot of companies, it may be better to come to an informal understanding that if the brochures you leave on the premises wind up sending business your way, you'll be glad to talk up their service too.

6.3.2   Networking

Your Warm Market

Your "warm market" is anyone who knows you — family, friends, the people you sit next to at the Rotary luncheon, the fellow you served with on the Red Cross blood drive committee. People you already have a relationship with are more likely to be receptive to your request for an appointment to make a PowerPoint presentation or to explain the scope of your services in detail. If you telephone them, they'll take the call.

If you choose your networking venues carefully, chances are your warm market will include people who are decision makers and who have contracting authority. They can hire you, or they can recommend that you be hired to perform your service for their company.

Once you've identified an organization's decision makers, even those you may not have met personally, you can send them a brochure and pitch letter or a press kit to introduce your services to them. If your materials have a top-notch look – and they should – you're in a good position to follow up by phone to arrange a meeting.

If you don't get a meeting on your first try, don't worry. Be persistent. Every time your company's services are cited in the press, that's an opportunity for you to make a copy of the story and attach a note saying something like, "Just a reminder that we're available for your image-consulting needs — confidentiality guaranteed." And every so often, make another phone call. Eventually, when that company needs an intervention for a computer-programmer-turned-information management vice president whose table manners need upgrading, you'll be the one to call.

Join Organizations

Local organizations can offer wonderful opportunities to network and establish contacts. A valuable form of networking is through a networking club. Some of these are general business groups, but many have a target group of clients and include one member from different industries (e.g. insurance, financial planning, law, professional photography, real estate, etc.) to reach those in the target group. Each member of the club is expected to bring a certain number of leads to the group each week or month. Make sure the members represent the kind of people who might become clients for you, or who would know others who could benefit from your services.

One way to find a networking club is through word of mouth. You can also look for them online. Business Network International (**www.bni. com**) has more than 2,300 chapters in cities around the world. In addition to networking clubs, consider joining groups that members of your target market belong to. For example, if you want to work with singles, get involved with singles organizations. If you want to work with women in business, consider joining the National Association for Female Executives (**www.nafe.com**).

If you work with corporate clients, consider joining your state or local chamber of commerce. Membership fees are usually based on a sliding scale. In addition to being able to attend regular meetings and scheduled events, you will be listed in their member directory. There are additional benefits of membership, such as discounts on insurance and the use of chamber facilities for holding seminars and related events. Visit **www.chamberofcommerce.com** to find contact information for your local chamber.

Effective Networking

To make the most out of your membership in an organization, there are several things you can do to raise your profile, including:

- Serve on a committee

- Write articles for the association newsletter

- Offer to give presentations on topics of interest to the members

- Do volunteer work that will bring you into contact with other members

- Run for election to the Executive Committee

Trade Shows

Conventions and industry trade shows are well suited to rubbing shoulders with prospective corporate clients.

When you socialize and trade business cards at these events, you're putting yourself in the position of (1) identifying who at a company is in a position to make an image consulting contract decision and (2) having a real live person to talk to when you follow up the next week on the telephone or with a direct-mail package and a proposal to make a presentation. You can see that this is also a method of avoiding having to make cold calls.

Budget concerns may force you to be very selective about which organizations and/or meetings that you will attend. Use the *Encyclopedia of Associations*, a multivolume directory organized more or less by industrial group and specialty interest and available in most public libraries. Some library Internet hookups provide free access to the online version of EA. A typical entry describes the scope of interest of the organization, including the titles of relevant trade publications, and lists the site and dates of meetings as far as three years out.

Trade publications are valuable sources of current industry trends and issues, as well as the names and photographs of key industry players whom you might meet at a convention. Let's say you're looking for business from the supermarket industry and you attend the Supermarket Synergy Showcase in Las Vegas (**www.nationalgrocers.org**).

If you're armed with information about what was in the latest issue of, say, *Frozen Food Age*, you're going to have something to talk about that's of interest to the industry people. If you begin with what they want to talk about, you can steer conversation toward what you offer.

Trade Show News Network (**www.tsnn.com**) provides cross-industry information on shows by industry, location, and year. You can click your way to contact information for the show organizers.

If you decide that you actually want to take a booth at a trade show to make your presence known to an industry, you'll definitely want the convenience of this Internet site. But a booth of your own is a down-the-road option if you're just starting out. Before you become an exhibitor yourself, it's a good idea to attend a dozen or so shows to get a picture of how they work.

Be sure not to lose sight of your marketing agenda when you actually get to these meetings and conventions. Come armed with plenty of business cards, as well as notepad and pencil, or a PDA that will let you write electronic notes to yourself. These notes will help you follow up after the event with your networking partners. Prompt follow-up is essential for maintaining your company's visibility with prospects.

Your 30-Second Commercial

Whether you're talking up your practice at a convention or a Toastmasters breakfast, there are certain techniques you can use to improve your effectiveness. When you decide to take the marketing plunge, prepare what's called the 30-second pitch or elevator pitch. That's the name given to what you first say to prospects you meet in person to give them a coherent idea about your business, your brand, yourself.

This concise self-introduction aims to fill another person in on what you do and to sell the other person on the benefits of working with you. In a minute or so, you answer some basic questions another person may have about you and your profession.

The elevator pitch has become such a standard feature of business strategies that contests are held to evaluate which ones work best. It's been touted as a secret of success for venture capital and job seekers and brand-name developers. Some experts have expanded the idea to as much as 90 seconds, but the time frame is less important than the fact that the people you meet may give you only a very limited chance to talk about yourself. So you've got to be effective in a small amount of time.

You can learn more about this technique online. One good source of information is **www.bolmer.com/Articles/Career/90SecondSell.html**.

Here is an example of a commercial an image consultant could use at an event:

> "Hi, my name is Jennifer Jones. I am an image consultant with experience in all areas of consulting, but I'm most often asked about body language, conversation, dining etiquette, and wardrobe. Over the past fifteen years, I have conducted several seminars for major corporations in the United States and Canada, and I have also provided one-on-one consultations to businesspeople as well as actors looking to improve their image and marketability. It's a real pleasure to meet you today."

One thing you need to take away from this method of personal contact is that it's just part of the process of in-person marketing. It's an icebreaker that gets you started. You have to finish the job. Be prepared to converse coherently beyond the initial spiel, which means listening and responding appropriately to the person you're speaking with.

Also keep in mind that if you're at a convention where you may be talking to 50 or 60 or 100 people in a day, it's probably good business not to rely on just one 30-second opener. You need variety not just for its own sake but because you'll encounter multiple personalities, and you'll want to adjust your approach accordingly.

Follow-Up Tips

Follow-up is the other side of the networking coin. Make sure that if you say you'll send a brochure to someone, you do so, and quickly.

Include a transmittal note on your letterhead that reminds addressees of your meeting and notifies them that you'll be following up yet again to set an appointment. Reinforcing your in-person presentation with strong on-the-record materials doesn't need to be confined to the corporate market. However, image consultants have the most to gain from the corporate market's perception of their value and professionalism.

The thought of doing follow-up correspondence with dozens or even hundreds of people the day after a convention might seem daunting. But you can use your computer to streamline the process if you do some pre-event planning. It can be especially useful if you're a one- or two-person shop.

What you can do is ramp up your word processing program or database program into high gear. Here's the word processing approach, using the mailmerge function of Microsoft Word. Other word processing programs have the same capabilities. Directions on your computer should tell you everything you need to know. Here's the drill:

- Create a data source file. This will contain personalized records of individual contacts. Follow directions for naming fields that specify individual information (Name, Address, Telephone, etc.).

- Create a form-letter text file. This is a "boilerplate" follow-up letter. Follow word-processor directions for making this file into a mailmerge file. That will include keying this file to the data source file. Now the two files will work together.

- Determine places in the text where you can insert personalized (field) information in addition to the normal mailmerge/database contact-information fields (First Name, Last Name, Company Name, etc.).

- In the data source file, create personalized fields with unique names (Company Name, Personal1, Personal2, etc.). These fields will hold the unique information that can be merged into the form letter to personalize it. Follow mailmerge instructions for creating and inserting these fields at appropriate places in the boilerplate form letter.

- As you meet people at the event, make notes on their business cards or in a notebook about specifics, keeping in mind the Personal mailmerge/database fields you've created in your boilerplate text.

- Enter contact and personalized information into the appropriate mailmerge/database fields in the data source file.

- Once you've entered the data and saved the data source file, open the mailmerge letter and link it to the data source file. Then print out your letters and labels.

Keep in mind that it's best to set up the template and the boilerplate language before you attend the convention. You should give some thought to how you want the letter to be worded so that your personalized datafields and the general language fall where they should.

You can see from the sample letters included on the next few pages, which were created from the same form-letter boilerplate, that the mailmerge document can function as a general template and as a personalized communication at the same time.

You may want to rewrite the text of your follow-up form letter from time to time, but once you've created the template and data source file, you can use and reuse and update the data for all kinds of correspondence without having to reinvent the follow-up-letter wheel every time. The personalized data, once entered, can be plugged in as needed.

Sample Letter #1 shows you what your boilerplate form letter will look like onscreen after you've created it according to your word processor's instructions. The words enclosed in arrow brackets and in boldface type are the datafield names, which are defined in the data source file. When you're ready to do your mailing, you'll link this document to the data source file to produce Letters #2 and #3.

Sample Letter #2 and Sample Letter #3 illustrate how flexible a form letter can be. It's not immediately obvious that these two letters have a common ancestor. The unique information, in bold (for illustration purposes only), reflects data stored in the datafields of the source file.

Sample Letter #1

(Stored in the computer)

Date

«Title» «FirstName» «LastName»
«JobTitle»
«Company»
«Address1»
«Address2»
«City», «State» «PostalCode»

Dear «Personal1»:

It was a pleasure to chat with you at the «Personal2» in «Personal3». «Personal4».

Your comments about «Personal5» were especially interesting. As we discussed, I think FremontImageCo can help give «Company» a vital edge in «Personal6». As you'll see from our brochure, part of our expertise is «Personal7».

Please do call me with any questions you may have about the scope of services FremontImageCo provides. I'll follow up with you «Personal8», to set a time when we can make a presentation to you. Meanwhile, we wish «Company» the best of continued success.

Sincerely,

Frank Fremont
President

Sample Letter #2

(Personalized mailmerge letter)

[On Your Letterhead]

Date

Mr. Bradley Smith
Chief Operating Officer
Accent Grocery Stores
1550 Carson Building, Suite 700
Kansas City, MO 12345

Dear Brad:

It was a pleasure to chat with you at the Supermarket Extravaganza Expo in Las Vegas last week.

Your comments about Accent Grocery's plans for expansion into Iowa were especially interesting. As we discussed, I think FremontImageCo can help give Accent Grocery Stores a vital edge in helping your advance people be more effective in their presentations to city planners and other officials. As you'll see from our brochure, part of our expertise is coaching managers in voice, diction, and body language.

Please do call me with any questions you may have about the scope of services FremontImageCo provides. I'll follow up with you next Friday, the 19th, to set a time when we can make a presentation to you. Meanwhile, we wish Accent Grocery Stores the best of continued success.

Sincerely,

Frank Fremont
President

Sample Letter #3

(Personalized mailmerge letter)

[On Your Letterhead]

Date

Ms. Evelyn Jenkins
Human Resources Manager
Percy & Co., Ltd.
1440 Simms Blvd.
Triangle Square South
Scarsdale, NY 54321

Dear Ms. Jenkins:

It was a pleasure to chat with you at the Rotary luncheon in Clarksville on Tuesday. Like you, I believe that providing scholarships is the best work that Rotary does.

Your comments about the issues involved in the coming labor negotiations were especially interesting. As we discussed, I think FremontImageCo can help give Percy & Co., Ltd. a vital edge in helping Percy's managers deal with the press if a strike should occur. As you'll see from our brochure, part of our expertise is crisis management and media strategy. We've coached many corporate spokespersons on facing reporters and a bank of microphones.

Please do call me with any questions you may have about the scope of services FremontImageCo provides. I'll follow up with you sometime before next Tuesday's Rotary luncheon, to set a time when we can make a presentation to you. Meanwhile, we wish Percy & Co., Ltd. the best of continued success.

Sincerely,

Frank Fremont
President

If you've never worked with mailmerge or databases before, you may have to practice manipulating datafields and boilerplate text. But once you've taken the time to nail down the function, you'll never look back. You'll be able to use it for all kinds of documents: correspondence, lists, envelopes, mailing labels, contracts, etc. The payoff comes in efficiency and in time saved.

6.3.3   Speaking and Seminars

Give a Speech

Even if you don't join an organization, you may still be able to connect with their members and get new business by being a speaker at a break-fast meeting, luncheon, or workshop.

Seek out opportunities to spread the image gospel at meetings of organizations like Toastmasters, Rotary International, Lions International, and Kiwanis Clubs. The Federation of Women's Clubs and the National Association of Women Business owners, both headquartered in Washington, D.C., have chapters located in large and midsize cities all over the country.

- *Lions Clubs International*
  www.lionsclubs.org

- *Kiwanis*
  www.kiwanis.org

- *Rotary International*
  www.rotary.org

- *National Association of Women Business Owners*
  www.nawbo.org

- *General Federation Of Women's Clubs*
  www.gfwc.org

Go online to research both the national organizations and the local chapters to get a picture of what the groups' missions and objectives are and — most important — to identify officers and board members.

You can also ask friends and acquaintances if they belong to any groups that have presentations from speakers. Contact people in local chapters who are in charge of programs and explain that you can give a speech on, say, budget-smart dress-for-success strategies.

It may take some time to develop a PowerPoint presentation (with before-and-after pictures of actual clients and other visual aids that enliven your presentation), but once you've rehearsed your program, you can easily transfer it from venue to venue.

While you probably will not be paid for your presentations, it can be an excellent opportunity to promote your business. Your company name may be published in the organization's newsletter, it will be mentioned by the person who introduces you, you can distribute business cards and brochures, and you can mingle with attendees before and after your presentation. (You may get a free breakfast or lunch too!)

If you give a good talk and offer useful advice, you will be seen as an expert. As long as there are people in the audience who need image consulting services, this can be an excellent way to attract clients.

Teach a Class

Teaching a class can be a great way to earn extra money, establish your reputation, and meet prospective clients. You don't need a degree to teach adults — just lots of enthusiasm and knowledge.

The first step is to review the current catalog of continuing education courses offered by local colleges, universities and other organizations that provide adult education classes in your community. Call and ask for a print catalog if they do not have course information at their website. Once you have reviewed their current list of courses, come up with some ideas for new courses. (They already have instructors for any courses that are in their catalog.)

Once you have an idea for a new course in mind, call the college or organization and ask to speak with whoever hires continuing education instructors. They will tell you what you need to do to apply.

Your Own Workshops or Seminars

While teaching continuing education courses can be rewarding, it normally takes months for a new course to be offered (and there's always the chance the continuing education program may decide not to offer it). If you'd like to start presenting courses right away, consider designing and giving your own workshops or seminars.

You will need to choose a date and time (evenings are usually best for businesspeople) and a location. You might approach a strategic partner, such as a salon, about holding the seminar there. Or you could book a meeting room at a hotel or conference center.

You will then have to decide how much to charge. Consider making the fee comparable to continuing education courses offered in your community. Or it may be free if you are offering it in conjunction with a strategic partner.

If you are working with a strategic partner, they will likely market it to their customers. However, they will expect you to do some marketing yourself, and you will be responsible for getting registrations yourself if you hold it at another location. The following is from the *FabJob Guide to Become a Motivational Speaker*, which gives detailed advice on how to market a seminar:

When preparing your marketing materials, remember to focus on communicating all the benefits of attending. As well as the information, benefits of attending a seminar may include: a fun night out, a chance to network, or personal advice from an expert. The other items you might put in a brochure include:

- Who should attend

- When and where the seminar takes place

- The speaker's credentials

- Testimonials

- That enrollment is limited (mention if past seminars sold out)

- A call to action, such as "Register now"

- How to register, including your phone number and web address

Brochures with this information can also be used to market seminars to the public. The ideal brochure for a public seminar is one that can double as a poster (e.g. printed on one side of a colorful 8 1/2" x 11" sheet). If permitted, try posting them at bulletin boards, especially in bookstores and college campuses — two places you're likely to find people interested in seminars.

6.3.4   Advertising

Yellow Pages

Image consultants can be found in the Yellow Pages under categories like business consulting, training, and, of course, image consulting.

Before you buy a Yellow Pages ad, you should carefully investigate the costs compared to the potential return. Many consultants find a Yellow Pages ad does not make the phone ring off the hook with clients. If someone does respond to your ad, they may be "shopping around," so you must be prepared to invest time and advertising dollars if you use this method of advertising.

To minimize your risk, you might want to consider starting with a small display ad, such as a 1/8 page ad. If you can get your hands on a previous year's edition of your local Yellow Pages, compare the ads for other image consultants from year to year. If you notice others have increased or decreased the size of their ads, this can give you an indication of what might work for you. Also, if you meet other image consultants at networking events, you can ask how well their Yellow Pages ads are working for them.

You can either design the ad yourself, have the Yellow Pages design it for you, or hire a designer. Take a look at the ads in the events category of your current Yellow Pages for ideas. If you are interested in advertising, contact your local Yellow Pages to speak with a sales rep. Check the print version of your phone book for contact information.

Magazine and Newspaper Advertising

Advertising can be expensive, and may not generate the results you want unless you do it repeatedly. (It has been estimated that people need to see an advertisement three to seven times before they buy.)

Therefore, if you choose to buy advertising, it will probably be most cost effective to place ads in local magazines or newspapers aimed at your target market. A discreet ad in a local singles publication is one place to start. Make sure it's a display ad. Classifieds are cheaper, but don't forget that you're selling image. Smaller publications will cost less than advertising online and in big metro dailies.

You could advertise in big-city glossy magazines. In such publications a display or classified ad in or near the personals section might be useful. However, make sure that your practice is structured in a way that's consistent with advertising in a glossy city magazine.

If most of your client pool consists of marriage-minded singles, then a glossy city magazine ad might be perfect for you. But if your client base consists of trial lawyers or oncology patients, it probably won't work.

You have to match your advertising to your target market. Here are some tips for effective advertising:

- Make your ad about your customers. Explain how they can benefit from your services rather than just listing the services you provide.

- Make them an offer they can't refuse. Your ad should describe a service or special promotion that makes you stand out from your competition. It should also include a call to action (i.e. saying "Call today" or including a coupon that expires by a certain date).

- Make sure you're available for people who respond to your ad. If someone wants to talk to you but keeps getting your voice mail, they may give up.

- Make long-term plans for your advertising program. Chances are that running an ad only once won't give you as much business as you would hope. Develop a long-term advertising strategy and stick with it.

However, you will get much better results if you can manage to get free publicity in those publications, instead of paying for advertising.

6.3.5 Free Publicity

There is a way to get a lot of exposure without buying ads: free publicity. Actually, it's not entirely free, since you may have to spend some money setting up the publicity opportunity. But when you do receive publicity, you achieve a measure of credibility and seriousness that standard advertising cannot buy you.

Position yourself with the media as an image expert. Take a tip from such esteemed organizations as the Brookings Institute and RAND Corporation, which routinely send the media a catalogue of pictures and contact information about scholars who are "available" to provide commentary on public-policy issues — taxes, health care, etc.

To facilitate this project, put together a press kit (see below), including a photograph of yourself, that announces your availability to comment on the image issues that your practice covers. This may get you quoted in the newspaper, on radio, or on TV; reporters and news editors are always looking for expert input to their stories.

Obviously this strategy doesn't just apply to marketing to sales reps. However, this kind of visibility gives you the chops that may be especially important to this segment of your market.

Creating a Press Kit

Your publicity machine begins with a press kit. A press kit is what companies or their PR firms send to media outlets to explain what the company sells, who its major officers are, and its plans for the future. It's distributed to media outlets that can use it to assist reporters in writing stories about the company or calling on company personnel for expert commentary.

Press kits have evolved to include certain elements that reporters expect to see. They are static in some ways and changeable in others. For example, a backgrounder that explains the history of a company probably won't change much, though it may be updated from time to time. Press releases that are included in a kit may change constantly because the information they contain is time sensitive.

You don't have to send a reporter or editor a new one every time you want to make contact. Instead, you'd send a press kit the first time you make contact, then send individual press releases on their own by either e-mail or snail mail.

Press kits typically contain the following elements:

Current Press Release

This is a notice of something the company has done or is doing that's newsworthy. Maybe you're announcing that you're making yourself available to the media as an expert commentator. Maybe you've donated $5,000 to the United Way. Maybe you're scheduled to speak at the Woman's Club. That stuff is news, or at least you present it as newsworthy. The point is to get your company's name before the press.

Press releases should always be dated, even if they include the words "FOR IMMEDIATE RELEASE." They also typically close with a standard paragraph restating the basic line of business of the company.

Here are some tips for writing a good press release:

- Make sure the press release is newsworthy. For example, you could write about an upcoming event you'll be speaking at.

- Give your press release a strong lead paragraph that answers the six main questions: who, what, where, when, why, and how.

- Include factual information about yourself and your services. Remember, a press release should read like a news story, not an advertisement.

- Keep it short. Aim for a maximum of 500 words.

- Include your contact information at the end of the press release so that reporters and readers can get ahold of you.

You can find more information about writing a press release at **www.publicityinsider.com/release.asp**.

A sample press release is included on the next page.

Biography

This is a narrative of the owner's resume, of the partners, or of other key executive personnel in the company.

Photographs

Traditionally, black and white glossy photos or color slides are used for art. Today, however, you might opt for a CD, which can be scanned digitally into print. For an introductory press kit, include a photograph of yourself so that reporters and editors can put a face with the name. Or you could consider before-and-after photographs of clients (you'll need written permission), which would show that you get results.

Business Card

Always include a standard business card. The card should include all of your contact information: business name, address, telephone number(s), e-mail address, and web address. Some companies get business cards made up in the form of a punch-out Rolodex card. Print shops are very familiar with how to make these. If you opt for them, save money by getting competitive bids.

Sample Press Release

FOR IMMEDIATE RELEASE

Image Workshop Offered at Local Woman's Club

SEATTLE, October 15, 2011 — With presentation of his seminar "Walking the Walk," Frank Fremont once again proves why he is one of the most sought-after image consultants in the Pacific Northwest. Using the techniques of classical acting training, as well as research into nonverbal communication, Fremont and two colleagues at FremontImageCo will conduct a JobFinder workshop for Junior Achievement students participating in the Greater Seattle Career Festival. The workshop, aimed at helping Junior Achievers maximize their prospects for employment after high school, will be the program for the Junior Achievement Honors Luncheon held at Woman's Club next Thursday at 12:30 p.m.

From his vantage point as executive director of the Lexington Regional Theatre Group in Lexington, Kentucky, Fremont was for 12 years in a position to spot the strengths and weaknesses of actors who auditioned and worked at the award-winning "Lex." He realized that actors weren't the only people who needed guidance and support in optimizing their ability to present themselves optimally and communicate their talents and objectives effectively. That was the origin of FremontImageCo, a full-service image-consulting firm run on the principle that putting the best foot forward can't be left to chance when the fate of organizations and the people they employ is at stake. "And it starts with the people who want to get the best job they can," declares Fremont. "We show them what they need to do to accomplish that."

Fremont's image- and career-upgrade workshops are in high demand by corporations across the Pacific Rim. FremontImageCo assists executives and management trainees in optimizing their career opportunities and their ability to interact with mass-media outlets. "If you want to succeed in your job, how you present yourself is just as important as what you say," Fremont explains. "That's why we're in business. And that's why we want to give the kids a leg up on building their careers."

FremontImageCo, a full-service image-consulting firm with an impressive corporate client list, is located at 15552 Sand Point Circle, Bellingham, WA 99999.

###

CONTACT: Bobbi Landau, (555) 123-4567

Previous Press Coverage

This aspect is cumulative. As you get publicity, photocopy the stories and add them to the press kit. Companies that have already gotten press coverage are credible resources and therefore more likely to get into print in the future.

Backgrounder

As the term implies, this document (no more than two double-spaced pages) describes highlights of the company's founding and history.

Fact Sheet

This is a one-page executive summary of highlights of the company. It's in list format and is usually no more than one page. An example is on the next page.

Writing Articles

Another related media strategy for being perceived as an expert would be to write articles or a column on an image-related issue. You might have to start small — perhaps a community newspaper or even a throwaway shopping circular. You may even have to pitch five or six publications.

But if you're effective, you'll develop a following, and you should be able to upgrade to a magazine or daily newspaper published in your area.

You might not get paid very much for the articles — maybe not at all if you go with a throwaway. But being in print in virtually any respectable publication lends you the kind of credibility that a full-page ad in *Vogue* or *Maxim* can't buy you even if you could afford it.

If writing isn't your strong suit, you could pay for ghost-writing services from a freelance writer. PR firms also routinely offer articles under their clients' bylines to trade and commercial publications. Hiring someone to do the writing will cost you money, but your objective is the payoff in credibility with client prospects. The benefit of having PR professionals do the writing for you – and handle the job of finding placements – is that they may be able to place the articles with targeted trade publications.

Sample Fact Sheet

Ericson Image
c/o Michelle Ericson
100 Fifth Street, Suite 231
Sunnyday, California 90210
Phone: (555) 123-5555

The Company:

A full-service image-consulting firm founded in 2002.

The Mission:

To assist individual and corporate clients on optimizing and professionalizing their public presentation.
Services:

- Wardrobe consultation and shopping assistance

- Cosmetics and hair consultation

- Diet and exercise consultation and support

- Verbal and nonverbal communication skills

- Etiquette skills training

Pricing:

- No-fee initial consultation

- Project pricing based on needs assessment

Company Personnel:

- Three executive consultants

- Two associate consultants

- Support staff

Management:

President:	Michelle Ericson
Vice President, Account Service:	Donald G. Payton
Vice President, Operations:	Melissa Cortez

Contacting the Media

Most magazines and newspapers publish contact information for their editors. Newspapers may have dozens of editors, so make sure you send your submission to the right one. For example, you would want to contact the Business Editor for your new business announcement, and the Fashion Editor if your specialty is wardrobe consulting.

As an alternative to writing a press release, you could call the editor or send him or her a brief "pitch letter" to suggest an idea for a story. If you want a few pointers on writing pitch letters, try visiting **www. publicityinsider.com/pitch.asp**.

7. Success Stories

In chapter four, we explained how to conduct informational interviews with image consultants. Well, while we encourage you to get out there and talk to others in the field, allow us to introduce you to some of the most successful consultants in the field. Sit back, pick up some advice, and get to know these amazing people.

7.1 Meet Jon-Michail

Jon-Michail
Image Group International
Victoria, Australia
www.imagegroup.com.au

Known as an advisor's advisor, Jon-Michail, AICI, CIP, is one of the world's top image consultants. The founder and CEO of Image Group International, based in Australia, he runs the Institute for Image Management. Together they form a multi-million dollar corporate image advisory and coaching organization.

The vice president of marketing for the Association of Image Consultants International (AICI), Jon-Michail calls himself an image coach. "That is the title I use for myself," he says. "Our work is really transformational. I am not your typical image consultant you will find around the world."

Established in 1989, Image Group International has representatives in 12 countries, including New Zealand, Southeast Asia, the United Kingdom, and the United States. "Our specialty is the executive world and the top-end. When the client comes to see us we basically walk the walk and talk their language," he says.

Jon-Michail suggests new image consultants pick out one or two specialty areas. "It could be grooming; protocol and etiquette; wardrobe; presentation skills, etc.," he says. "That is normally how people start, and then depending how eclectic you want to become in your skill-base, how much study you want to do, and how serious you take the business you are in, you can continuously grow and add to that list."

However, Jon-Michail warns that doesn't mean an image consultant can be all things to all people. "I think it's important to know when to take control in that area and don't overdo it."

Networking is a good way to build a client base. Meet with business organizations, business clubs, chamber of commerce, and personal develop groups, he says, or create seminars or workshops for business and local community groups. Focus these sessions on your area of expertise. A limited advertising local campaign may reap rewards as well, he says.

The business involves a certain amount of psychology, Jon-Michail stresses. "You need excellent intuitive skills to get a very quick sense of where the client is coming from, and you need good interviewing and listening skills to get a sense for where they want to go," he says. You also need to be able to pick up "holes" in the information you are given. "Any good expert in any particular area can do that. We would regard that as excellent value addition, adding to the whole consultation session."

Another tip Jon-Michail offers is to form alliances with providers that serve the same type of clientele you serve. "Investigate whether they are willing to play win-win with you, which means you are going to be taking clients to them but are they also willing to reciprocate with you. So it is not always one-way traffic," he adds.

You should also take a look at their client demographic, he adds, and see how it fits with yours. "If you want your service to be fairly up-market and you are operating with an alliance of fairly low-end style, that then can be incongruent with building your business."

As a past fashion designer with Christian Dior, Jon-Michail once owned a medium-sized manufacturing firm and a small chain of stores. However, he says most image consultants don't come from the fashion world. The majority of people that attend his institute are business professionals. Jon-Michail himself studied international business management at Monash University, Australia, and has experience in corporate communication and marketing.

He says it's important to learn the business of image consulting. "There is no point in getting trained in anything if you aren't going to learn the business of how you are going to make a living out of this," he says. "It is important to learn the business with someone who has already done it and has the stats on the wall. Go and get coached yourself."

A mentoring relationship is a good idea, and newcomers to the field can find contacts through AICI. They can also attend training programs run by an image consultant. "Get the hidden nuggets you would get from someone who is in the field,"' he says.

He points to the skill of setting your fees. "Someone outside the industry will give you one example; someone inside the industry will give you another one," he says. "Setting fees is a common one in any industry and the educational programs don't teach anything around that area."

A past winner of the International Image-Maker of the Year Award (USA), Jon-Michail was the Australian Achievers Award 1999 recipient and 2001-2002 Hong Kong Bank International Business Award winner.

7.2 Meet Evangelia D. Souris

Evangelia D. Souris
OPTIMUM, International Center
for Image Management
Boston, Massachusetts
www.optimumimageic.com

Evangelia D. Souris has only been working full-time in the world of image consulting for a few years but she is already flying high. The founder of OPTIMUM, International Center for Image Management in Boston, Mass., Souris was the 2003 recipient of the Association of Image Consultants International Rising Star Award. The honor is voted on by the board and given to someone who shows excellent direction and insight within the image industry.

With an undergraduate degree in political science and history, and a master's in administration and law, Souris worked for 13 years in government. She was the assistant treasurer for the city of Natick, Mass. and prior to that for the town of Weston, Mass. While pursuing this line of work, she also began to look at how to best portray the image of government employees to the public. That road took her into a part-time career in image consulting.

"I did freelance image consulting on evenings, weekends, and during vacations," she says. In 2002 she opened OPTIMUM, and she now specializes in corporate image, men's professional image, and public figures. Souris is also a sought-after keynote speaker and seminar/workshop leader.

While working part-time in the field of image consulting, Souris advertised as an image consultant in business magazines and journals. At the time, she focused on wardrobing and did fashion consultations. She recommends that newcomers to the field pick an area within image consulting and become an expert.

There are a variety of ways to get your name out into the public arena, Souris says. One method she used is to write articles for association newsletters. Publications put out by professional associations and organizations are a good place to get published when you are starting out, she says. Contact the editor and pitch an idea, and be prepared with an outline. Make sure you choose a topic specific to the group of professionals the organization serves, and not a subject that simply promotes your business.

"You have to pick something that has a need and answer it, and it should be something that would apply to that audience," she says. For example, for an organization that caters to business professionals, you could write about how to create the perfect first contact for a business presentation or a job interview, she says. Your article could cover the topic by explaining how nonverbal skills are important, including dressing, appearance, posture, poise, and body language. You would write about the basic tools needed to prepare a presentation. You also could answer the practical questions in your articles, Souris says, like how to dress for a meeting with the financial sector.

"Writing articles is an excellent way for people to know you, and it will not only help you get new clients but also create credibility for yourself," she says. "You will be received differently if you have been published or taken an extra step to do research and pick a specialty."

To be considered an expert, Souris warns, you need to be an adept researcher. Interview top professionals in human research departments and career development firms as well as college professors, she says, so the advice you are giving is relevant to the market. Read everything you can that relates to your field in trade magazines and newspapers, she adds.

If an association is looking for a keynote speaker, Souris says, offer your services. "It is not always about the money. Because if that is your main objective, the message of what you are saying will be lost."

Volunteer work can help you hone your skills, she says. For example, Souris gave free personal development workshops at a homeless shelter for women. "That is an area that I have not exactly specialized in yet. I knew I could do it, but I needed to fine-tune it, so I volunteered to do workshops at the shelter," she says. A good way to find out how your audience is receiving you is to include written evaluations. That strategy offers you a way to learn your weaknesses.

Don't be afraid to network with other image consultants, Souris says. "There are a lot of image consultants out there who wouldn't mind answering questions or having you do an internship with them. Have them teach you everything they know. If you ask the right person, they will take you under their wing," she says. "They get something out of it and you get the free learning."

7.3   Meet Gloria Starr

Gloria Starr
Global Success Strategies, Inc.
Charlotte, North Carolina
www.gloriastarr.com

With more than 20 years experience in the field of image consulting, Gloria Starr has risen to the top of her profession. She has a sparkling reputation with the likes of Destiny's Child, Levi Strauss, 3M, and Celebrity Cruise Lines on her client list.

She is a sought-after speaker who has given seminars in Hong Kong, Singapore, South America, Italy, Canada, the United States, and South Africa. She is also a featured expert on *Style By Jury*, a show airing on Canada's W Network. Starr's company, Global Success Strategies, Inc., is based in Charlotte, North Carolina.

Starr began her business while employed as a floral designer and adjunct professor, teaching continuing education and small development programs at several U.S. and Canadian colleges and universities.

She says her interest in image consulting was sparked when she had her own color analysis done. "I was amazed at the difference it made," she said. "I could instantly see that I looked better, and it would make shopping so much easier (with) no more fashion mistakes."

Working part-time in the field, Starr opened the doors to Global Success Strategies, Inc. in 1981, and by 1983 was working full-time in what she describes as the field of impression management.

Image consultants can come from a wide variety of backgrounds, Starr says, and there are no formal, academic degree programs. However, there are several ways to learn about the field and become a success. "Purchase every book relating to this industry," she says. "Have a quest for knowledge and never stop learning." Finding a "master" in the field to study under is also an option.

Many image consultants, like Starr, teach classes and head training programs. Starr offers several tips about selecting the right program: "Look at their client list and talk with them. See if their program really meets your criteria." Look for someone who has been in business for a number of years and has proven themselves, she adds.

From a florist to a retired CEO of a manufacturing company in Moscow that employed 65,000 people to an advertising firm owner in Hong Kong, the variety of Starr's pupils shows that the field truly is open to people with differing experiences. "It's not even about their interest in fashion," Starr says. "I'm not in the 'fashion' industry as such, but do offer advice to people who want to look their best through their image, etiquette and social graces, and their communication skills."

It is a great time to get into the field, she adds. "This is the busiest time in my 20-plus years. People are looking for the edge in business," she says. "Presenting themselves for success by dressing well and using appropriate business and dining skills opens the doors for greater recognition and success."

And while Starr's reputation has allowed her to work her transformation powers on the elite, she says there are many ways to build up a client list. "Get your name out there," Starr says. "Do some complimentary color analysis for people of influence."

Finding such people is easier than you think, Starr says. "We all have friends who have influence within their own company, church group, or places like that," she explains. "You would be amazed at the people who would be thrilled about that idea. Demonstrate for them some of the advantages of having some image work done and the changes it can make, and they will get all excited about it, and book you."

Strategic alliances with other professionals such as clothing retailers and hairdressers are important as well. Taking dry runs without clients can help the new image consultant decide with whom to forge strategic partnerships.

"I never tell them when I go into the store initially what I do, so their personnel will treat me as an everyday customer," Starr explains. "Depending on how they treat me, then I would make a decision on whether I will use that person. So, do they have a good eye for color? Are they friendly? Are they pushy? Do they know their merchandise?"

Starr also suggests networking by joining professional organizations. Starr is a professional member of the National Speaker's Association, the Florida Speaker's Association, and a charter member of the Society for the Advancement of Consulting. She is also the chairperson for the Professional Emphasis Group of Consultants.

"Network continually. Position yourself as the expert of choice," she says. "Write articles for magazines and trade journals, and treat your clients well to build a solid referral system."

7.4 Meet Dianne Daniels

Dianne Daniels, AICI
Image and Color Services
Norwich, Connecticut
www.imageandcolor.com

As a woman in the male-dominated field of information, Dianne Daniels says she got mixed messages regarding her image as a strong businesswoman and leader. Those experiences led her to a session with an image consultant and eventually a new career. "The changes that were made were not big huge changes but it made such a difference for me," Daniels recalls. "It helped my self-esteem and self-confidence and I said, 'I want to do this for other people.'"

Daniels, AICI, has been an image consultant for more than five years. Her business, Image and Color Services, located in Norwich, Conn., caters to life and business coaches, consultants, and solo practitioners. "Being a solo entrepreneur myself, I understand the challenges they face," she says. "Solo entrepreneurs are often such hard-working people that they sometimes neglect themselves and they may not realize that their professional image affects their bottom line directly."

Before her business took off, Daniels worked on friends and family for free. Practicing your craft is critical, Daniels stresses. "Whether that means you are volunteering your time, you are working with friends and family, or you are working with a women's center or a shelter, it is valuable hands-on experience that you can get," she says. "Then you can take that experience and leverage it to get paying clients."

Parlaying volunteer work into paying jobs is achievable. "The people that organization is helping, their clients, or their constituents, they might not be the ones to pay you for your services, but the people that work there might be," she says. "And they will know other people in the business world and then they can recommend you to those other people."

Daniels also recommends that new image consultants pick a specialty area. "People are looking for specialists. If you are a generalist, than how do you target that market? For someone just starting out in business that is an overwhelming prospect," she says. "If you specialize in one group of people to begin with – and that does not necessarily mean that is the only group of people you will ever work with, but it is a way to get started — get deep into that market, and become a specialist for that market. You will find that expansion will come naturally."

Daniels began by working with other small businesspeople as opposed to chambers of commerce, which she says tend to target larger businesses. "If you can find a small business-oriented group, that is a great way to start," she says. "Groups like that are always looking for public speakers. That is one of the main ways I have built my business." She points out that there are local associations of accountants, attorneys, real estate agents, and coaches, places where 70 to 80 percent of the people may be in your target market, depending on your niche.

Another way to build up a clientele is to write articles for local papers or post articles on announcement lists on the Internet. Daniels says these lists can be found by doing a search on an Internet search engine. "Do a search for 'article announcement lists.' You will bring up a whole host of sites where you can write a small article, 300-800 words, and post them so they can be printed or included on a website freely," she says.

"You don't get paid for these, but your name, contact information, and website can be listed, and people will pick up these articles and print them. I have had people call me for speaking engagements based on an article I have written, which can then turn into clients."

Using this strategy, Daniels has become a sought-after speaker. She was a keynote speaker for annual CoachVille Conference in Orlando Fla. in June of 2004. With more than 65,000 members worldwide, CoachVille (**http://learning.coachville.com**) is a coaches training firm whose network includes personal, professional, and corporate coaches. Daniels called the invitation to speak there one of the highlights of her young career.

Another way to make a name for yourself is by teaching locally, according to Daniels. "Get your expertise out there by teaching classes at local community colleges. It usually does not require a degree," she says. "If you have experience under your belt, you can do that. If you have worked with 15 or 20 or 25 people, then you have the subject material to put together a class on. That is something I have done to help my business and my public image."

Helping others shape their image, Daniels says, is extremely rewarding. "It is an absolutely wonderful profession," she adds. "I don't think we can have too many people there helping men and women increase their self-esteem and self-confidence."

7.5 Meet Michelle T. Sterling

Michelle T. Sterling, AICI
Global Image Group
San Francisco, California
www.globalimagegrp.com

Michelle T. Sterling, AICI, knew early in life that she had an interest in fashion, but it took a turn in banking to give her the skills she needed to succeed as an image consultant.

"As a child I was preoccupied with personal image, and how you present yourself, especially going through puberty, being a minority growing up in the United States," says Sterling, the principal and founder of Global Image Group in San Francisco.

"That was something I was always very cognizant of. Image was really important to me as a child, and as I got older into my teens I discovered that I really liked working in fashion, in retail, working with clothes, working with people, and really putting looks together for individuals."

A graduate of prestigious Wellesley College in Massachusetts, Sterling began her professional career as an investment banker. "That actually really gave me the work ethic I needed to succeed as an entrepreneur," she says. "Many consultants fail to realize that you are actually running a business and that you should do the research on how to run an appropriate business."

Sterling was formally trained in image, etiquette, communication and relationship management. The ColorStyle Institute in Menlo Park, California, trained her in color theory and the art of personal style. She is also a graduate of the Dale Carnegie Performance Training program.

She has affiliations with several top fashion houses such as Giorgio Armani, Salvatore Ferragamo, and Cartier.

Building strategic alliances with retailers and other providers means knowing yourself. "The stores I have selected are specific to me," says Sterling who describes her style as classically elegant. "For a new image consultant to come into the market, they will have their own personal style they are comfortable with."

Every image consultant is unique, Sterling stresses. "They should have their own specialization. They should niche themselves instead of going after a broad market. I have done it," she says. "For someone just entering, they should start with a smaller portion of different types of services — just do color or style, work on people's closets, or do personal shopping."

When you get into the field it is helpful to know what other image consultants are in your area and their specialties. "Learn who has a reputation for different services," she says. "If you are only doing style and you are not really that savvy on color, then it is good to know someone who knows a lot about color so you can refer clients to them. It really is about establishing a relationship." She suggests setting up an interview with consultants and managers of other service providers to find out if they are a good match with you.

Sterling attracted her first clients by networking. She attended gatherings with groups such as Commonwealth Club, Women in Business, and Women in Consulting. Associations related to marketing and law are good choices as well, she says, as are fashion parties and other social events.

"Every social event I went to, I marketed my business," she says. "Being successful in this industry equates to 80 percent marketing and 20 percent consulting."

However, following her lead may take you down a different path. "Pounding the pavement is different for everyone," she explains. "And people need to do the research about which organizations and associations work for them and join them. Start with the Internet and look for associates, social clubs, and networking groups in your area."

Sterling has served on the Executive Board of the Association of Image Consultants International (AICI) San Francisco chapter and is a Passport Holder of the National Speakers Association Northern California (NSA/NC) chapter.

Sterling suggests developing a 30-second "elevator pitch" and then practicing it over and over again until you have perfected it. "Whenever you meet someone new, it is an opportunity for you to network and market your business," she says.

Offering just a taste of complimentary advice can be a boost to your business as well. "Give everyone you meet a bit of advice about what they are wearing," she says. "A consultant will know what type of information adds value to a client if they have been trained and understand the basics of style. And credibility comes from crafting an elevator speech that builds up your credentials. This is unique to each individual and it takes time to learn the language and market yourself."

7.6 Meet Brenda York

Brenda York
Academy of Fashion and Image
Washington, D.C.

It was Brenda York's love of fashion that guided her into a career as an image consultant more than 25 years ago. Today, while fashion still plays a big part in her career, it's her drive to help others succeed at becoming image consultants that keeps her focused and playing at the top of her game.

York is the founder and director of the Academy of Fashion and Image, a training school that she opened only five years after starting her image consulting business — another indication that she's one of the industry's great innovators.

"The academy grew out of the fact that, when I started as an image consultant, there was no place to get proper training and certification," she says. "While you can learn on the job, having the proper training and documentation gives clients confidence that you've put in the time, energy, and effort, and have the knowledge needed to justify charging $75 to $100 an hour."

"When I helped to pioneer the first image consulting association (Association of Fashion and Image Consultants, or AFIC) in Washington, D.C. in 1983, the purpose was to bring image consultants together, because there was no professional association at the time. I've always found associations to be an invaluable source of support and business contacts," she explains.

As it turned out, York's hunch that there was a desire for a professional association was right, and the AFIC boasted more than 400 members within four years of its inception. The association York helped start has since merged with the Association of Image Consultants International (AICI), with chapters around the globe.

While the academy is York's primary focus these days, she does continue to actively practice as an image consultant, and fondly remembers how she got started in the business.

"After I had a child," remembers York, "I wanted to open a business where I could work from home, have the flexibility to be a mother, and utilize my extensive background and skills in fashion and cosmetics gained working for major retailers like Estée Lauder and Liz Claiborne. Image consulting seemed like the natural fit and progression."

With no avenues for formal training available to her, York attacked her new profession head-on, by envisioning what she wanted her consulting practice to be and going after it. She made her vision more concrete by developing a business plan that included detailed descriptions of potential clients, niche markets and fees. Once the plan was in place, York "just went after her clients."

This direct approach saw York finding her first clients through networking with different business associations, but it was her work giving seminars on the importance of image to real estate associations, the hospitality industry and retailers that really made things click. In fact, York's early approach to landing clients is something that she reiterates to her students and others interested in a career as an image consultant.

"When networking introduce yourself in a way that people will come up to you at the end and say 'I want to know more about what you do.' To do this, present yourself as a professional with the right look and knowledge required of the business. Most importantly, though, arrange to give seminars to businesses, associations — anyone who's interested in establishing or promoting an image for herself or business. All it takes is a single phone call."

York adds that providing seminars early in your career may mean doing these on a pro bono basis, but it's an excellent self-marketing tool and many of these seminars result in revenue-generating business from attendees and their recommendations. She recalls giving one seminar at a women's shelter at which the participants were so appreciative that many promised to pay her when they had the ability to do so.

Another piece of advice that York offers budding image consultants is to keep an eye on current and emerging fashion trends around the world.

"As image consultants we have to understand that you can't tell someone from New York to assume an image more suited for Texas, or someone from Japan [where there is a preference for basic black and white] to start wearing floral prints. You have to understand the culture that you're working in, and how that culture drives fashion and image."

Although York has seen the business of image consulting evolve and reinvent itself as frequent as fashion trends, even after more than a quarter-century in the business she continues to view image consulting as an excellent career choice.

"One of the greatest things about imaging consulting is that you can grow old in it. So many industries don't want you when you're over 40, but image consulting is an industry in which you can stay in fashion and do it as long as you want. In fact, you get better at it with age and experience."

8. Resources

AICI Reading List

Below is a required reading list for the 2006 Association of Image Consultants International certification exam, as well as some advanced level reading, reprinted with permission of AICI. Please note that this list may change in the future.

The Business of Being an Image Consultant

- *The AICI Code of Ethics, AICI Member Directory and Resource Guide* **www.aici.org**

- *The Perfect Fit: How to Start an Image Consulting Business,* by Lynne Marks, AICI, CIP and Dominique Isbecque, AICI, CIP

- *How to Get Your Point Across in 30 Seconds or Less,* by Milo Frank

Color

- *Color With Style,* by Donna Fuji

- *The Triumph of Individual Style,* by Carla Mathis, AICI, CIP

- *Color Me Beautiful's Looking Your Best: Color, Makeup and Style,* by Mary Spillane and Christine Sherlock

Women

- *Wardrobe Strategies for Women,* by Judith Rasband, AICI, CIM

- *Flatter Your Figure,* by Jan Larkey

- *Plus Style,* by Suzan Nanfeldt

- *The Triumph of Individual Style,*
  by Carla Mathis, AICI, CIP

- *Always in Style: The Revised Edition of the Acclaimed Classic on Creating Your Personal Style,*
  by Doris Pooser

- *Does This Make Me Look Fat?*
  by Leah Feldon

- *Looking Good: A Comprehensive Guide to Wardrobe Planning, Color, and Personal Style,*
  by Nancy Nix-Rice and Pati Palmer

Men

- *Dressing The Man: Mastering the Art of Permanent Fashion,*
  by Alan Flusser

- *Life Branding - How to Maximize Your Potential with the Abundance Lifestyle Coaching System,*
  by Jon-Michail

- *Men's Wardrobe (Chic Simple),*
  by Kim Johnson Gross

Personal Style

- *What's My Style,*
  by Alyce Parsons, AICI, CIP, with Allison L. Better

- *Brenda's Wardrobe Companion,*
  A Guide to Getting Dressed from the Inside Out,
  by Brenda Kinsel

- *In the Dressing Room with Brenda,*
  by Brenda Kinsel

- *10 Steps to Fashion Freedom:*
  Discover Your Personal Style from the Inside Out,
  by Malcolm Levene & Kate Mayfield

Business Dress

- *The New Professional Image:
  From Business Casual to the Ultimate Power Look,*
  by Susan Bixler and Nancy Nix-Rice

- *Business Casual Made Easy,*
  by Ilene Amiel, AICI, CIP, and Angie Michael, AICI, CIP

Grooming: Hair, Skin, Makeup

- *Bobbi Brown Beauty,*
  by Bobbi Brown

- *From Head to Soul for Women,*
  by Dr. Joyce Knudsen, AICI, CIM

- *From Head to Soul for Men,*
  by Dr. Joyce Knudsen, AICI, CIM

Etiquette and Protocol

- *Managing Your Image Potential,*
  by Catherine Bell, AICI, CIP

- *Five Steps to Professional Presence,*
  by Susan Bixler

- *Business Etiquette for Dummies,*
  by Sue Fox

Advanced Level Reading

Business of Being an Image Consultant

- *The Seven Habits of Highly Effective People,*
  by Stephen Covey

- *Image Consulting for the 21st Century,*
  by Brenda York-McDaniel

- *Working From Home,*
  by Paul and Sarah Edwards

Color

- *Pantone Guide to Communicating with Color,*
  by Leatrice Eiseman

- *The Secrets of Color and Style,*
  by Diana Olson

Women

- *Fabulous Fit,*
  by Judith Rasband

- *Visual Design in Dress (3rd Edition),*
  by Marian Davis

Men

- *Red Socks Don't Work,*
  by Kenneth J. Karpinski

Grooming: Hair, Skin

- *The Total Look,*
  by Ian Mistlin

Etiquette

- *The Etiquette Advantage in Business,*
  by Peggy Post & Peter Post

- *Complete Business Etiquette,*
  by Barbara Pachter and Marjorie Brody

Body Language and Verbal Communication

- *Voice Power,*
  by Renee Grant-Williams

Other

- *Fairchild's Dictionary of Fashion,*
  by Dr. Charlotte Calasibetta

- *Fairchild's Dictionary of Textiles, 6th edition,*
  by Isabel Wingate

- *Co-Active Coaching: New Skills for Coaching People
  Toward Success in Work and Life,*
  by Laura Whitworth, Karen Kimsey-House, Phil Sandahl,
  & Henry Kimsey-House

Bridal

- *My Bride Guide: A Wedding Planner for Your Personal Style,*
  by Judith Ann Graham

- *How to Buy Your Perfect Wedding Dress,*
  by Ronald Rothstein and Mara Urshel

Save 50% on Your Next Purchase

Would you like to save money on your next FabJob guide purchase? Please contact us at **www.FabJob.com/feedback.asp** to tell us how this guide has helped prepare you for your dream career. If we publish your comments on our website or in our promotional materials, we will send you a gift certificate for 50% off your next purchase of a FabJob guide.

Get Free Career Advice

Get valuable career advice for free by subscribing to the FabJob newsletter. You'll receive insightful tips on: how to break into the job of your dreams or start the business of your dreams, how to avoid career mistakes, and how to increase your on-the-job success. You'll also receive discounts on FabJob guides, and be the first to know about upcoming titles. Subscribe to the FabJob newsletter at **www.FabJob.com/newsletter.asp**.

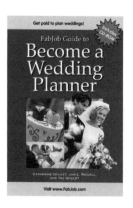

Does Someone You Love Deserve a Dream Career?

Giving a FabJob® guide is a fabulous way to show someone you believe in them and support their dreams. Help them break into the career of their dreams with more than 75 career guides to choose from.

Visit www.FabJob.com to order guides today!

More Guides to Build Your Business

Increase your income by offering additional services. Here are some recommended FabJob guides to help you build your business:

Get Paid to Give Etiquette Advice

Imagine having a rewarding career teaching people essential skills they need to succeed in business and in life. In the **FabJob Guide to Become an Etiquette Consultant** you will learn how to:

- Become an expert in business, dining, social, children's or international etiquette

- Coach individuals on proper etiquette

- Create a part-time or full-time job as an etiquette consultant

- Start an etiquette consulting business, price your services, and find clients

- Present etiquette seminars or workshops and corporate training programs

Get Paid to Shop

Imagine having a creative high-paying job shopping for fashions, housewares, gifts, or almost anything else you love to shop for. In the **FabJob Guide to Become a Personal Shopper** you will discover:

- Step-by-step instructions for personal shopping from identifying what people want to finding the best products and retailers

- How to get discounts on merchandise

- How to prevent purchasing mistakes

- How to get a job as a personal shopper for a boutique, department store or shopping center

- How to start a personal shopping business, price your services, and find clients

Visit www.FabJob.com to order guides today!

More Fabulous Guides

Find out how to break into the "fab" job of your dreams with FabJob career guides. You can choose from more than 75 titles including:

Get Paid to Apply Makeup

Imagine having a fun high-paying job that lets you use your creativity to make people look good. In the **FabJob Guide to Become a Makeup Artist** you will learn:

- How to apply makeup to best suit someone's coloring, skin type, face shape and features (plus what to have in your makeup kit)

- How to choose a training program

- How to get a job as a makeup artist for a salon, spa, retail store, or cosmetics company

- How to get freelance work as a makeup artist for advertisements, magazines, movies, music videos, runway shows, TV, theater and more

Open Your Own Day Spa

As a spa owner you could have a profitable business helping people experience more happiness, health, and well being. In the **FabJob Guide to Become a Spa Owner**, you will learn:

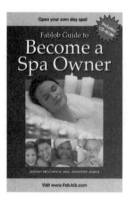

- Your options for opening a new spa, buying an existing spa, or starting a mobile spa business

- Different types of spa and salon services and how much to charge (plus tips on selling retail products)

- How to create a business plan and get financing

- How to choose a location, design your layout, hire staff, and find suppliers

- How to market your spa to attract customers, including tips on booking groups

Visit www.FabJob.com to order guides today!

About The Editors

 **Tag Goulet** is a leading expert in careers and interpersonal communications, who has consulted for multinational corporations and conducted training programs for American Management Association International. Tag's career articles have been read by millions of people worldwide at websites such as AOL.com, CNN.com, and Microsoft's MSN, and have appeared in newspapers and online through Career-Builder in the United States, Sun Media in Canada, and Metro News in Europe. As a career expert she has been featured in media from ABC and Oprah.com to *Entrepreneur* and *The Wall Street Journal* online and in many popular women's magazines including *Woman's Day* and *Woman's World*. Tag is a contributor to more than a dozen books including *USA Today* and Amazon.com bestsellers, and she has spoken before hundreds of thousands of people in dozens of cities over the past 15 years. Currently, Tag is co-CEO of FabJob Inc., an award-winning publishing company whose website **www.FabJob.com** was named "the #1 place to get published online" by *Writer's Digest*. She is also a part-time university instructor of interpersonal communications.

Rachel Gurevich is former senior development editor for FabJob Inc., where she had the opportunity to work on over 20 books in various stages of the editorial process. With the *FabJob Guide to Become an Image Consultant*, she brought together the contributions of dozens of writers and experts to create a cohesive and comprehensive guide. Her writing has appeared in more than 20 different publications and she is the author of two books. She was an assistant editor for more than three years for what is now known as the SheKnows Network. Currently she is a writing instructor for Long Ridge Writers Group, and provides freelance writing and editorial services. More information about Rachel can be found at her website: **www.rachelgurevich.com**.

About the Writers

The *FabJob Guide to Become an Image Consultant* was written by an experienced team of professional writers with expertise in the topics covered in this guide, including beauty, business, careers, communication, fashion, and lifestyles.

Caryne Brown is an editorial consultant and business planner based in Los Angeles. As Senior Editor of *Entrepreneur Magazine*, she wrote or supervised editing of more than 60 how-to books, and developed distance-learning courses in business planning and entrepreneurial management. Topics of business manuals she has written include image consulting, start-up basics, and increasing sales. As "Ask the Experts" columnist for *Income Opportunities Magazine*, she answered reader inquiries on small business management. She was a founding editor of *Woman's Enterprise*, and her numerous other writing credits include *American History, Architectural Digest, Bon Appétit, Ironman,* and *Shape*.

Craig Coolahan is a freelance writer and editor with degrees in Journalism and English. A former newspaper reporter, he has written hundreds of articles for a variety of publications including the *Times Higher Education Supplement*. He has edited two how-to books which received excellent reviews in newspapers and magazines across the U.S. and is a former instructor of Job Search Skills for a business training institute.

Holli Cosgrove is a former editorial director of Ferguson Publishing Company, publishers of *The Encyclopedia of Careers and Vocational Guidance*. She worked on the 9th edition as assistant editor and guided the 10th and 11th editions as editorial director. Prior to working at Ferguson, she spent four years at Encyclopaedia Britannica as an indexer and research editor.

Rennay Craats is a freelance writer and editor in Calgary. Trained in journalism and communication, she has written and edited newspaper and magazine articles on a wide variety of topics ranging from archaeological digs to profiles of humanitarians. Her writing on image includes a feature on the men's spa experience for *American Health and Fitness* and articles on cosmetic dentistry and other topics for a daily newspaper. She has written career profiles for a website maintained by the Government of Michigan, and prepares promotional material through her company, Boomerang Communications.

Carol Marshall is a full-time newspaper reporter, and freelance writer and editor. Based in southeast Michigan, she specializes in career guide writing, and has written and contributed to guides for aspiring careerists in fields ranging from education to consulting to the funeral profession.

Marly Miller is currently Creative Services Manager within the Corporate Integrated Marketing Group of a leading magazine publishing company in New York City, NY. Her current work is geared toward the men's lifestyle category for two top national magazines and she previously worked with a series of women's special interest magazines. She is a guest lecturer in various New York City classrooms on the topics of marketing in the corporate environment. She is a freelance writer in her spare time and her writing projects have ranged from fashion to business.

Marsha Miller is a certified professional image and marketing consultant. She has written a biography and a handbook for job seekers as well as articles for *Woman's World* and *Southern Theatre*. She has a BS in Communication and teaches writing and personal development to college students.

Cal Orey is an accomplished author and journalist who holds a master's degree in English (Creative Writing) from San Francisco State University. Over the past 15 years, she has written hundreds of articles for national magazines and websites, specializing in topics as diverse as beauty, health, nutrition, and relationships. Her articles have appeared in publications such as *Woman's World, Woman's Day, Men's Fitness*, as well as in *Complete Woman*, of which she also is a contributing editor. Ms. Orey is also the author of *The Healing Powers of Vinegar* and *Doctors' Orders: What 101 Doctors Do to Stay Healthy* (both published by Kensington). She lives in northern California.

Stephanie Scott is a New York City-based beauty editor with *Essence Magazine*. She has researched three books, *Lloyd Boston's Men of Color, Lloyd Boston's Makeover Your Man: A Woman's Guide to Dressing Any Man in Your Life,* and *Mikki Taylor's Self Seduction: Your Path to Inner and Outer Beauty*. She enjoys public speaking and cooking in her spare time.

Susan Shelly is a freelance writer, researcher, and editorial consultant. A former newspaper reporter and columnist, she has written freelance material for an online news service and for various magazines, newspapers, businesses, and agencies. She has written or co-written 20 books, 11 of which are Complete Idiot's Guides. The guide topics include Being a Successful Entrepreneur and Networking for Novices.

Kim Tobin has a master's degree in Journalism, and experience as a group editor for a New York retail weekly, a freelancer for various national trade monthlies, and a marketing manager at a national television shopping network.

Susan Wessling is an award-winning writer and editor whose work has been recognized by the National (U.S.) Newspaper Association and The New England Press Association. Her articles have appeared in a number of New England newspapers, U.S. and international magazines, and numerous education, health, and sports websites including Encyclopaedia Britannica's online encyclopedia. She has interviewed some of the top image consultants in the world. Wessling lives in central Massachusetts with her partner, Pat, their son Stephen, and Irish Setter Clancy.

Acknowledgements

Thank you to the following experts (listed alphabetically) for generously sharing advice through personal interviews and/or consenting to reproduction of written material in this FabJob guide. Opinions expressed in this guide are those of the respective writers and not necessarily those of individuals interviewed for the guide.

- Association of Image Consultants International
  www.aici.org

- Catherine Graham Bell
  Prime Impressions
  www.prime-impressions.com

- Marjorie Brody
  Brody Communications Ltd.
  www.brodycommunications.com

- Karen Brunger
  International Image Institute
  www.imageinstitute.com

- Maureen Costello
  Image Launch
  www.imagelaunch.com

- Jenny Cutler
  Image Counts

- Georgia Donovan
  The Clothes Doctor
  www.georgiadonovan.com

- Juanita Ecker
  Professional Image Management
  www.professionalimagemgt.com

- Louise Elerding
  Fashion Feng Shui International
  www.fashionfengshui.com

- Susan M. Fignar
  Pur*Sue Image Consultant Services
  www.pur-sue.com

- Debra Fine
  The Fine Art of Small Talk
  www.debrafine.com

- Marion Gellatly
  Powerful Presence
  www.powerful-presence.com

- Steve Jaffe
  Jaffe & Co. Strategic Media Relations
  www.stevejaffepr.com

- Lori B. Johnson
  Your Best Image Personal Image Development
  www.yourbestimagepid.com

- Lisa Kaufman
  Marketing Director for Dr. Stephen T. Greenberg
  www.greenbergcosmeticsurgery.com

- Dr. Joyce Knudsen
  The ImageMaker, Inc.
  www.imagemaker1.com

- Teresa Lopuchin
  Self Image

- Charli Mace
  ColorTools.com
  www.colortools.com

- Lynne Marks
  London Image Institute
  www.londonimageinstitute.com

- Sherry Maysonave
  Empowerment Enterprises
  www.casualpower.com

- Jon-Michail
  Image Group International
  www.imagegroup.com.au

- Larry Oskin
  Marketing Solutions
  www.mktgsols.com

- Donna Panko
  Professional Skill Builders, Inc.
  www.professionalskillbuilders.com

- Diana Reynolds
  The Eye Boutique
  www.eyeboutique.com

- Barbara Quayle
  The Associates Image Enhancement
  and Support Center

- Jennifer Robin
  Clothe Your Spirit
  www.clotheyourspirit.com

- Toy Russell
  Toy Russell Inc.
  www.toyrussell.com

- Karen M. Shelton
  HairBoutique.com
  www.hairboutique.com

- Lauren Solomon
  LS Image, Inc.
  www.lsimage.com

- Evangelia D. Souris
  Optimum International Center for
  Image Management
  www.optimumimageic.com

- Anne Sowden
  Here's Looking at You
  www.hereslookingatyou.ca

- Gloria Starr
  Global Success Strategies
  www.gloriastarr.com

- Michelle T. Sterling
  Global Image Group
  www.globalimagegrp.com

- Michael Thurmond
  6 Week Body Makeover
  www.bodymakeovers.com

- Anna Soo Wildermuth
  Personal Images Inc.
  www.personalimagesinc.com

- Brenda York McDaniel
  Academy of Fashion and Image